boilerplate MW00568228

Hands-On
Microsoft Windows NT 4.0
Server with Projects

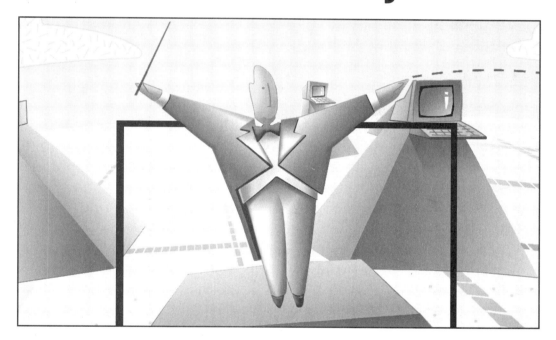

Michael J. Palmer

COURSE TECHNOLOGY

ONE MAIN STREET, CAMBRIDGE, MA 02142

an International Thomson Publishing company I(T)P®

Cambridge • Albany • Bonn • Boston • Cincinnati • London • Madrid • Melbourne • Mexico City
New York • Paris • San Francisco • Singapore • Tokyo • Toronto • Washington

Hands-On Microsoft Windows NT 4.0 Server with Projects is published by Course Technology.

Managing Editor:	Wendy Welch Gordon
Product Manager:	Richard Keaveny
Associate Product Manager:	Susan Roche
Production Editor:	Nancy Shea
Marketing Manager:	Tracy Wells
Manufacturing Supervisor:	Susannah Lean
Development Editor:	Cindy Brown
Copy Editor:	Anna Huff
Composition House:	GEX, Inc.
Cover Designer:	Doug Goodman
Text Designer:	David Reed

© 1997 by Course Technology—I(T)P®

For more information contact:

Course Technology
One Main Street
Cambridge, MA 02142

International Thomson Publishing Europe
Berkshire House 168-173
High Holborn
London WCIV 7AA
England

Thomas Nelson Australia
102 Dodds Street
South Melbourne, 3205
Victoria, Australia

Nelson Canada
1120 Birchmount Road
Scarborough, Ontario
Canada M1K 5G4

International Thomson Editores
Campos Eliseos 385, Piso 7
Col. Polanco
11560 Mexico D.F. Mexico

International Thomson Publishing GmbH
Königswinterer Strasse 418
53227 Bonn
Germany

International Thomson Publishing Asia
211 Henderson Road
#05-10 Henderson Building
Singapore 0315

International Thomson Publishing
Hirakawacho Kyowa Building, 3F
2-2-1 Hirakawacho
Chiyoda-ku, Tokyo 102
Japan

Trademarks

Course Technology and the open book logo are registered trademarks of Course Technology.
I(T)P® The ITP logo is a registered trademark of International Thomson Publishing.
Some of the product names and company names used in this book have been used for identification purposes only and may be trademarks or registered trademarks of their respective manufacturers and sellers.

Disclaimer

Course Technology reserves the right to revise this publication and make changes from time to time in its content without notice.

0-7600-5008-2

Printed in the United States of America

10 9 8 7 6 5 4 3 2 1

RELATED TITLES IN THE NETWORKING SERIES

INTRODUCTION

Many opportunities exist for capable network and server managers in business, government, and educational organizations. The field of network and server management is expanding rapidly as more and more uses for today's networking technologies are discovered. Most importantly, networks allow people within and between organizations to share software applications such as word processors, spreadsheets, personal databases, and electronic mail. Today, new, versatile networks are also being used for more mission critical functions sculpted around client/server, Internet, and intranet applications. Network and server managers play a key role in setting up and administering all of the services that make organizations more efficient.

Microsoft Windows NT Server is one of the most dynamic and popular network operating systems on which to build the services that are essential to today's businesses. As a result, there is a significant and growing demand for people with NT Server expertise. The primary aim of this book is to help the reader to become a network or server manager who is able to install and manage Windows NT Server 4.0 on a local area network and thus meet the need for people with NT Server expertise. A second purpose of this book is to help prepare those interested in certification as a Microsoft Windows NT Server 4.0 Product Specialist or a Systems Engineer for the Windows NT 4.0 certification exam. Consistent with these goals, this book provides hands-on training in the following areas:

- Setting up hardware and software for network servers and client workstations
- Installing and configuring NT Server 4.0
- Designing a basic network and understanding the components
- Configuring network protocols
- Setting up and managing user accounts
- Setting up and managing user groups
- Using the NT Server administrative wizards and administrative tools
- Establishing server management policies
- Managing security, access rights, and permissions
- Creating directory structures
- Creating and managing network shares
- Setting up and managing network printers
- Auditing resources
- Implementing server and workstation backups and restores
- Setting up domains and domain controllers
- Monitoring an NT server
- Tuning and troubleshooting techniques

Microsoft Certification

Microsoft Certification is an important accomplishment which is valued by many employers. This book has been written with the objectives of Microsoft Certification in mind in order to make this book suitable to be used as a preparation tool when studying for Microsoft

Certification exams. If you are interested in finding out more about the requirements and objectives of Microsoft Certification, please consult Microsoft on the Web at **http://www.microsoft.com/train_cert/cert/certif.htm**

Approach

Hands-On Microsoft Windows NT 4.0 Server with Projects is designed to help students learn about Windows NT 4.0 through hands-on application. A running case throughout the book places students in the workplace. Beginning with the basics—which include the fundamentals of networks, servers, and client workstations—this book proceeds to cover all of the necessary material to teach a student to be a fully prepared Windows NT 4.0 Server technician.

Each chapter in *Hands-On Microsoft Windows NT 4.0 Server with Projects* includes chapter objectives, a chapter summary, definitions of key terms, and student exercises. Chapter 1 introduces the student to NT Server capabilities, file servers, and networking capabilities. It closes with a brief tour of Windows networking. Chapter 2 provides a foundation to understand networking components, topologies, and network design. How to determine the costs of networking is also presented. Chapter 3 focuses on preparing and sizing the file server hardware, including making it network-ready. Chapter 4 shows how to prepare the network client (workstation) and topics covered include selecting a client operating system, sizing the client, and client setup to connect to the server. Part of the setup is to configure the network interface card, driver, and designate protocols to use on the network. In chapter 5 students focus on the server installation. The chapter begins by teaching the student to plan ahead for each installation step. Then, students go through an installation step-by-step, including using the NT Server Setup Wizard. Chapter 6 shows students how to set up and manage domains through an in-depth discussion of domains, domain models, and trust relationships. In Chapter 7 students learn how to set up and manage user accounts, logon scripts, user groups, rights, and home directories. The administrative tools and the administrative wizards are demonstrated for managing user accounts and groups. Chapter 8 shows students how to design a directory structure, set up attributes, set up permissions, create a share, install applications, and manage the Registry. Chapter 9 focuses on network printing, including print spooling, printer setup, printer drivers, the Printer Setup Wizard, and creating a printer share. In chapter 10 students learn about monitoring NT servers, including how to use a range of monitoring tools, and stop and start services. Students also are introduced to event logs and receive tips on tuning the server through paging. Chapter 11 contains a range of information about server maintenance and more tips on server tuning. In this chapter students learn to manage event logs, perform disk maintenance, set up fault tolerance, determine which level of RAID to use, set up and manage backups and restores, create a tape rotation method, and set up a UPS. Chapter 12 discusses server and network troubleshooting, including how to use the diagnostic tools, how to troubleshoot through additional server tuning, and approaches to solving a range of problems including memory, disk, printer, and network problems. Students also learn how to recover from a major hardware failure in this chapter.

Text and Graphic Conventions

Wherever appropriate, additional information and exercises have been added to this book to help students better understand what is being discussed within the chapter. Students are made aware of additional material through the use of icons. The icons used in this textbook are described below.

Located at the end of each chapter is a continuing running case that is indicated by the Project icon. In this extensive case example, students are asked to implement the skills explained in the chapter at the fictitious Holland College. This case is distinct from the one that runs within the chapters themselves and allows students to implement what they have learned independently.

Special attention has been paid in this book to networking language and the definition of terms. To help reinforce for students the key terms and concepts, definitions are provided in both the text of the chapter, in end-of-chapter reviews, and in specially marked text boxes denoted by the Definition icon.

The Note icon is used to present additional helpful material related to the subject being described.

Based on his years of teaching experience, the author has placed notes in the margin next to concepts or steps which often cause students difficulty. Each caution box anticipates the student's mistake, and provides methods for avoiding the same problem in the future.

As an experienced network administrator, the author has practical experience of how NT works in real business situations. Tip boxes provide students with suggestions on ways to attack problems they may encounter in a real world situation.

Each hands-on activity in this book is preceded by the hands-on icon and a description of the exercise that follows.

Knowing about trends in the computer industry can help students see the current and future value of the concepts and techniques that they are learning in the chapter. Trend boxes provide students with information about relevant trends in the computer industry.

Features

To ensure that students comprehend the concepts discussed in this book and how they are applied in real business organizations, this text incorporates the following features:

Extensive illustrations that reflect real-life examples. To help students more fully understand the material being explained, each chapter contains numerous illustrations that reflect situations students might encounter in a real-life situation.

Chapter Objectives. Each chapter begins with a detailed list of objectives that allow students to see at a glance what topics will be covered in the chapter. The objectives lists also provide students with a useful review and study aid.

Summary of Windows Functions. Reflecting the author's commitment to helping students gain a comprehensive knowledge of the subject matter, following each chapter is a summary that recaps the topics learned in the chapter.

Key Concepts Summary. Throughout each chapter key terms are clearly introduced in bold type and defined when they are first used. At the end of each chapter, a Key Term Review List provides students with a useful review and study tool of the terms explained in the chapter.

Review Exercises. To help students assess their comprehension of the material, each chapter concludes with a series of questions that ask them to apply the material in a real life situation. Instructors have the flexibility to ask students to submit their answers for grading.

Hands-On Exercises. Each chapter concludes with a hands-on project that reflects the skills learned within that chapter. Through these end of chapter hands-on assignments, students practice building a server from the ground up and gain valuable practical experience.

The Supplements

All of the Supplements available with this book are provided to the instructor on a single CD-ROM.

Instructor's Manual.   The Instructor's Manual that accompanies this textbook was written by the author and has been quality-assurance tested. It includes:

- Additional instructional material to help for class preparation including suggestions for lecture topics and suggested lab activities

- PowerPoint Slides for classroom presentations, including HP OpenView to view the slides without PowerPoint Software, which are referenced in the proposed lecture topics

- Solutions to all end of chapter materials including the Project assignments

Course Test Manager 1.1.   Accompanying this book is a powerful assessment tool known as the Course Test Manager. Designed by Course Technology, this cutting-edge Windows-based testing software helps instructors design and administer tests and pre-tests. In addition to being able to generate tests that can be printed and administered, this full-featured program also has an online testing component that allows students to take tests at the computer and have their exams automatically graded.

Acknowledgments

Sharing ideas through writing is exciting and exacting work. So also is the field of computer science, where file server technology has grown from a questionable notion to a solid reality. It is a pleasure to participate in the growth of this field and watch new ideas come alive. This book is intended as a building block for students sharing in the growth and making their own contribution.

Many people have contributed to make the book possible and to whom I want to express a deep and heartfelt thanks. Wendy Welch Gordon, managing editor at Course Technology, has provided much support and encouragement. Cindy Brown has played a vital role as developmental editor, bringing cohesiveness and clarity to this book. She also is a remarkable adviser and technical reviewer. Richard Keaveny of Course Technology is a catalyst who plays a large role in making projects succeed. Nancy Shea and Susan Roche of Course Technology deserve many thanks for their editorial and production work on both the book and supplementary materials. I also wish to thank Patty Stephan, Tracy Wells, Susannah Lean, Lyle Korytkowski, Greg Bigelow, and Doug Goodman of Course Technology for their work on the project.

Special thanks go to the technical reviewers of this book who are Robert Bruce Sinclair of the University of Wyoming, Floyd Winters of Manatee Community College, and Nick Symiakakis. They have carefully read the chapters, checked for accuracy, and provided many excellent suggestions to improve the presentation. I truly appreciate their comments and ideas which I believe have enriched the book.

Dedication

To my children Kristy and Shawn who are a great source of joy; and to my wife Sally and parents Ed and Helen Palmer for their encouragement past and present.

TABLE OF CONTENTS

HANDS-ON
MICROSOFT WINDOWS NT 4.0
SERVER WITH PROJECTS

READ THIS BEFORE YOU BEGIN

To the Student

This book comes with an NT Server installation simulator, available from your instructor that enables you to practice the installation steps from any computer with Windows 3.1 or higher. Each chapter in the book ends with review questions and hands–on assignments for a project. When you complete the hands-on projects you can submit them on separate pages, the assignment pages at the end of each chapter, or by way of electronic file. The Student Work Disk contains a Microsoft Word file for each end of chapter project. You can record your answers in the space provided within the file and submit them to your instructor by disk, through the network, or through e-mail.

To the Instructor (Please refer to the Instructor's Resource Kit that accompanies this text for more details.)

Setting up the classroom or lab file server. To complete the assignments in the book, the students will need access to a file server. To maximize the learning experience, it is recommended that you have a file server which can be dedicated for classroom use. The server need not be an expensive model, but should be on Microsoft's Hardware Compatibility List. Also, it is recommended that you have cards which the students can use to practice installing in the server, such as a network interface card, SCSI adapter, and tape controller card. You will need a copy of Microsoft Windows NT Server 4.0 with enough access licenses for all students and instructors in the class. Each student will need an account on the server with administrator privileges.

Internet assignments. Some project assignments require Internet access for information searches. These assignments are not mandatory, however, the assignments will help train the student in using this resource as a prospective network manager.

Accepting assignments electronically. The project files on the Student Work Disk are in Microsoft Word format. This enables you to accept assignments electronically, if appropriate to your classroom setting. For more details, please refer to the Instructor's Manual.

System Requirements

The recommended software and hardware configurations are as follows:

Workstations

- Windows 3.11 or higher (Windows 95 or Windows NT Workstation are preferred)
- 386 or higher processor with 4 MB of RAM (486 or higher preferred with 8+MB of RAM)
- VGA monitor
- Mouse
- Network interface card cabled to the classroom file server
- Hard disk with 10 MB free
- At least one high density 3.5-inch floppy disk drive
- Internet access and a browser (for selected research assignments)

File Server

- Listed in Microsoft's Hardware Compatibility List
- 32-bit bus computer with an 80486 25 MHz or faster processor
- VGA or better resolution monitor
- Mouse
- High density 3.5-inch floppy disk drive
- CD-ROM drive
- 16 MB or more memory
- One or more hard disks with 500 MB or greater
- Network interface card for network communications
- Tape subsystem (preferred)
- Printer (to practice setting up a network printer)

MICROSOFT WINDOWS NT FILE SERVERS: AN OVERVIEW

Sara Martin has worked for two years as the PC coordinator for Nishida and McGuire, a prosperous law firm with two senior partners, three partners, and two associate attorneys. There are five support staff including Sara. An organizational chart of the office is shown in Figure 1-1.

The firm offers a variety of legal services including criminal law, civil litigation, bankruptcy, wills, estates, federal taxes, real estate, and business law. Management decisions are made by a management group consisting of the two senior partners and the three partners. The support staff are Sara, the office manager, a business administrator, and two paralegals. The office manager coordinates all business functions of the office including the budget, the accounting functions, ordering supplies, and the computer resources. The business administrator directly handles the day-to-day accounting functions such as billing clients, keeping the financial information, and paying the firm's bills. Sara's job is to support all computer resources. The paralegals provide legal assistance to the attorneys, including research, preparing legal forms, scheduling court dates, and performing secretarial functions.

AFTER READING THIS CHAPTER AND COMPLETING THE EXERCISES YOU WILL BE ABLE TO:

- UNDERSTAND MULTI-USER COMPUTING.
- DESCRIBE THE ADVANTAGES OF FILE SERVER COMPUTING AND NETWORKS.
- UNDERSTAND THE CAPABILITIES OF WINDOWS NT SERVER.
- COMPLETE A COMPUTER SOFTWARE AND HARDWARE INVENTORY.
- EXPERIENCE MICROSOFT WINDOWS COMPUTING, SUCH AS HOW TO SHARE A DRIVE, HOW TO MAP A DRIVE, AND HOW TO VIEW COMPUTERS ON THE NETWORK.

A week ago, the firm's senior partners, Anne Nishida and Kent McGuire, met with Sara's manager, Kristin Walters, to discuss how they might expand computer operations. Kristin recommended the firm install a computer network. As office manager, Kristin had already been reading about computer networking and discussing the possibilities with Sara. The senior partners liked the idea of a network and promoted Sara to network administrator. Sara's new responsibilities include laying the groundwork for future networking at Nishida and McGuire.

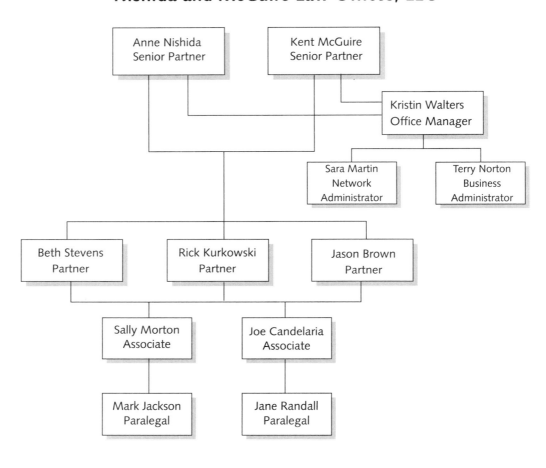

Nishida and McGuire Law Offices, LLC

THE FIRM'S EQUIPMENT

Sara's first assignment as network administrator is to inventory the present equipment and to show how networking will help the firm make better use of their computers.

Each person in the firm has Microsoft Windows on an 80486 or Pentium computer, except for Jason Brown, who has an old 80386 with DOS-based word processing software. Each member of the firm has an ink jet or dot matrix printer. There are two laser printers, one connected to Mark Jackson's computer and one to Jane Randall's.

Whenever someone needs a high-quality printout for legal forms, briefs, or billings, they carry a disk to Mark or Jane to print on one of the laser printers. Jane also has a modem in her computer to access the Internet for legal research.

Sara has decided to perform her inventory using an Excel spreadsheet. She has checked throughout the office and recorded basic information about CPU type, memory, disk storage, and printers (see Table 1-1).

Table 1-1

Nishida and McGuire computer equipment inventory

Owner	CPU	Memory	Disk Storage	Printer	Other Equipment	Operating System
Jason Brown	80386	1 MB	120 MB	Dot matrix	None	DOS 6.2
Rick Kurkowski	80486SX	1 MB	200 MB	Dot matrix	None	Windows 3.1
Kent McGuire	80486SX	4 MB	200 MB	Ink jet	None	Windows 3.1
Joe Candelaria	75 MHz Pentium	8 MB	500 MB	Dot matrix	None	Windows 3.11
Mark Jackson	75 MNz Pentium	8 MB	500 MB	300 dpi laser	None	Windows 3.11
Sara Martin	90 MHz Pentium	16 MB	850 MB	Dot matrix	None	Windows 95
Sally Morton	80486	4 MB	250 MB	Dot matrix	None	Windows 3.1
Terry Norton	90 MHz Pentium	8 MB	1.09 GB	Ink jet	None	Windows 95
Jane Randall	80486	8 MB	200 MB	600 dpi laser	14.4 modem	Windows 3.11
Anne Nishida	100 MHz Pentium	8 MB	1.2 GB	Ink jet	None	Windows 95
Beth Stevens	80486	4 MB	250 MB	Dot matrix	None	Windows 3.11
Kristin Walters	90 MHz Pentium	8 MB	1.2 GB	Ink jet	None	Windows 95

Sara also has inventoried the software that is used on each person's computer. The firm uses word processing, spreadsheet, accounting, and legal forms and legal time accounting software (see Table 1-2).

Table 1-2

Nishida and McGuire computer software inventory

Owner	Word Processing	Spreadsheet	Accounting	Legal Forms	Legal Time Accounting
Jason Brown	WordPerfect	Lotus 1-2-3			
Rick Kurkowski	MS Word	MS Excel			
Kent McGuire	MS Word	MS Excel			
Joe Candelaria	MS Word	MS Excel			
Mark Jackson	MS Word	MS Excel		Wills and Bankruptcy Forms	
Sara Martin	MS Word	MS Excel			
Sally Morton	WordPerfect	Lotus 1-2-3			
Terry Norton	MS Word	MS Excel	Great Plains		Time Accounting
Jane Randall	MS Word	MS Excel		Contracts and Tax Forms	
Anne Nishida	MS Word	MS Excel			
Beth Stevens	MS Word	MS Excel			
Kristin Walters	MS Word	MS Excel			

SHARING RESOURCES

While compiling the equipment inventory, Sara has been thinking of ways to share computer resources. For example, members of the law office frequently walk to other offices to share disk files containing briefs and other information. When someone needs to print on a laser printer, he or she must go to Mark's or Jane's office. Some organizations call this "sneaker-net." A difficulty with sneaker-net is that it creates frequent interruptions. Mark and Jane are often interrupted when someone needs a printout. Sally is interrupted when Rick brings her the latest brief to review on disk. Sneaker-net also makes an organization vulnerable to computer viruses that damage operating systems and files.

Sara realizes a great deal of time would be saved if people could share files from a single computer. Time also would be saved if print files could be sent to the laser printers without taking Jane and Mark away from their work.

Sara recognizes that the law office is potentially a multi-user environment and could benefit by having a central resource computer for sharing files and programs. Several people could log in to the computer at the same time. For example, Rick could make the file containing his brief available for Sally to view at her convenience. Anne could view Terry's accounting information on a client without interrupting Terry in his office.

How File Servers Are Used

Sara's assignment to find out about networking led her to a seminar on networks and sharing computer resources. In the seminar, she learned that the computers in her office could be linked by means of a **computer network**. The network consists of communication cabling similar to telephone wire or the wire used in cable TV. Computers are cabled together and linked to a **file server**.

File servers are single computers that provide multi-user access. Often the server is simply an 80486 or a Pentium computer. The server can allow access for as few as two users or for several hundred users. Figure 1-2 illustrates a multi-user file server.

A **computer network** is a system of cables, communication devices, computers, printers, and software linked to enable the exchange and sharing of information. The exchange of information is made possible by a network operating system, which is software that enables communication and data sharing between computers. Windows NT Server is an example of a network operating system.

A **file server** is a network computer that makes software applications, data files, and network utilities available to other network computers. For example, a file server with the NT Server operating system can make available applications such as Microsoft Word or Word documents. One or more computers, called **workstations** or **clients**, connect to the file server to obtain Microsoft Word, word processing files, and other information.

Figure 1-2

A multiuser
server

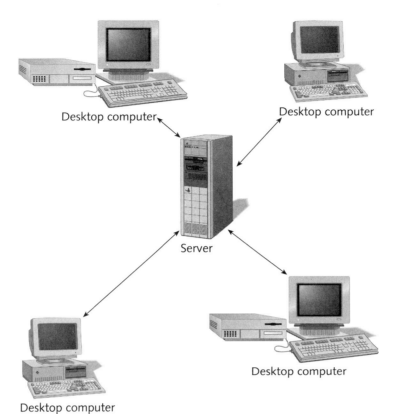

Desktop computer

Desktop computer

Server

Desktop computer

Desktop computer

In the seminar, Sara learned that file servers and networks offer several advantages. For the Nishida and McGuire law offices, these advantages include the following:

- All attorneys can share computer files. For example, Joe may be asked to start a brief for Beth. Once Joe is done, he can put the brief on the file server. When she is ready, Beth can access the brief and add her portion. Later, Kent can look over the brief before Beth submits it to the court.

- The laser printers in Mark's and Jane's offices can be shared by means of the file server. Anyone in the office can print a document on these printers. The printers also can be located away from their offices to prevent interruptions.

- All members of the office can have electronic mail (e-mail) and send messages to other office members through the network and file server. For example, when Beth is ready for Kent to review her brief, she can send him an e-mail message.

- The office can share software applications, such as the time accounting package or word processing. This provides an opportunity to have everyone on the same software (and the benefits of common support for one software package).

- All computers can be backed up more easily. Currently, the office has one tape drive for backups. Once each week, Sara takes the tape drive from office to office to back up each computer. With a network and file server, the backups can be done from one location and regularly scheduled to run from the server. The server can be backed up, too.

- The sharing of computer resources can be arranged to reflect the workgroups within the office. For example, the five managing partners work together to make management decisions and share information. They could belong to a special workgroup for the firm's management.

- The Microsoft Windows users would be able to take better advantage of Windows features such as forming workgroups and managing shared software.

- Sara can save time when installing future software upgrades. For example, if the office decides to implement the latest version of Microsoft Word, Sara will upgrade only the software at the server. Each Word user can upgrade his or her version from the server.

MICROSOFT NT SERVER CAPABILITIES

Sara attended another seminar to learn about the features of Microsoft NT Server 4.0. NT Server was recommended to Sara by another network administrator because it has all the advantages described in the preceding section about multi-user file servers. NT Server has several other capabilities, too:

- It is scalable, which means the server can grow as Sara's office grows. As more applications are run from the server, Sara can purchase more powerful hardware to meet the office needs. NT Server 4.0 can run on servers with 1 to 32 CPUs, depending on the capability of the hardware.

- NT Server uses the Microsoft Windows interface, which makes it intuitive to set up and manage.

- The server can communicate with different types of workstations having different operating systems. The firm's 386, 486, and Pentium computers all will connect to NT Server. Also, the systems used in the office—DOS, Windows 3.1, Windows 3.11 (Windows for Workgroups), and Windows 95—all will communicate with NT Server. Other systems, such as OS/2, Macintosh, and UNIX, can connect, too.

- One file server can handle electronic mail, file sharing, printer sharing, information databases, software applications sharing, and network communications.

- NT Server can be used with other Microsoft Backoffice products. These include Microsoft Mail Server, the Internet Information Server (for Internet communications), System Management Server to help manage user workstations and software applications, and SQL Server for large databases.

- The server setup is performed mainly from one CD-ROM.

- Files can be made secure to ensure only the appropriate people can read sensitive information, such as information about cases, clients, or finances.

- NT servers are reliable. They can be set up with protection to ensure data are not lost should a hard drive fail. Redundant directories and hard drives can be established to prevent loss of data. NT also has file system recovery options. These features are called **fault tolerance**.

Fault tolerance is protection built into a software or hardware system to prevent loss of data or computer services due to problems such as hardware failures and power outages.

- Management of the server can be performed from one location.

- NT Server has many built-in performance monitoring tools to help quickly troubleshoot any problems.

ALTERNATIVE SERVER SYSTEMS

Sara obtained literature on two other systems, Novell NetWare and Digital Equipment Corporation's (DEC) PATHWORKS. Both systems offer networking capabilities such as file and print services, security options, messaging facilities, and Internet services. Sara has concluded that NetWare is closer to meeting the firm's needs than PATHWORKS, because NetWare is designed for large and small PC-based offices. PATHWORKS is particularly suited for organizations already using DEC equipment.

Sara has decided that Windows NT Server meets the firm's needs best because they already use Microsoft products. Members of the office will be able to build on the Windows-based skills they have already.

WINDOWS ENVIRONMENTS

As Sara has learned in her work with computers, the Microsoft Windows environment is a significant advantage over systems without a **graphical user interface (GUI)**. Graphical user interfaces are designed to be easy to learn and use, with pictures and icons as graphical representations of the activities the user wants to perform.

 Graphical user interfaces are designed on the idea that "a picture is worth a thousand words." These interfaces use small pictures, called icons, to represent a computer task that can be performed by clicking the icon with a mouse. GUIs also use a standard set of visual tools such as pull-down menus, toolbars, and check boxes. Some example icons are:

 = open a file; = save to disk; = print; = exit an application.

By contrast, a non-GUI environment like DOS presents the PC user with a command-line prompt and a blank screen. To copy a file from drive C to a floppy disk in drive A, you enter a command such as the following:

```
C:\>copy \apps\work\court.doc a:
```

With Windows 95 or NT, on the other hand, you simply drag the icon representing the file you want to copy to another icon representing drive A. Unlike with DOS, using Windows doesn't require you to remember or to look up commands, or to be skilled as a typist.

Sara also has found that Windows is much easier to support than DOS. For example, the new versions of Windows, such as Windows 95 and Windows NT Workstation, solve the memory limitations of earlier PC operating systems. Windows applications are installed by running a setup program that automatically copies files and system **drivers**. This is much easier than manually copying files and setting up drivers, as in some DOS applications.

 Drivers are files that enable software to communicate with printers, screens (monitors), disk drives, and other computer components.

Basic Windows skills are easy to learn, such as using the menu bar and toolbar, dragging and dropping objects, and so on. Once these skills are mastered, the user can quickly adapt to any new Windows application. The learning curve is reduced because Windows applications are designed with many functions in common. For example, the menu bar in Windows software has common options that appear in a standard order such as File, Edit, View, Window, and Help. Below the menu bar are the icon tools in the toolbar. The icon for printing is a picture of a printer, and the icon to save a file to disk is a picture of a disk. Save and print functions are activated by clicking the appropriate icon.

The toolbar Save and Print buttons work the same way in Microsoft Word, Microsoft Excel, and third-party Windows software such as Lotus 1-2-3. Figure 1-3 illustrates the Microsoft Word menu bar and toolbar.

Figure 1-3

Microsoft Word menu bar and toolbar

Pull-down menus are another intuitive feature of the Windows interface. For example, Figure 1-4 shows a pull-down menu for the Edit option on the menu bar. When a user selects the Edit option with the mouse, a pull-down menu appears.

Figure 1-4

Pull-down menu in Microsoft Word

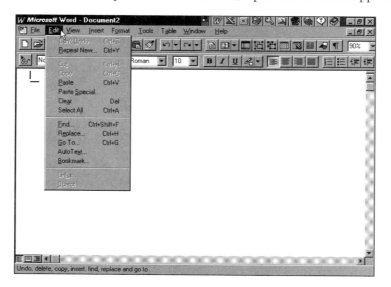

Another Windows GUI feature is the Shortcut bar that comes with Microsoft Office. The Shortcut bar is a series of icon buttons for often-used applications. Notice the Shortcut bar in the top right corner of the screen shown in Figure 1-4. This contains icons for starting Microsoft Word, Excel, PowerPoint, Schedule+, Access, Explorer, Bookshelf, Getting Results Book, Office Compatible, and the Answer Wizard. The shortcut bar can be customized to display any of the most frequently used applications. Its purpose is to save you time in starting an application or when switching between applications.

The Shortcut bar illustrates a critical difference between Windows and DOS environments. With Windows, you can run several applications at the same time, using tools such as the shortcut bar to quickly switch between applications. With DOS, you are limited to running one application at a time.

WEB INTEGRATION

Sara is interested in providing Internet services to her office to enable the lawyers to perform research for cases and to communicate with other lawyers around the country. Eventually, her firm could develop a Web page to describe the legal services they offer. The firm is considering branch offices in two other cities, and a Web site would enable the new offices to access information on the main office server.

Sara likes the option to develop Web services through NT Server. NT Server comes with built-in Web server software called Internet Information Server (IIS). IIS gives Sara the ability to take advantage of **intranet** software as well as **Internet** software.

The **Internet** is a collection of more than 60,000 smaller networks tied together around the globe by a vast array of network equipment and communications links.

An **intranet** is a private network within an organization. It uses the same Web-based software as the Internet but is highly restricted from public access. Intranets are currently used to enable managers to run high-level reports, to enable staff members to update human resources information, and to provide access to other forms of private data.

NT Server has a built-in service called Index Server. This software automatically indexes the content of information created for intranet access within a company. Index information is created for **HyperText Markup Language (HTML)**, text files, or Microsoft Office documents, such as Word. The Index Server enables quick searches for the indexed topics while using low network overhead.

HyperText Markup Language (HTML) is a formatting process used to enable documents and graphics images to be read on the World Wide Web. HTML also provides for fast links to other documents, to graphics, and to Web sites. The World Wide Web is a series of file servers with software, such as IIS, that make HTML and other Web documents available for workstations.

To create Web pages and to help manage Web sites, Sara can use Microsoft's FrontPage, a Web publishing package bundled with NT Server that shares the "look and feel" of Microsoft Office applications.

Microsoft is making a strong commitment to Web development, and many other Windows software vendors are offering companion Web products. For example, Crystal Reports offers products to design reports for intranet and Internet use, and PeopleSoft has introduced Web-based accounting capabilities.

SCALING UPWARD FOR THE FUTURE

The managing partners in the firm want to find a system that can grow as their firm's needs grow. In her seminars, Sara learned that scalability is important because network and file server demand start to grow almost as soon as the equipment and software are installed. People quickly determine new ways to use the systems and want more and more capability.

At Nishida and McGuire, client databases are growing and there's an increasing need for more tracking of financial distributions and obligations. It's likely the firm will develop new databases, such as research databases to track changes in the law and new court decisions.

When the firm opens its branch offices, there will be more lawyers and legal staff to support on the file server. Some of these branch office members will want remote access to the server through telephone lines or through the Internet.

NT Server can be scaled to handle the firm's growth. The operating system can support from 1 to 15,000 user connections. It works on both single-processor and multi-processor computers.

NT Server can handle small and large databases. Microsoft Access is an example of a small database system that works with NT Server. Larger database capabilities are fulfilled by relational database systems such as Microsoft SQL Server, Oracle, and Sybase. A single database on an NT server can hold more than 200 GB of information and have more than 5,000 users accessing it at the same time.

Another area of growth is the need to communicate with a wider range of computers and networks. Microsoft NT communicates with IBM, Novell, UNIX, Banyan, DEC, and other systems. Also, it can be accessed by client computers with any of the following operating systems:

- MS-DOS
- Windows
- Windows for Workgroups
- Windows 95
- Windows NT Workstation
- Macintosh
- UNIX

Sara's research shows that several thousand applications currently work with NT and that new ones are being added regularly. NT Server runs on more than 5,000 different computers.

TOURING NT SERVER

Sara's friend Ryan Young is the network administrator for the law firm Wilson, Morton, and Holt. Ryan's firm has an NT Server network that is a year old. Before the network was installed, Ryan attended an NT Server class. During the past year, he has become a skilled NT Server administrator.

Ryan and Sara met five months ago at a reception held by his firm. They became good friends because they share an interest in computer technology. When Ryan has a question he often calls Sara to consult; Sara does the same with Ryan. As part of her research, Sara asks Ryan to give her a quick tour of the NT Server at his firm.

To start, Ryan shows Sara a list of network computers by clicking the Network Neighborhood icon on his PC desktop (see Figure 1-5). The resulting screen shows all logged on computers for his firm. Each computer has a name that was chosen by the user. Ryan's computer name is TECHIE. The most senior partner in his firm has the computer name BOSS.

Figure 1-5

Windows desktop icons

Next, Ryan clicks the My Computer icon (see Figure 1-5). This shows his connection to the file server, as well as pictorial representations of his A, C, and D drives. The file server is connected to a logical drive called G. When Ryan clicks the file server icon, Sara could see a list of the files and folders on the server. **Folders** are directories that contain files.

Ryan discusses with Sara how easy it is to share folders and their contents with others on the network by using the Sharing option on the File menu. Ryan goes into the Windows Explorer to show Sara another way of viewing folders and files (see Figures 1-6 and 1-7). Using Explorer, he displays the folders on his C drive as well as the connections to the file server, known as mapped drives. Ryan has drive G mapped to the software applications directory on the file server so he can load applications, such as Microsoft Excel. This saves disk space on his computer, since the program files can be loaded into the computer from the file server instead of from his crowded hard drive.

Figure 1-6

The Windows NT Explorer option on the Programs menu

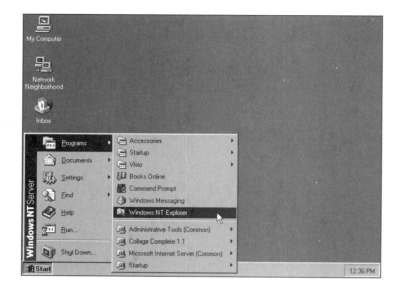

Figure 1-7

The NT Explorer display

From the Windows Explorer screen, Ryan shows Sara how to map a network drive. He clicks the Tools option on the menu bar, displaying a pull-down menu with options to map or disconnect a drive (see Figure 1-8). After selecting the option to map a drive, Ryan selects drive letter H for the new mapping and associates it with the CONTRACTS folder on the file server.

Definition

A **mapped drive** is a disk volume or directory that is shared on the network by a file server or workstation. It gives designated network workstations access to files and data on its shared volume. The workstation, via software, determines a drive letter for the shared volume, which is the workstation's map to the data.

Figure 1-8

Mapping a drive

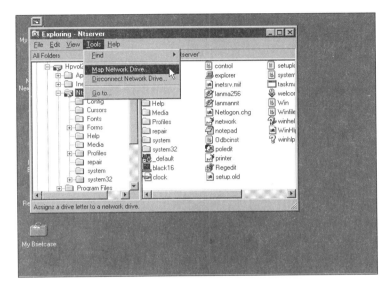

Next, Ryan demonstrates electronic mail. He clicks the Inbox icon to start Microsoft Exchange. On the menu bar, he selects the Compose option and then chooses the New Message option. On the message screen, he enters the destination address, the subject of the message, and the message text. He sends the message to himself by selecting the File option on the menu bar and selecting Send from the pull-down menu. Figure 1-9 shows the message screen Ryan uses.

Figure 1-9

Ryan's Microsoft Exchange test message

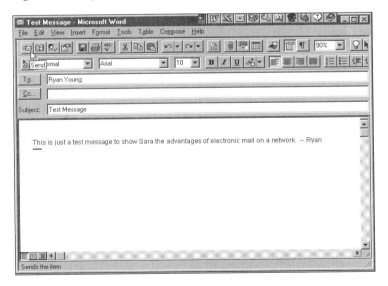

Ryan and Sara wait a few minutes for the sent message to appear in Ryan's electronic Inbox. When the message appears, Sara sees the message header with Ryan's name, the subject of the message, the time it was sent, and the size of the message. Ryan tells Sara to double-click the message header so she can read the message text.

RESULTS OF SARA'S FIRST ASSIGNMENT

When Sara returns to her office, she sends the hardware and software inventory spreadsheets to Kristin. Accompanying the spreadsheets, she sends a memo describing the advantages of networking and NT Server as the network operating system. Sara's memo is shown in Figure 1-10.

Figure 1-10

Sara's memo

INTEROFFICE MEMORANDUM

TO: KRISTIN WALTERS

FROM: SARA MARTIN

SUBJECT: ADVANTAGES OF NETWORKING AND NT SERVER

CC: ANNE NISHIDA AND KENT MCGUIRE

ADVANTAGES OF NETWORKING

Networking solves many problems we have been experiencing with our computer resources. The following is a list of several problem areas we can solve:

- We can have better communication in the office with electronic mail. This will eliminate problems with telephone tag and lost or misplaced messages.

- Several weeks ago Joe Candelaria's hard drive failed. He lost some important files because he did not have a recent backup. Networking enables us to schedule regular backups from one location.

- People will no longer have to spend time going between offices to share files and other information. The files can be put on a network file server for common use, or files can be sent through the mail.

- No one will have to leave his or her office to send a printout to the laser printers. We all can share these printers from the network.

- I can perform many of the PC software maintenance activities from my office, instead of going from computer to computer. This will save me time and I can provide new services to the office much faster.

- Networking will enable us to be ready for a connection to the Internet, improving research and communications.

- Networking also will solve many file sharing and communication problems when our new branch offices are opened.

Figure 1-10

Sara's memo
continued

ADVANTAGES OF NT SERVER

Microsoft Windows NT Server 4.0 is a very powerful network operating system that will work well with the Microsoft products we currently use. I have listed below some of the benefits of Microsoft NT Server:

- As most of the office already uses Microsoft Windows, NT Server will be familiar to us because it is Windows-based.

- As we grow, NT Server will grow with us. We will not have to purchase a different system as we have larger software and hardware needs. This system also will grow with us as we open branch offices.

- We can use all of our existing computers with NT Server.

- The NT Server will work on computer hardware that fits into our budget. We will need only one server to meet our computing goals.

- Most commonly used software packages already run on NT Server.

- NT Server is a tested technology. It has the security and maintenance capabilities we need for our office.

- Web server and Web building software are included with the operating system.

- We can set up and manage the NT Server software ourselves, using our existing office personnel.

Kristin is impressed by Sara's research but wants to know more about what type of network should be installed. Kristin also wants to present some installation cost estimates to the senior partners. She asks Sara to outline the networking options and to prepare a list of costs.

In Chapter 2 you will follow Sara as she explores the different types of networks and networking costs.

KEY CONCEPTS SUMMARY

This chapter includes many introductory key concepts that are used throughout the text. The following is a summary of these concepts.

client   This type of computer logs into another computer, such as a file server, to obtain software applications, files, and data.

computer network   Computers can be linked to one another by attaching them to communication cabling and providing a means for them to communicate with one another to trade information. When this happens, they compose a computer network.

drivers   Computers are able to communicate with devices like printers, monitors, and hard disk drives through files called drivers.

fault tolerance   Redundant software or hardware that reduces loss of data and computer services due to a system or hardware failure.

file server   A network computer that provides other computers access to files, software applications, and data.

Graphical User Interface (GUI)   A GUI workstation environment uses mouse systems, icons, and graphics to run computer operations.

Hypertext Markup Language (HTML)   HTML is a text formatting process that enables text and graphics to be read on the World Wide Web.

Internet   A global network of thousands of smaller networks and computers connected by an array of communications equipment.

intranet   A private network that uses the same software and communication interfaces as those available on the Internet.

multi-user   A multi-user operating system permits two or more people access at the same time. Microsoft's NT Server and Novell's NetWare are two examples of multi-user network operating systems.

workstation   Workstations are systems that have a CPU and provide a range of software to a user for a complete working environment. The software may reside on the workstation or it may be obtained, along with other files, from a file server or other host system.

SUMMARY OF WINDOWS FUNCTIONS

Several Windows functions and menu options have been presented in this chapter. These are summarized in the paragraphs that follow.

folder   In Windows 95 and Windows NT 4.0, Microsoft introduces the folders concept. Folders were formerly called directories, such as in the File Manager in Windows for Workgroups. A folder is represented in My Computer or the Explorer as a graphical picture of a file folder. Just as a real file folder might hold several documents, a Microsoft folder can store several files.

mapped drive This type of drive is not in the computer physically. It is a drive that is shared on the network. By using the Explorer, you can map a drive so your computer treats that drive similarly to one of its own drives. A drive letter is assigned to the mapped drive so you have a way to reference the drive.

menu bar This is a common feature in Windows software. The menu bar is at the top of the screen display and contains a series of pull-down menus. Common pull-down menus are File, Edit, View, Window, and Help. For example, options to open, save, or exit your work are offered on the File pull-down menu.

Microsoft Exchange This software enables you to send and receive electronic mail across a local area network or through the Internet. You can attach a file, such as a word processing or spreadsheet file, to send along with your message. Objects such as a picture, a voice message, or a blueprint can be attached as well.

My Computer You can view all your mapped drives, the Microsoft Control Panel (discussed in Chapter 2), and information about printers from this icon. The icon usually appears on the left side of the screen in Windows 95 and Windows NT 4.0. If you click one of these icons, you will "drill down" to more information, such as the list of folders and files on drive C.

Network Neighborhood You click this icon to display all the logged on computers in a network. If a computer has a shared folder, you can click the icon for that computer and the shared information is available for you to view. If you have been granted access by the owner of the folder, you can run software, view files, and even copy files from the shared folder.

pull-down or drop-down menu This kind of menu is offered on the menu bar. When you click a menu bar selection, such as File, a menu of options drops down vertically. You can select any of the options by clicking the specific option.

Windows Explorer This option is on the Windows 95 and Windows NT 4.0 Start menu. You use the Explorer to see the folders and files on your computer's A, C, and other local drives, including the CD-ROM drive. You can also use the Explorer to see the folders and files on network drives you have mapped to your computer. The following general housekeeping functions are available from the Explorer:

- Create folders.
- Copy, move, and delete folders or files.
- Create shortcuts for accessing software.
- Start programs.
- View files.
- Find files.
- Associate an application with a file.
- Map or disconnect a drive.

REVIEW QUESTIONS

1. What is scalability? Why is it important?

2. Which of the following is not an advantage of using a network?

   a. Electronic mail

   b. Sharing files

   c. Mapping drives

   d. Managing memory on your computer

3. Only 80486 or Pentium computers can connect to NT Server.

   a. True

   b. False

4. What type of drive on your computer is a network drive?

   a. Drive A

   b. A mapped drive

   c. A CD-ROM drive

   d. The main drive

5. A _____ menu is obtained from a menu bar selection in Windows.

   a. Pull-down

   b. Virtual

   c. Inbox

   d. Realistic

6. Which of the following can be inserted into a Microsoft Exchange message?

   a. A picture

   b. A text file

   c. A spreadsheet

   d. All of the above

7. What would you use to view files in Windows?

   a. My Computer

   b. File displayer

   c. Explorer

   d. Both a and c

8. Personal computers can be backed up through a network.

   a. True

   b. False

9. What tools and software come with Windows NT for Internet and intranet applications?

10. What would you use to map a drive in Windows?

    a. Explorer

    b. Exchange

    c. Inbox

    d. Mapper

11. NT Server's file recovery capability is an example of

    a. File rollback.

    b. Backup technology.

    c. Fault tolerance.

    d. All of the above.

12. File servers are an example of a _____ system.

    a. Multi-user

    b. Multimedia

    c. Single-user

    d. Hard-drive

13. Windows applications are installed using

    a. Setup.exe.

    b. Install.bat.

    c. Begin.com.

    d. Win.ini.

14. Which of the following is an example of a database that will work with NT Server?

    a. Microsoft SQL Server

    b. Access

    c. Oracle

    d. All of the above

15. Which of the following enables Windows to communicate with a printer?

    a. An install

    b. An initialization file

    c. A font

    d. A driver

16. Which of the following operating systems can connect to NT Server?

    a. UNIX

    b. Windows 95

    c. Macintosh

    d. All of the above

17.   Which of the following contains files in a Windows system?

a.   A folder

b.   A partitioned data set

c.   A display icon

d.   An account

THE HOLLAND COLLEGE
PROJECT: PHASE 1

Holland College is a liberal arts college with 2,200 students. You have recently been hired as the new PC coordinator reporting to the director of information systems, Bob Watson. The college has two computer labs, but neither one is networked. The math and science lab has 22 computers: ten 80386 computers each with 4 MB of memory and twelve 80486 computers with 8 MB of memory each. The 80386 computers have 120 MB of hard disk space and the 80486 computers each have 250 MB. The English and writing lab has 35 computers. This relatively new lab is equipped with 24 Pentium computers with 16 MB of memory and 1.2 GB of hard disk storage. The lab also has eleven 80486 computers with 8 MB of memory and 500 MB hard disks. One year ago the college made a decision to standardize on Windows. The 80386 computers are using Windows for Workgroups. The 80486 and the Pentium computers are running Windows 95.

The computers in the math and science lab have Microsoft Word, Microsoft Excel, Microsoft Access, MathCAD, AutoCAD, SAS (for statistics), a C++ compiler, and Visual Basic. The computers in the English and writing lab have Microsoft Office (Word, Excel, Access, and PowerPoint), Lotus 1-2-3 for Windows, and WordPerfect for Windows.

The administrative offices are equipped with standalone PCs that were purchased by the vice president of administration, Reuben Asimow (see the Holland College organizational chart in Figure 1-11). The managers under Reuben each have Pentium computers with 16 MB of memory and 1.08 GB of hard disk space. Janice McKinney (Payroll) and Ryan McKim (Budget) have 80486 computers with 16 MB of memory and 550 MB hard disks. Dave Whitefeather (GL/AP) and Randy Thomas (Accounts Receivable) have Pentium computers with 8 MB of memory and 1.2 GB hard disks. Each of these computers is equipped with Microsoft Office and Windows 95.

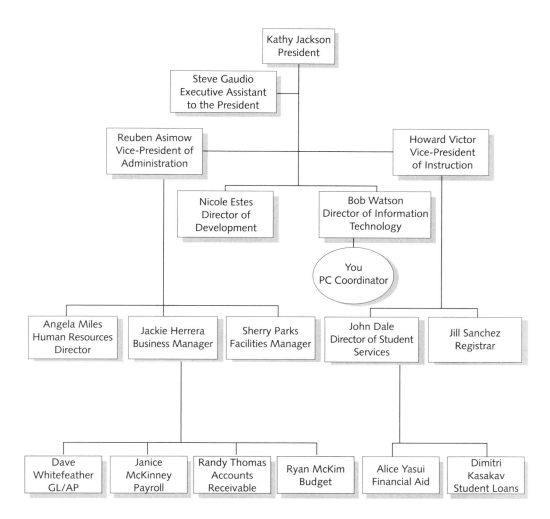

Figure 1-11

Holland College organizational structure

Howard Victor is the vice–president of instruction. He has purchased Pentium computers for his administrative staff members, John Dale (Student Services), Jill Sanchez (Registrar), Alice Yasui (Financial Aid), and Dimitri Kasakav (Student Loans). Their Pentium computers have 16 MB of memory and 2 GB hard disks. Howard also has a Pentium computer with 32 MB of memory and a 2 GB hard disk. These computers have Microsoft Office and Windows 95. Further, Alice Yasui and Dimitri Kasakav use PC-based financial aid packages.

The development director, Nicole Estes, has an 80486 computer with 16 MB of memory and a 250 GB hard disk. Nicole uses Microsoft Office and Windows 95.

Steve Gaudio, the executive assistant to the president, has an 80486 computer with 16 MB of memory and a 250 GB hard disk. The president, Kathy Jackson, has a Pentium computer with 32 MB of memory and a 2 GB hard disk. Steve and Kathy use Microsoft Office and Windows 95. Steve also keeps a FoxPro database with information about the college's board of trustees and influential alums.

The PCs in your office area are Pentiums. Bob Watson has 32 MB of memory on his and you have 16 MB, and you each have 2 GB of hard disk storage. Both of you have Microsoft Office, Windows 95, and the C++ compiler.

Administrative computing is handled by a DEC VAX computer with direct lines into the computer from each office. Also, the VAX is home to a foundation and development software package used by Nicole Estes. Each administrative computer user has a VT terminal emulator, ProVT, to make his or her PC act as a terminal for access to the DEC VAX.

The college also has a Sequent computer for academic use. Lines to the Sequent computer go into the computers in the labs. The labs use the same VT terminal emulator as the administrative offices.

President Jackson is very interested in having e-mail on campus for all faculty, staff, and students. She also wants to have a Web page for the college to help attract students. Kathy knows there are advantages to having a network but would like to know more. She has asked Bob Watson to have you investigate networking for the campus. She would like to begin preparing a recommendation for the board of trustees.

 ## ASSIGNMENT 1-1

Describe how a network would benefit the following groups:

- The management team of Kathy Jackson, Reuben Asimow, Howard Victor, and Nicole Estes

- The midlevel management group of Angela Miles, Jackie Herrera, Sherry Parks, John Dale, Jill Sanchez, and Bob Watson

- The Business Office under Jackie Herrera

- The students and faculty who use the labs

- The registrar

- You, as the PC coordinator

 ## ASSIGNMENT 1-2

Perform an inventory of PCs on campus. Create three spreadsheets showing the owner (user), CPU, amount of memory, amount of hard disk space, and operating system. Complete one spreadsheet for the math and science lab, one for the English and writing lab, and one for the administrative offices.

Inventory of Administrative User PCs

Owner	CPU	Memory	Hard Disk Space	Operating System

Inventory of PCs in the Math and Science Lab

CPU	Memory	Hard Disk Space	Operating System

Inventory of PCs in the English and Writing Lab

CPU	Memory	Hard Disk Space	Operating System

ASSIGNMENT 1-3

Create an inventory of the software used. Because the campus has standardized software, record in the spreadsheet below the name of each software package and the locations where it is used.

Software Package	Location of Use

ASSIGNMENT 1-4

Document why Microsoft Windows NT Server would be appropriate for Holland College. How would this software help students? How would it help the faculty? How would it help the staff?

 ### ASSIGNMENT 1-5

Describe the benefits of e-mail for Holland College. How would Internet access benefit the college?

 ### ASSIGNMENT 1-6

Use e-mail to contact an NT Server user or administrator at another college. How has the presence of a file server helped that college? Is the college experiencing any growth problems on its network? (If you know of a business that uses NT Server you may contact them instead.)

 ### ASSIGNMENT 1-7

Access the Internet and investigate two or three college or university Web pages. Describe one of the Web pages. In your opinion, how does the existence of Web pages help these colleges?

 ### ASSIGNMENT 1-8

If today you were asked to install a portion of a network on the Holland College campus, describe what area should be networked first. Base your recommendation on which area would have the most immediate benefit. Also describe why this area should be the first to be networked.

LAN CONFIGURATIONS AND PROTOCOLS

After taking the brief tour provided by Ryan, Sara is ready to work more with Windows NT Server 4.0. She foresees applications that will help make the attorneys and office staff more productive. Right now, there is a great need for file and printer sharing, NT security, and electronic mail. She also wants to use mapped drives as a way to share information. The NT Explorer interface with My Computer, the Network Neighborhood, and the Inbox has the advantage of being familiar to Sara because it is similar to the Windows 95 Explorer interface she uses now.

Sara needs to learn more about networking before she can create a budget for the installation of her own network. She needs to investigate several areas such as cabling, how to connect equipment to a network, and how to design a network, as well as understanding how data are sent on the network. Sara's boss, Kristin, wants Sara to obtain more network experience, and with Kristin's encouragement, Sara has enrolled in a three-day networking outreach class for computer professionals offered by the local community college.

The first day of class covers networking basics such as local area networks, wide area networks, and network cabling. The second and third days of class cover topics such as network communications and basic network design.

AFTER READING THIS CHAPTER AND COMPLETING THE EXERCISES YOU WILL BE ABLE TO:

- UNDERSTAND THE COMPONENTS OF A LAN.
- DESCRIBE THE DIFFERENCE BETWEEN COAXIAL AND TWISTED-PAIR CABLING.
- COMPREHEND THE USE OF ETHERNET AND TOKEN RING NETWORKS.
- UNDERSTAND NETWORK TOPOLOGIES.
- LIST THE BASIC DESIGN PRINCIPLES OF NETWORKING.
- BUDGET FOR AND DETERMINE THE COST OF A NETWORK.
- SET UP NETWORK COMMUNICATIONS IN WINDOWS.

LANS EXPLAINED

In the networking class, Sara learns about **Local Area Networks (LANs)**. She understands that a LAN is a network within a small area such as an office, a building floor, or throughout a building. LANs connected throughout large regions form **Wide Area Networks (WANs)**. Some examples of WANs are corporate LANs connected between cities, college networks that connect satellite campuses, and the Internet.

LANs have the following three basic components:

- Workstations
- A network operating system
- Cabling

As mentioned in Chapter 1, workstations are the personal computers linked by the network. In Sara's law firm, these computers are listed in the inventory from Table 1-1. Sara's network will have 12 workstations.

The **network operating system** is the software that enables file servers and workstations to communicate and share resources and files. Sara plans to use Windows NT Server 4.0 as the network operating system for her firm. The file server will consist of NT Server on a networked computer.

The workstations and file servers are physically connected to the LAN by communication **cabling**. The most common type of cable used in a small LAN is twisted-pair. Coaxial cable, though still popular, is generally used in older LANs. Fiber-optic cabling is used primarily to connect computers that demand high-speed access to large files. Sara may consider fiber-optic cabling in the future if her firm later decides to implement high-speed networking. Figure 2-1 shows the three basic network components.

 Network cabling is the communication medium that carries data signals from point to point. Some examples of cabling media are wire, glass fibers, and plastic fibers. Data signals also are transmitted through radio waves, although radio waves are not technically considered cabling.

Figure 2-1

Basic network components

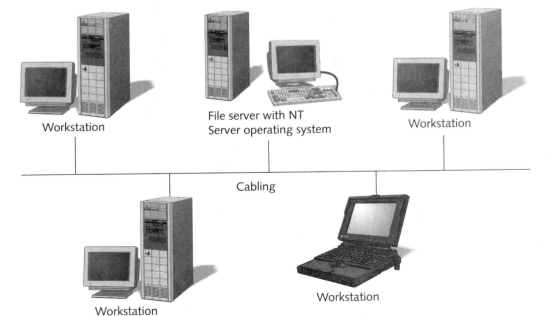

Workstation

File server with NT Server operating system

Workstation

Cabling

Workstation

Workstation

COAXIAL CABLE

Coaxial cabling is similar to television cable. However, unlike with television cable, the electrical characteristics of network cable must be very precise and meet the specifications established by the Institute of Electrical and Electronics Engineers (IEEE). These specifications require cable to have 50 ohms of resistance. Network coaxial cabling is labeled with the notation "RG–58A/U" (Radio Grade 58) to show it is 50-ohm cable. Network administrators call this cable 10BASE2, which means it has a maximum theoretical network speed of 10 megabits per second (10 Mbps), can have wire runs up to 200 meters, and uses baseband-type (BASE) data transmission. Baseband communications means there is only one data communication path per cable, as opposed to broadband communications where there can be several communication paths on one cable. However, these distinctions are becoming blurred as new networking equipment is developed.

Although 10BASE2 cable runs can be up to 200 meters, 185 meters is preferred to allow for extra cabling needs required by network equipment. It is important to carefully follow cable specifications to ensure reliable data communications.

Coaxial cabling has a copper or copper-clad aluminum conductor at the core and an insulating material that surrounds the core. A woven mesh aluminum sleeve wraps around the insulating material and is covered with an outside polyvinyl jacket for insulation. Coaxial cable comes in a variety of colors. Figure 2-2 illustrates coaxial cable.

Figure 2-2

Coaxial cable

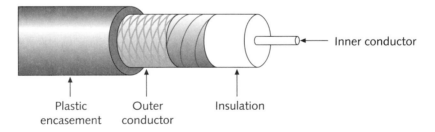

Coaxial cable is attached to computers and network devices by using a T-connector. The bottom of the T is connected to the computer or network device. Sara learns more about terminators and network devices later in the class. For the present, the instructor passes around a T-connector with a terminator (see Figure 2-3) for the class to examine.

Figure 2-3

T-Connector with a terminator

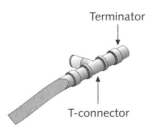

TWISTED-PAIR CABLE

Sara learns that twisted-pair cabling is presently preferred to coaxial. Resembling telephone wire, twisted-pair is more flexible than coaxial cable for running through walls and around corners. If it is attached to the right network equipment, this cable can be adapted for high-speed communications of 100 Mbps. For most applications, the maximum length to extend twisted-pair is 100 meters.

Twisted-pair cabling is connected to network devices with RJ-45 plug-in connectors, which resemble the RJ-11 connectors used on telephones. These connectors are less expensive than T-connectors and less susceptible to damage when moved. They also are easy to connect and allow more flexible cable configurations than coaxial cable.

The two kinds of twisted-pair cable are shielded and unshielded. Unshielded cable is preferred because of its lower cost and reliability. Sara's instructor shows the class twisted–pair cable (shown in Figure 2-4) as he describes the different cabling systems.

Figure 2-4

Twisted-pair cable

Shielded twisted-pair (STP)

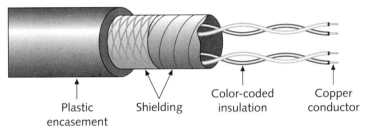

Plastic encasement   Shielding   Color-coded insulation   Copper conductor

Unshielded twisted-pair (UTP)

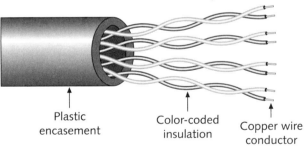

Plastic encasement   Color-coded insulation   Copper wire conductor

SHIELDED TWISTED-PAIR CABLE

Shielded twisted pair (STP) cable consists of pairs of insulated solid wire surrounded by a braided or corrugated shielding. Braided shielding is used for indoor wire and corrugated shielding is used for outside or underground wiring. Shielding reduces interruptions of the communication signal caused by **radio frequency interference (RFI)** or **electromagnetic interference (EMI)**. Twisting the wire pairs also helps reduce RFI and EMI, but not to the same extent as the shield. This type of cabling is used in situations where heavy electrical equipment or other strong sources of interference are nearby. The original types of STP, type 1 and type 2, transmit at the relatively low speed of 4 Mbps. Type 2 cable is a combination of shielded and unshielded pairs and is used mainly indoors. Newer STP cabling is used in high-speed networks.

Radio frequency interference (RFI) is electrical "noise" or the interruption of a signal due to radio waves emitted by a television, computer monitor, or other electrical device. **Electromagnetic interference (EMI)** is caused by magnetic fields created by power sources and circuits in electrical devices.

UNSHIELDED TWISTED-PAIR CABLE

Unshielded twisted-pair (UTP) cable is the most frequently used network cabling because of its low cost and relatively easy installation. UTP is telephone wire consisting of wire pairs within an insulated outside covering. As with STP, each inside strand is twisted with another strand to help reduce interference to the data-carrying signal. The individual strands are insulated, but there is no shielding surrounding the bundle of strands. An electrical device called a media filter is built into the workstation and file server connections to reduce EMI and RFI.

UTP is popularly called 10BASET cable, which means it has a transmission rate of 10 Mbps, uses baseband communications, and is twisted-pair. This version of UTP is also called type 3 cable. Type 4 UTP has a transmission rate of 16 Mbps and type 5 has a 100-Mbps transmission rate. Table 2-1 shows the most frequently used twisted-pair cable types as specified by the IEEE.

Table 2-1

Twisted-pair
cable types

Twisted-Pair Type	Shielding	Transmission Rate
1	Shielded	4 Mbps
2	Combination	4 Mbps
3	Unshielded	10 Mbps
4	Unshielded	16 Mbps
5	Unshielded	100 Mbps

NETWORK INTERFACE CARD

The device used to connect a workstation, file server, or other network equipment to the cable is called a **network interface card (NIC)**. The NIC contains a transmitter/receiver, or **transceiver**, for sending and receiving data signals on the cable. Each NIC comes with a set of software drivers to encode and decode the data so they are readable by the workstation or file server. NICs also have built-in memory chips to provide temporary storage while the data are waiting to be transmitted or to be sent to the station's CPU for processing.

Computers on Ethernet networks use NICs designed for coaxial, twisted-pair, or fiber-optic cable. Some NICs come with adapters for both coaxial and twisted-pair cable (see Chapter 3 for more information on NICs). Many vendors sell computers with the NIC already installed, for college and business customers. Figure 2-5 on the next page shows examples of Ethernet NICs.

Figure 2-5

3COM'S
EtherLink XL
PCI network
interface cards

ETHERNET LAN COMMUNICATIONS

Sara is learning about several methods of LAN communication. The method used most is called **Ethernet**. This method divides data into small increments called **packets**. When a workstation or a file server wants to send information on the network, it sends the information in a series of packets.

A **packet** is a carrier signal that contains a data unit formatted to be sent along the network communication cable.

Ethernet communications are known as Carrier Sense Multiple Access with Collision Detection (CSMA/CD). This means that each computer listens for the data carrier signal on the cable before it sends. Only one workstation or file server can send information at one time. For example, if Sara, Beth Stevens, Jason Brown, and Rick Kurkowski have their computers connected on a small network with a file server, only one computer can send information at a time.

If Beth wants to obtain a Word contract file from the server, her computer will first check the network cable to determine whether any other computer is sending information. If no computer is sending, then Beth's computer is clear to go ahead. Every computer has an equal opportunity to send data as long as the cable is not busy. If Beth's computer should start transmitting at the same time as another computer, then a packet "collision" occurs on the cable. Both computers will sense the collision and stop sending. Each computer waits a different amount of time before again checking the cable for traffic. Like a customer who is given a number for his or her turn at the post office, the computer with the shortest wait time has the first opportunity to send its message. Figure 2-6 shows an example where Beth's computer is sending, while the other computers are in wait states.

Figure 2-6

Beth's
computer
sending on an
Ethernet
network

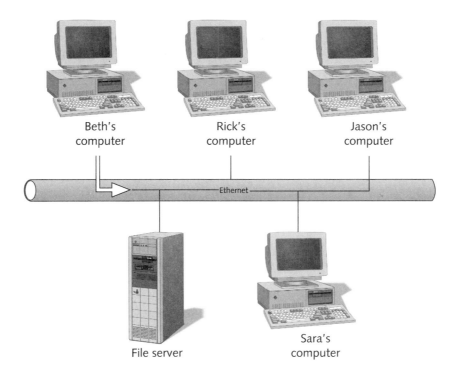

Beth's computer Rick's computer Jason's computer

Ethernet

File server Sara's computer

In class, Sara asks how packets get to the right place on the network. The instructor explains that network computers have addresses just like houses on a city block. A letter carrier is able to deliver the mail because each letter contains an address that corresponds to a specific house. Similarly, each computer has a network interface card with a unique address burned into a computer chip (see Figure 2-7 on the next page) by the manufacturer. When a packet is constructed, the packet contains the address of the sending computer and the address of the destination computer. The packet travels the length of the network until it is received by the destination computer. Every computer on the network, unless it's turned off, is constantly monitoring to see whether a packet is addressed to it. When a packet is received, an acknowledgment is sent to the originating computer. The acknowledgment is like the notice a postal customer receives to verify successful delivery of a registered letter.

Figure 2-7

Network
computers with
unique
addresses

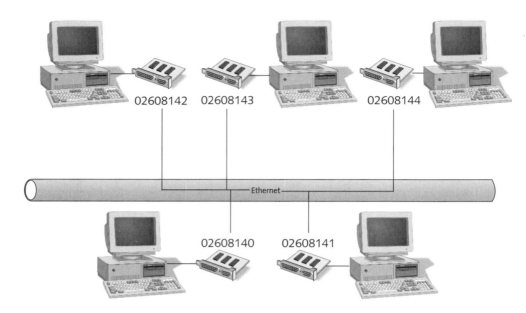

02608142   02608143   02608144

Ethernet

02608140   02608141

If there is no receipt acknowledgment, the packet is sent again after a designated period of time. If there is still no acknowledgment, a message will appear on the sending computer to communicate the problem. For example, if the destination computer is called LAW1, then the message might be, "LAW1 is not responding."

Standard Ethernet communications are at 10 Mbps and use coaxial or UTP cable. Newer high-speed Ethernet communications are called fast Ethernet, with a transmission speed of 100 Mbps.

 Don't expect Ethernet communications to occur at the maximum speed. The true speed is lower due to collisions and wait times after collisions.

TOKEN RING LAN COMMUNICATIONS

Token ring communications are an alternate way to send data on a network. The token ring method involves passing a token around to each network station. If a station has the token, that station can send data to the network. The token is passed from station to station until one station holds the token and starts transmitting. No other station can transmit until the station with the token is finished and places the token back on the network.

Token ring requires the use of a **multistation access unit (MAU)** for communications. The MAU is a central hub that ensures the token is passed from station to station. The first token ring networks transmitted data at 4 Mbps. Improvements in token ring technology have resulted in transmission speeds of 16 Mbps.

 A **multistation access unit (MAU)** transfers tokens and data packets from station to station on a token ring network. All token ring workstations and file servers must connect to an MAU, which amplifies the data signal and ensures that the signal reaches the destination.

In the early stages of networking, token ring communications were more reliable than Ethernet. Ethernet communications were subject to excessive collisions and difficulties in locating network problems. The absence of data collisions in the token passing method, and the physical design of token ring networks have made them very reliable.

Today, modern design techniques and advances in Ethernet technology have made Ethernet popular among network administrators. Ethernet networks are used extensively because they can be upgraded for fast Ethernet as network demand grows.

THE DESIGN OF NETWORKS

Sara's instructor explains three ways to design networks: bus, ring, and star. Each design method, or **topology**, affects how network cable is run through a building and the transmission path for the data. A topology has physical and logical characteristics. The physical side consists of the cabling layout, sometimes called the cable plant. The layout may be decentralized, with cable running between each station on the network, or the layout may be centralized, with each station physically connected to a central device such as an MAU. Centralized layouts are like a star with individual fingers reaching out to each network station. Decentralized layouts resemble mountain climbers, each at a different location on the mountain but all joined by a long rope.

The logical side of a topology involves how the signal travels along the network. For example, a token ring signal logically travels around the network in a ring-like fashion and therefore qualifies as a logical ring topology. However, because it requires an MAU to transmit the signal around the ring to each station, it also has a centralized physical star layout.

Usually **topology** is defined as the physical cable layout of a network. However, it is important to recognize the logical characteristic of a topology, which consists of the signal path along the network.

The instructor mentions that the physical star topology is preferred over the others because it uses twisted-pair cable and is easiest to troubleshoot.

BUS TOPOLOGY

The bus topology consists of running cable from one PC or file server to the next, similar to a city bus route. A city bus has a starting point and an ending point on its route, and along the way it visits each possible pick-up station.

In a bus topology, a 50-ohm terminator is connected to each end of a bus cable segment. Like the city bus, a data packet stops at each station on the line. Also like the city bus, a packet has a given amount of time to reach its destination, or it is considered late.

The terminator is critical on bus networks because it signals the physical end to the segment. Without a terminator, a segment violates IEEE specifications and signals are unreliable.

A bus network segment must be within IEEE length specifications to ensure packets arrive in the expected time. For Ethernet communications, the maximum cable length for RG-58A/U wire is 200 meters. Figure 2-8 shows an Ethernet bus network.

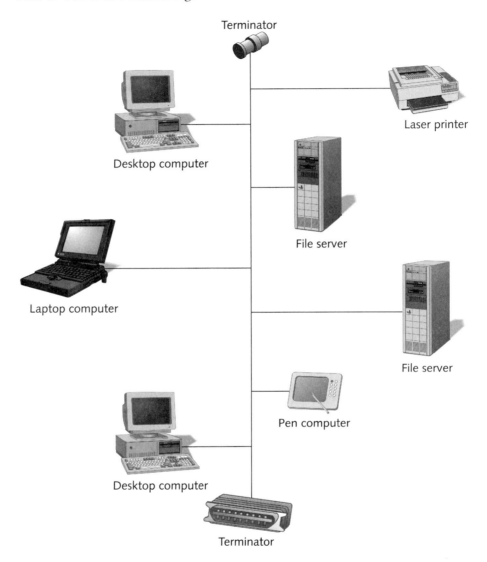

RING TOPOLOGY

The ring topology is a continuous path for data with no logical beginning or ending point. Workstations and file servers are attached to the cable at points around the ring (see Figure 2-9). When data are transmitted onto the ring, they go from station to station until the destination is reached. Because the destination may be reached before the data have gone full circle, the data often do not pass through all stations.

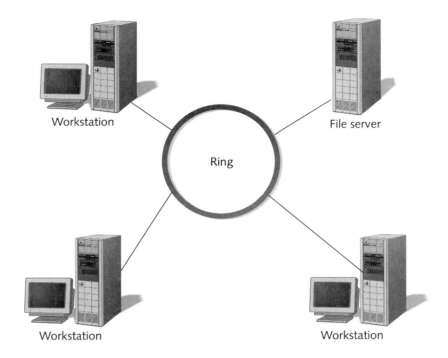

Figure 2-9

Ring topology

Workstation

File server

Ring

Workstation

Workstation

STAR TOPOLOGY

The star topology is in the shape of a physical star. This is the oldest communications design method, with its roots in telephone switching systems. Although it is the oldest design method, advances in network technology have made the star topology a good option for modern networks. The star topology is used in both Ethernet and token ring networks.

On Ethernet networks, the center of the star is an intelligent concentrator or hub. A concentrator links each star segment into a logical bus network. A hub performs the same function but can have several add-on modules for different types of networks, such as to link a token ring network with an Ethernet network. Hubs also may have modules to link individual LANs, such as LANs on different floors or in different buildings. For example, a router module in a hub can join LAN A and LAN B. The router module also can be used to determine which packets from LAN A are allowed to reach LAN B and vice versa.

Each branch of the star topology is a separate segment that can link one or more network stations to the network. Workstations and file servers are connected to the concentrator or hub by communication cable. Termination of each star segment is handled within the concentrator or hub. Figure 2-10 shows the Ethernet star topology with network stations connected to a concentrator.

Figure 2-10

Ethernet star topology with a concentrator

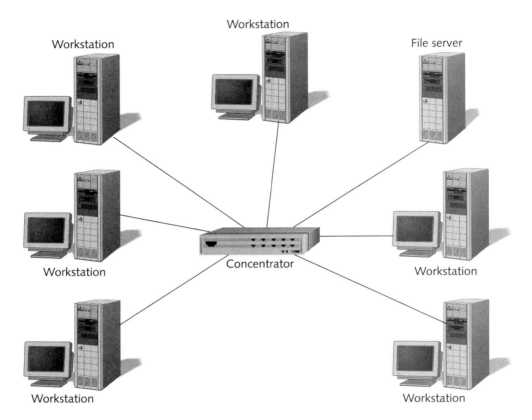

Figure 2-10 Ethernet star topology with a concentrator

Due to the use of MAUs, token ring networks are physically designed in a star fashion. Each workstation or file server is connected to a central MAU. The MAU sends data from station to station, making the data move in a logical ring fashion. The ring-like path is made possible because individual segments are not terminated inside the MAU. Figure 2-11 illustrates a star topology used for a token ring network.

Figure 2-11

Token ring star
configuration
with an MAU

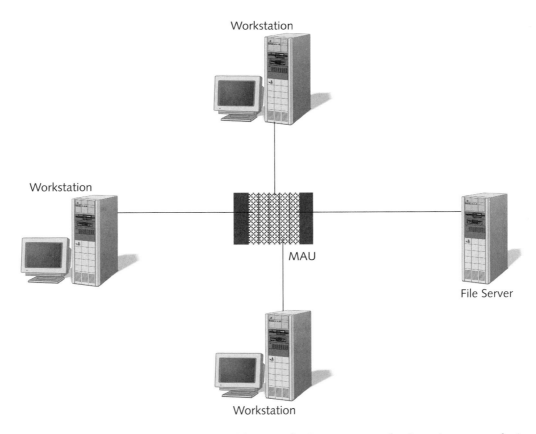

Sara comments in class that the physical layout of Ethernet star and token ring networks is the same. The differences are twofold: 1) the type of adapter card used to connect a workstation or file server to the network and 2) the device used at the center of the star (concentrator versus MAU).

ADVANTAGES OF STAR DESIGNS

Now that the class is over, Sara has purchased a modem for her computer and has decided to gain access to the Internet through CompuServe. She is reading the CompuServe networking forums and Internet newsgroups to find out more about which design topology works best. Through these discussion groups she is finding that many new networks are Ethernet instead of token ring. Ethernet is often mentioned as the preferred choice because of the abundance of network equipment options and the expansion options to fast Ethernet.

Also, many of the network administrators said they were using the star topology for new networks. She found the star design is popular because of the advantages of concentrators and UTP wire. For example, concentrators are available with "intelligence" built into the system. The software in the concentrator can be used to monitor the network and report problems to the network administrator's workstation. This software can be used to determine whether a workstation's NIC is malfunctioning and then to turn off the cable segment to that NIC so communication is preserved for the other computers on the network.

The advantage of the Ethernet star design is that identification of a malfunctioning station is easier than with the traditional Ethernet bus design. Once the malfunctioning station is identified, it is easy to isolate the station without affecting other computers on the network.

This is because only one or more computers are attached to a star segment. Sara believes this is better than interrupting all computers on a segment when it is necessary to remove a broken NIC in a station.

NETWORK COSTS

Sara's research via the Internet reveals that the disadvantage of the star design is cost. An Ethernet bus design is less expensive than the star because of the concentrator. A star-based concentrator costs $2,000 to $3,000. This cost is not part of the bus design, because the concentrator is not needed.

Even though the cost is more, Sara decides to recommend the star topology to Kristin Walters. She believes it will prove to be less expensive in the long run. As new developments occur in networking, Sara will have a network ready to take advantage of them. Also, she feels that the problem diagnostics available through the concentrator will save time in locating and troubleshooting problems. The reduced downtime will save the firm money in lost productivity.

To determine the costs of a network installation, Sara researches the following items:

- Amount of UTP cable needed
- Cable installation costs
- The cost of one concentrator
- NIC costs
- The cost of a file server
- The NT Server license cost

She prepares a table of the costs and includes this information in a memo to Kristin. Figure 2-12 is the memo that Sara prepared. She has included the purchase of two extra NICs so she has some spares on hand in case any fail.

Figure 2-12

Sara's
recommendations
to Kristin

INTEROFFICE MEMORANDUM

TO:	KRISTIN WALTERS
FROM:	SARA MARTIN
SUBJECT:	NETWORKING COSTS
CC:	ANNE NISHIDA AND KENT MCGUIRE

LAN DESIGN RECOMMENDATIONS

I have been researching LAN design options and costs in preparation for our LAN installation. The most feasible LAN designs for our needs are an Ethernet bus design or an Ethernet star design. The advantage of the bus design is that the initial installation costs are low. However, with the bus design, network problems can be difficult to find. Lengthy downtime of the entire network would prove to be costly if we have a network problem that takes several hours to locate and fix.

The star design is more expensive in the beginning than the bus. The advantage of the star design is the flexibility of using a concentrator or hub to link all network stations (PCs, file server, and other equipment). Network problems are easier to find on a star network because of the design configuration and because concentrators and hubs have network monitoring capabilities. In the long run, I believe we will save money implementing the star. The savings will come as we reduce computer downtime to a minimum by faster isolation of problems, and because we will be better able to take advantage of network equipment advances in the future.

Along with the star design, I recommend the purchase of unshielded twisted-pair cabling. This cabling is flexible to run through the building and is reliable for network communications. Also, the flexibility of this type of cabling in a star design will mean savings on installation costs.

NETWORKING COSTS

Below I have presented a spreadsheet with the projected networking costs for the firm.

Equipment	Cost per Unit	Amount	Total Cost
Network cable	$.08/ft.	500 ft.	$ 40
Cable installation	$4,500	1 floor	$4,500
Concentrator	$2,895	1	$2,895
Network interface cards	$ 99	15	$1,485
File server hardware	$7,295	1	$7,295
NT Server licensing	$ 140	20 licenses	$2,800
Grand Total			**$19,015**

SETTING UP THE NETWORK

The Nishida and McGuire law offices are located in a 10-story building downtown. The firm occupies the fifth floor of the building. Each person in the firm has his or her own office except Mark Jackson and Jane Randall. Their desks are at the entrance to the firm.

Figure 2-13

Sara's proposed network

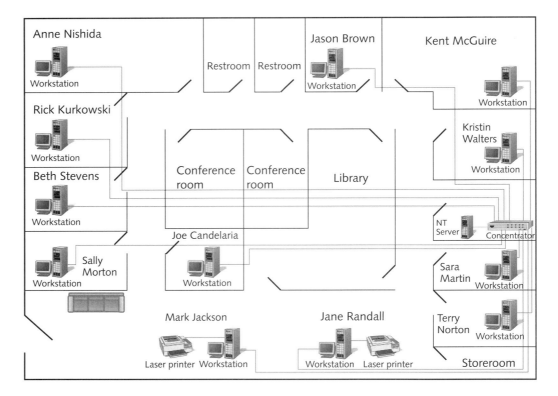

Sara has prepared a drawing of the firm's offices. Figure 2-13 shows Sara's network diagram with the proposed cable runs for each station. It also shows the locations of the file server, the concentrator, and the laser printers.

In designing the network, Sara is concerned about the security of the file server and the concentrator. These are single points of failure on the firm's network. If either piece of equipment is damaged, the entire network will be out of service.

Sara's design places the concentrator and file server in an empty storeroom. This location will help reduce the possibility of damage to either machine, because they will be away from the office traffic.

A lock will be placed on the door so the server and concentrator can be secured to authorized access only. The storeroom will be cleaned and equipped with air conditioning and heating like the rest of the office to give the network computer equipment a clean environment with a constant temperature. The UTP cabling to each office will be **punched down** in the storeroom, making it a wiring closet for the firm.

A **punch down** is a centralized wiring panel located in an area called a wiring closet.

NETWORK PROTOCOLS

In the networking class, Sara learned that data communication on a network is made possible by **protocols**. Protocols are guidelines for communications between computers, similar to a set of rules that govern language. The Internet has made Transmission Control Protocol/Internet Protocol (TCP/IP) the international language of network communications. TCP/IP is really several protocols bundled into one universal protocol. For example, the TCP portion of the protocol establishes a communication session, ensures the session continues successfully, and closes the session when the communication is done. Another portion of the protocol puts the data to be transmitted into small data packages called datagrams. The IP protocol handles network addressing and routing to ensure the data reach the assigned destination.

TCP/IP is used throughout the world on public and commercial networks. Besides rules for transmission of data, this protocol includes application services for transferring files and for sending e-mail. These services are called File Transfer Protocol (FTP) and Simple Mail Transfer Protocol (SMTP).

NETBEUI AND IPX

Microsoft Windows NT Server uses a communications protocol called NetBEUI, which is built on the NetBIOS Extended User Interface. NetBIOS was developed in the early 1980s for simple peer-to-peer communications between computers using MS-DOS. Developed in 1985, NetBEUI was designed from the NetBIOS concept for basic network communications on LAN Manager, an early Microsoft network operating system.

Sara learned in class that NetBEUI has strong positives and negatives. On the positive side it is compatible with millions of computers that use MS-DOS and Windows and works well on small, Microsoft-based networks like the firm's. A negative is that NetBEUI is not well suited for large networks because the protocol cannot be routed. This is a significant problem on a large network, where traffic on certain segments is controlled to reduce packet congestion. It means computers using NetBEUI cannot communicate with computers on network segments where congestion is reduced by routing packets along specific network pathways.

On networks where routing is needed, NT Server can be set up to use TCP/IP or IPX. Both protocols can be routed. IPX is the Internet Packet Exchange protocol. It is based on an earlier protocol developed by the Xerox Corporation called the Xerox Network System (XNS) protocol. Novell developed IPX for use with their network operating system, NetWare.

Sara will soon have an opportunity to set up protocols for workstations and the file server (in Chapters 4 and 5). For now, she knows from Ryan that they are set up from the Control Panel by selecting Start, choosing Settings, and then selecting the Control Panel. As practice,

Sara displays the Control Panel, as shown in Figure 2-14. She clicks the Network icon, which shows two workstations and a printer connected to a small cable.

Figure 2-14

Windows 95
Control Panel
with the
Network icon
selected

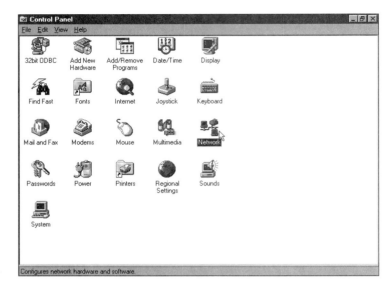

The protocol setup screen appears, as shown in Figure 2-15. Sara is not yet ready to change any settings, so she clicks Cancel on this screen.

Figure 2-15

Protocol setup
screen

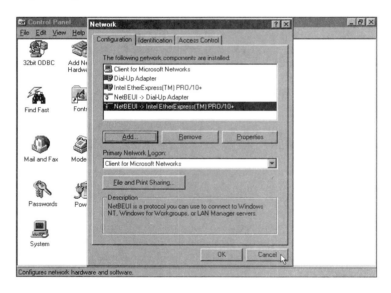

SARA'S NEXT ASSIGNMENT

Kristin reads Sara's memo and studies Sara's proposed cabling scheme for the office. After checking with the senior partners, Kristin asks Sara to contract with a networking company for the cabling installation. Kristin also tells Sara to order the concentrator.

Further, Kristin decides the next step is to look into the requirements for a file server. In Chapter 3, we follow Sara as she makes a file server selection for her firm.

KEY CONCEPTS SUMMARY

The networking concepts introduced in this chapter are summarized in the following list.

cabling Networks are linked by this communication media, which may be wire, glass fiber, or plastic fiber.

electromagnetic interference (EMI) Electrical interference or interruption is caused by magnetic fields such as a power source.

Ethernet This type of network uses carrier sensing and collision detection to determine whether a station can transmit data. Modern networking devices such as concentrators make Ethernet networks easier to maintain and to expand.

Local Area Network (LAN) This type of network links computers, file servers, printers, and other computer equipment in a distinct area, such as within a computer lab, a building floor, or throughout a building. The LAN enables data to be sent to its attached computers.

Multistation Access Unit (MAU) This device is used on token ring networks to connect all stations and transfer the data signal along the network.

network communications equipment This equipment helps link network stations, regulate network traffic, connect separate networks into one, and perform other network functions.

network interface card (NIC) This adapter card enables a workstation or file server to connect to a network and communicate with other network stations.

network operating system This software enables data communications and data exchange on a network, providing the software link between workstations, file servers, and other network components.

packet This network carrier signal contains data formatted to be transmitted over communication cable.

protocols Rules for sending and receiving data on a network. To communicate with one another, two network stations must be using the same protocol.

punch down A centralized wiring panel for communications networks.

radio frequency interference (RFI) This electrical "noise" is created by radio waves from television, computers, and other equipment and it can interrupt electrical transmissions and networks.

token ring This type of network uses a token to determine which network station has authority to transmit data. These networks are tied together by multistation access units.

topology The physical and logical layout of a LAN, such as bus, ring, and star. It affects the performance of the LAN and the future options for expansion.

transceiver This device transmits and receives signals. When used in a network interface card, the transceiver places outgoing data signals on the cable and picks up incoming signals.

Wide Area Network (WAN) Local and regional networks can be linked by network equipment to extend network communications across a campus, across a city, throughout a state or country, and to foreign countries.

SUMMARY OF WINDOWS FUNCTIONS

The Control Panel is a critical function that provides setup capabilities for many Windows services, such as communication protocols. The following is a summary of the Control Panel.

Control Panel This menu is used to set many options in Windows 95 and Windows NT. The network option in Windows enables you to set up communications through protocols, such as NetBEUI, TCP/IP, IPX. It also lets you set up communications with clients, file servers, and printers.

REVIEW QUESTIONS

1. Which of the following protocols is used for Internet communications?

    a. NetBEUI

    b. TCP/IP

    c. IPX

    d. XNS

2. Token ring communication uses _____ to enable data transmissions.

    a. Token passing

    b. CMOS

    c. CSMA/CD

    d. All of the above

3. Which of the following are components of LANs?

    a. Network operating system

    b. Workstations

    c. Cabling

    d. All of the above

4. RG-58A/U is which type of cabling?

    a. Twisted-pair

    b. Fiber-optic

    c. Coaxial

    d. Aluminum clad

5. Which of the following LAN communication methods uses collision detection to determine whether a station can send data?

    a. Token ring

    b. FDDI

     c. Ethernet

     d. Both a and b

6. 10BASE2 communications occur over which type of cable?

     a. Coaxial

     b. Fiber

     c. Twisted-pair

     d. None of the above

7. Which topology is terminated at the ends?

     a. Ethernet Bus

     b. Ring

     c. AT&T StarNet

     d. Token ring

8. How is data transmission rate measured?

     a. In ohms

     b. In amperes

     c. In megabits per second

     d. In nanoseconds

9. Type 3 twisted-pair cable has a data transfer rate of

     a. 4 Mbps.

     b. 10 Mbps.

     c. 22 Mbps.

     d. 100 Mbps.

10. A transceiver is used in which of the following?

     a. Network cable

     b. Network operating system

     c. Network interface card

     d. A CPU register

11. Data are sent in _____ on a network.

     a. Boxes

     b. Packets

     c. Packages

     d. Netcapsules

12. Which protocol(s) is (are) used by Microsoft NT Server?

 a. XNS

 b. IPX

 c. NetBEUI

 d. Both b and c

13. 10BASE2 cable must have an impedance of

 a. 50 ohms.

 b. 54 ohms.

 c. 75 ohms.

 d. 50–54 ohms.

14. Network addressing in TCP/IP is performed by which of the following protocols?

 a. TCP

 b. IP

 c. Datagrams

 d. FTP

15. What is the data transfer rate of an Ethernet network?

 a. 10 Mbps

 b. 50 Mbps

 c. 100 Mbps

 d. Both a and c

16. Which of the following data transfer rates are used in token ring networks?

 a. 4 Mbps

 b. 10 Mbps

 c. 16 Mbps

 d. Both a and c

 e. Both b and c

17. 100 Mbps is the data transfer rate for which of the following?

 a. Fast Ethernet

 b. Type 1 cable

 c. Token bus

 d. Both a and b

18. UTP cable has shielding.

 a. True

 b. False

19. The network protocol parameters in Windows 95 and Windows NT are set from

   a. The Applications menu

   b. The Programs menu.

   c. The Control Panel menu.

   d. The shortcut bar.

20. Data communications through an NIC are made possible by

   a. Software drivers.

   b. Network attributes.

   c. Control parameters.

   d. None of the above.

THE HOLLAND COLLEGE PROJECT: PHASE 2

In Chapter 1, Holland College President Kathy Jackson asked Bob Watson to have you begin preparing information about networking so she can make a recommendation to the trustees. President Jackson now would like more information about what type of network to install and about the costs of networking.

The Holland College administrative staff are housed in the two-story Hoyt Administration Building in the central part of campus. The main floor has the president's office, her executive assistant's office, the vice-presidents' offices, the development director's office, and the director of IT's office. The top floor has the offices of the human resources director, the facilities manager, the director of Student Services, and the registrar. The top floor also houses the business office staff (GL/AP, Payroll, Accounts Receivable, and Budget) and the Student Services staff (Financial Aid and Student Loans). It also contains Jackie Herrera and you.

The president is initially interested in having a network throughout the Hoyt Administration Building. She would like each administrative staff person to be linked to the network. This will enable them to communicate by e-mail and to share business information.

Because the college's vital business functions will rely on the network, the president wants a network that can operate 24 hours a day, 7 days a week. The management staff often need to prepare reports and obtain last-minute information to give to the trustees when the trustees meet on campus, once each month. Because the trustees meet over the weekend, the network and administrative systems must be available at all times.

During registration and when grades are prepared, the registrar and Student Services staff often work into the night. The computer systems must be available at these times for them to complete their work.

Because the network must be reliable and available, the president wants to invest in a network design that will meet these goals. She realizes that the college competes for students with other colleges and must provide first-rate business services to its students.

ASSIGNMENT 2-1

What type of network would you install in the Hoyt Administration Building? Why would you install this type of network? Please complete your answer to this assignment by addressing the following:

- Would you use an Ethernet or token ring network?

- What design method would you use: bus, ring, or star?

- What type of cabling would you use?

- Would you purchase any network communication equipment?

ASSIGNMENT 2-2

Figures 2-16 and 2-17 show the layout of the Hoyt Administration Building at Holland College. Use a pen or pencil and draw in the following to show how you would network the college (you may need advice from your instructor on how to link the floors):

- Cable runs

- Location of any network equipment

- Location of network printers

- Location of the file server

- Any physical security measures you would build in

Figure 2-16

Hoyt Administration Building first floor

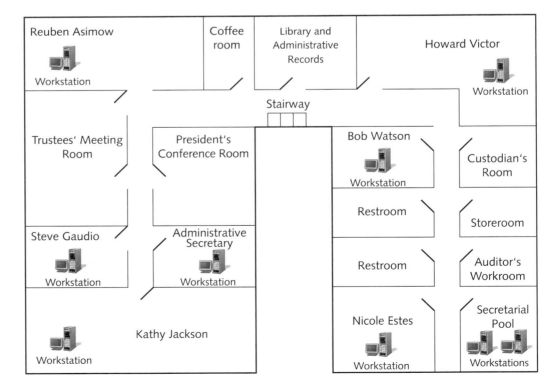

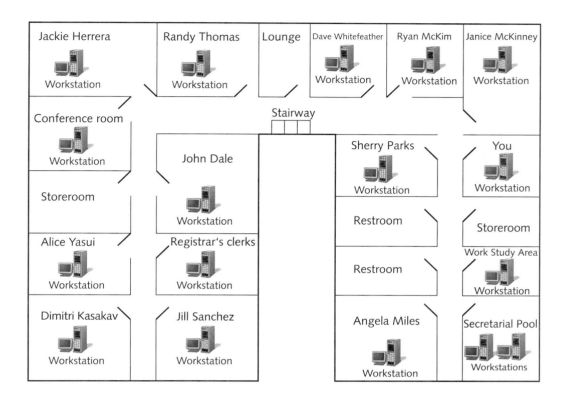

Figure 2-17

Hoyt
Administration
Building second
floor

 ## ASSIGNMENT 2-3

How many network interface cards will be needed to connect everyone (refer to Figure 1-11 in Chapter 1)?

 ## ASSIGNMENT 2-4

How many NT file servers will be needed for the offices on both floors? Why?

 ## ASSIGNMENT 2-5

Use the Internet or the library to research TCP/IP, NetBEUI, and IPX. What are the strengths of each protocol? What are the weaknesses?

ASSIGNMENT 2-6

Prepare a cost estimate of the equipment required to network the administration building. Please complete the spreadsheet provided for your cost estimate. Note that Bob Watson has measured distances in an effort to give you a hand. His measurements show you will need 1,200 feet of cabling, at a minimum.

Equipment	Cost per Unit	Number of Units	Total Cost

ASSIGNMENT 2-7

Prepare a memo to Bob Watson with your networking proposal. Explain the equipment you propose to purchase in Assignment 2-6. Why are you recommending this particular equipment? How will your recommendation help meet the president's stipulation that the network must be reliable? An example memo format is provided here.

HOLLAND COLLEGE INTEROFFICE MEMO

TO: BOB WATSON
FROM:
SUBJECT: NETWORKING COSTS
CC:

ASSIGNMENT 2-8

Bob Watson has asked you how to set up protocols in Windows. Experiment with setting up protocols. Next, prepare a brief set of instructions for Bob on how this is done.

CHAPTER THREE

SERVER HARDWARE

In Chapter 2, Sara learned the basics of networking theory and design. She found it valuable to learn the differences between Ethernet and token ring communications, and to understand how these differences will affect any future networking opportunities. The information she gathered on cabling is critical for monitoring the work of the cable installation contractor. With Kristin's approval Sara is using Network Cabling Specialists to perform the installation. She asks them to use UTP cabling and to follow the IEEE specifications. She shows them her cable-run drawings and reviews their suggested changes to meet local building codes.

During the installation, Sara frequently checks with the contractor to ensure the quality of the installation. For example, she asks the contractor to test cable distances and verify the results with her. The contractor provides a written guarantee for all the wiring and connectors and to ensure that each cable run is within the 100-meter limit.

Sara is ready to select the file server hardware. She seeks the advice of her friend Ryan Young at Wilson, Morton, and Holt, who advises her to purchase a server that can be expanded as the firm grows. He recommends seeking help from experienced network administrators on Internet news groups or online service forums, like the NT Server forum on CompuServe, where participants range from novices to experienced network administrators. Sara follows Ryan's advice by sending the message shown in Figure 3-1 to the forum participants.

AFTER READING THIS CHAPTER AND COMPLETING THE EXERCISES YOU WILL BE ABLE TO:

- SIZE AN NT SERVER FOR AN INSTALLATION.
- SELECT SERVER DISK STORAGE.
- CHOOSE SERVER MEMORY.
- SELECT A SERVER NIC.
- CHOOSE A TAPE BACKUP SYSTEM.
- INSTALL SERVER COMPONENTS.

Figure 3-1

Sara's message to the forum on how to select a server

> To: All
>
> From: Sara Martin
>
> Subject: Server Selection Issues
>
> Hello—I am seeking advice from experienced network administrators on what to consider when purchasing a server for running NT Server. I work for a law office that will have 12 users connected to the server. Eventually we will connect other, out-of-town offices, adding 20 or more users. All users have 486 or Pentium computers running Windows or Windows 95, except for one 386 computer running DOS applications.
>
> We use programs such as MS Word, MS Excel, MS Lotus 1-2-3, legal forms software, accounting software, and legal time accounting. I am new to network administration and would appreciate any advice you have to give about selecting a network server. Thanks for your help!

Sara received eight messages from her inquiry. Three messages appeared two hours after she sent the original one. All but one of the responses were from experienced network administrators. The exception was a message from a new administrator who had questions similar to Sara's. Figure 3-2 shows two of the messages Sara received.

Figure 3-2

Responses to Sara's forum question

> To: Sara Martin
>
> From: Jack Hardin
>
> Subject: Re: Server Selection Issues
>
> Hi, Sara—You're asking the same question I did two years ago when I set up my first server. Make sure you consider CPU performance and disk capacity and always buy your Pentium computers from well-known manufacturers. Also, be sure to buy plenty of disk space, because you'll need it as the server catches on. Personally, I like servers with SCSI-2 controllers because they are fast.
>
> Jack Hardin
> Johnson Glass Company

Figure 3-2

Continued

To: Sara Martin

From: Rachel Thomas

Subject: Re: Server Selection Issues

We have NT Server running on Intel multiprocessor file servers at our company. You probably don't need a server this big–but I'd pick a Pentium server from Microsoft's compatibility list. Also, make sure you purchase a 32-bit network interface card for the server.

Good luck! It sounds as though you are off to a good start by getting advice early on.

—Rachel Thomas at Scientific Instruments

After reading the forum responses, Sara made a list of the common topics that were mentioned. They were the following:

- NT Server compatibility
- CPU sizing
- Bus speed and expansion slots
- Disk storage
- SCSI-2 adapters
- Memory requirements
- Network interface card
- CD-ROM drive
- Tape drive

NT SERVER COMPATIBILITY

Just about everyone advised Sara to check Microsoft's hardware compatibility list (HCL), which comes with the NT Server software or is available on CompuServe, the Microsoft Network (MSN), or Microsoft's Web site, http://www.microsoft.com/.

Microsoft reviews all types of hardware to determine whether they will work with NT Server and NT Workstation. The compatibility list includes information on the following hardware:

- Single-processor computers
- Multiprocessor computers
- RISC computers

- Processor upgrades
- PCMCIA hardware
- SCSI adapters and drives
- Video adapters
- Network adapters
- Audio adapters
- Modems
- Printers
- Uninterruptible power supplies

Sara was advised to select well-known brand names and to avoid small companies that build individual computers from generic parts. Most established computer manufacturers have products compatible with NT Server, though their prices are somewhat higher than those of the smaller companies. Cutting expenses when buying server hardware could prove to be costly later on if it results in unreliable equipment and difficult software installations.

CPU SIZING

Most of the respondents suggested that Sara purchase a Pentium server with a CPU **clock speed** of 133 megahertz (MHz) or faster. The clock speed is the rate at which the CPU sends data through the **buses**, or data pathways, inside the computer. A high clock speed helps ensure the CPU does not become bottlenecked with more processing requests than it can handle.

At this time Sara projects the maximum use of the server to be 12 simultaneous connections. A single-processor Pentium computer will be enough to meet the immediate server needs. If the firm grows, then a 166 MHz or 200 MHz Pentium will be needed. The information that Sara gathered on CPU options is presented in the next sections.

80486 AND PENTIUM COMPUTERS

NT Server will work using an Intel-based 80486 CPU with a 33 MHz or 66 MHz clock speed. Many organizations have implemented 80486 servers with positive results. But the limitations of an 80486 become apparent as the server demand grows. The slower clock speed puts these servers at a disadvantage to a Pentium-based computer.

NT Server takes advantage of the Pentium's fast clock speeds to provide better server response. NT also uses Pentium features such as multithreading and multitasking. Threading involves dividing a program into parts that can run independently. **Multithreading** is the ability of a computer to run more than one program thread at a time. **Multitasking** means a computer can run two or more programs at the same time.

MULTIPROCESSOR COMPUTERS

If Sara decides to move up to a multiprocessor server, NT Server will be able to fully exploit the computer's capabilities. Many computer vendors make Pentium-based multiprocessor computers to be used specifically as servers. These computers, known as **symmetric multiprocessor (SMP)** computers, have two, three, four, or more processors to share the processing load.

RISC COMPUTERS

Should her office need the processing power in the future, they could purchase a **reduced instruction set computer (RISC)** to use as their NT Server. This type of computer uses fewer instructions per CPU operation than other large systems. With fewer instructions, there is less traffic along the CPU's bus, which speeds processing. Also, RISC CPUs come with clock speeds faster than those of most Intel-based servers. Some example RISC clock speeds are 266 MHz, 300 MHz, and 333 MHz.

Two other advantages of RISC servers are that they can issue four CPU instructions for each clock cycle and that they support larger buses (more traffic lanes for data) than Intel servers. Manufacturers of RISC computers that are compatible with NT Server include Acer, DEC, IBM, and NEC. As is true for Intel servers, RISC servers can be expanded to meet future demands.

A common business application for RISC computers is client/server computing. Large multi-gigabyte client/server databases require CPU power for data queries, updates, and high-volume user access. In these situations the RISC server is needed to prevent CPU bottlenecks.

BUS SPEED

Sara's Internet query resulted in several suggestions concerning the type of bus architecture to purchase in a server. Computers have two buses. The internal bus carries instructions about computer operations to the CPU. The external bus carries data to be processed, such as for mathematical operations. As Sara found out, the server's speed is influenced by the size of the bus. Pentium servers have a 32-bit bus and RISC servers have a 64-bit bus.

 To help you understand bus size, note that a single letter or number is composed of eight bits. A 32-bit bus can carry four letters or numbers at a time, while a 64-bit bus can carry eight.

NT Server is a 32-bit operating system, which means it can take advantage of a 32-bit or larger bus design. With this in mind, there are three bus types from which Sara can choose: **Extended Industry Standard Architecture (EISA)**, **Microchannel Architecture (MCA)**, or **Peripheral Computer Interface (PCI)**. All of these architectures are 32-bit. An EISA bus is older technology but has fast information throughput and supports the ability to have more than one process occurring at the same time. EISA internal and external buses support 8-, 16-, and 32-bit data transfer. The EISA bus permits several interface cards, such as two NICs, to transfer data without contention. This is possible through **bus mastering**, which enables some processing activities to take place on interface card processors instead of on the CPU.

Bus mastering is a process that reduces the reliance on the CPU for input/output activities on the computer's bus. Interface cards that have bus mastering can take control of the bus for faster data flow.

The MCA bus is used in Intel-based IBM computers. This bus has the same advantages as EISA, but it is capable of slightly faster data transfer rates. One advantage is that EISA is supported by many computer manufacturers that have defined this as a bus standard. A large variety of computer interface cards and add-ons are available for EISA because it is widely manufactured. A disadvantage of EISA and MCA is they are not as fast as PCI.

The newer PCI bus supports 32-bit and 64-bit data transfer. This architecture enables a much faster data transfer speed than EISA or MCA and nearly matches the speed of the CPU. Also, PCI has a local bus design that provides separate buses for disk storage and network interfaces. The local bus capability is designed to significantly speed the server by reducing contention on the bus. A disadvantage is that PCI adapters tend to be more expensive than EISA or MCA cards.

 PCI bus servers are a good choice to protect your server hardware investment as new resource-intense software applications continue to emerge, creating more demand for speed.

DISK STORAGE

Sara learns that choosing the right hard disk drive is just as important as selecting the right bus. Hard disk access on a file server is far more frequent than on a typical workstation. This constant activity leads to congested data paths and the malfunctioning of overused disk drive parts. In choosing a server hard drive, Sara needs to make decisions about capacity, contention, and redundancy.

DISK CAPACITY

Estimating hard disk capacity is not an exact science, and most network administrators calculate a general figure based on the total number of bytes needed. In Sara's case, she needs to determine her space requirements for software applications, user directories, shared files, databases, and NT Server operating system files. She develops an estimate using a spreadsheet, as shown in Figure 3-3.

Figure 3-3

Hard disk
space estimates

Operating System Files	Size
Microsoft NT Server	150 MB
Application Software	**Size**
Microsoft Word	12 MB
Microsoft Excel	14 MB
Microsoft Access	24 MB
Microsoft Exchange	100 MB
WordPerfect	10 MB
Lotus 1-2-3	12 MB
Great Plains general ledger	250 MB
Bankruptcy law forms	35 MB
Contracts law forms	42 MB
Tax law forms	41 MB
Wills law forms	45 MB
Legal time accounting	200 MB
User Directories	**Size**
Each user 50 MB * 12	600 MB
Total	1535 MB

In calculating hard disk space, Sara determines she will need 50 MB of space for each of the 12 Nishida and McGuire users. She arrives at this figure after talking with office members and estimating the size and number of files they want to share on the network. She realizes the hard disk space estimates should contain margins for error and for future growth. Sara estimates her margin of error to be 15%, which includes any requests she may get to enlarge user directories. Also, she knows that the legal time accounting and the GL accounting (Great Plains) databases will grow each new fiscal year on a regular basis. Therefore, she sets her growth margin to 25%. Sara's final hard disk capacity calculations (15% for error and 25% for growth) are: 1535 MB + (1535 MB * .4) = 2149 MB.

DISK CONTENTION

Disk contention is the number of simultaneous requests to read or write data onto a disk. On the firm's server, up to 12 workstations may have requests affecting data stored on disk. Disk contention can be reduced through the design of the server. The primary design issues are:

- Speed of the individual disks
- Speed of the disk controllers
- Speed of the data pathway to the disks
- Number of disk pathways
- Disk caching

The speed of the disk is called **disk access time**, measured in milliseconds (ms). This is the time it takes for the read/write heads on the disk to reach the data for reads or updates. A fast disk access time can reduce disk contention. Disk drives manufactured today have fast access times of 15 ms or less. Access time is important, but because most disks are built to be fast, it is not as important as how quickly the data reach the disk.

The speed of the data pathway or channel is called the **data transfer rate**, measured in megabytes per second (Mbps). The data transfer rate is determined by the type of disk controller used in the server. The **disk controller** is the board that acts as the interface between the disk drives and the computer. Figure 3-4 shows a disk controller. Many computer systems come with Integrated Device Electronics (IDE) or Enhanced Small Device Interface (ESDI) disk controllers. These controllers provide average data transfer rates and traditionally have been a viable choice for older servers.

Figure 3-4

Disk controller connecting a disk drive

Disk controller

Server

The best choice for a modern server is to implement a Small Computer System Interface (SCSI), which takes advantage of the 32-bit bus architecture of Pentium computers. SCSI interfaces rely less on the main system CPU than IDE and ESDI controllers, freeing the CPU for other work. Data transfer rate enhancements continue to be implemented for SCSI devices. The standard SCSI-1 interface has a data transfer rate of 5 Mbps, which is many times that of IDE or ESDI. Newer SCSI-2 interfaces come with narrow and wide bus options. The wide interfaces have about twice the data transfer speed, 20 Mbps, as the narrow ones, at 10 Mbps. The newer 64-bit SCSI-3 interfaces are made for RISC computers and have speeds up to 100 Mbps. Table 3-1 summarizes the SCSI interface speeds.

Table 3-1

SCSI interface data transfer rates

Interface	Data Transfer Rate
SCSI-1	Up to 5 Mbps
SCSI-2 narrow	Up to 10 Mbps
SCSI-2 wide	Up to 20 Mbps
SCSI-3 wide	Up to 100 Mbps

Several disk drives or other devices, such as a tape drive, can be daisy-chained on the cable of a SCSI interface, with wide SCSI-2 adapters providing the best performance. Also, it is important to be sure each device connected to the interface has a unique address, with the first device addressed as 0. Problems occur if two devices have the same address. The SCSI cable must be terminated with a SCSI terminator after the last device that is connected.

Computers designed as servers generally come equipped with SCSI-2 adapters. Watch for new developments with SCSI adapters including UltraSCSI implementations.

The controller of a SCSI device is directly attached to the device. This design makes it possible to mix different devices on the same interface. The SCSI interface plugs into one of the computer's open slots on the main board. A cable is run in daisy-chain fashion from the adapter to the controller card for each device, with a terminator at the last device. Several disk drives, a tape drive, and other SCSI devices can be attached to one adapter, as shown in Figure 3-5.

Figure 3-5

SCSI-2 adapter connected to two disk drives and a tape drive

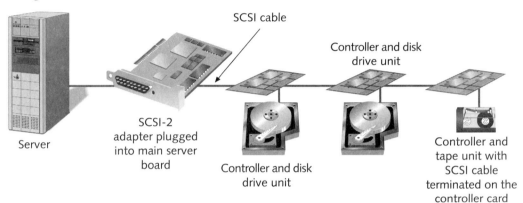

From the CompuServe forum discussions, Sara knows she has to be cautious about placing too much demand on access to hard disk storage. If she purchases only one drive, all the users will contend for data on that drive. If she purchases two drives to place on one SCSI-2 adapter, the data contention on the single pathway may be excessive. One solution is to purchase a server with a wide-bus SCSI-2 interface and put both drives on the same pathway. A better solution is to create two separate pathways with two wide-bus SCSI-2 interfaces, as shown in Figure 3-6.

Figure 3-6

Using two SCSI-2 adapters to create separate data paths for disk drives

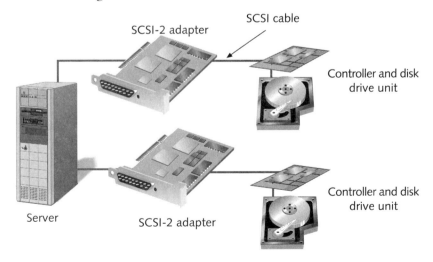

One method to significantly increase performance on a server is to purchase two or more hard disk drives and divide the flow of data between two or more data pathways by placing the drives on different adapters.

Although Sara only needs 2.2 GB for storage, most server hardware comes with larger hard drive capacity. Sara is considering the purchase of a server with two 4.3 GB disk drives and two SCSI adapters, for two data pathways. This gives the firm room to grow in the future, including the ability for users to store files on the server. Even though two disks and two adapters will increase the cost of the server, Sara believes the benefits she will get from increased performance will override the cost factor. Another advantage is that if one SCSI interface malfunctions, she can move its disk drive to the remaining interface for a fast recovery.

Disk caching is another way to improve disk response time. Cache is memory allocated to a device so the device can store frequently used information or the last information used. Because data access to memory is faster than access to disk, caching saves time. The purchase of a controller with a large disk caching capability will permit faster data access.

DISK REDUNDANCY

Sara's forum advisors suggested she plan for disk failures, because failure is a common risk on all computer systems. A scheme known as **redundant array of inexpensive drives (RAID)** provides several ways to prepare for disk failures. These include dual disk setups, dual disk controllers, and having several drives set up so that if one drive fails the remaining drives can reconstruct the information.

Sara decides to explore the RAID options later (in Chapter 11), after she acquires more experience with her server and understands the specific needs of her office. For now, she will purchase the two drives and controllers. For protection against disk failure, she elects to perform nightly tape backups of each disk attached to the system.

MEMORY REQUIREMENTS

Another factor that influences how well a server performs is the amount of memory available to the server. Some respondents advised Sara to use a minimum of 32 MB of memory while others suggested 256 MB. Estimating the amount of memory needed is not an exact science, but some basic rules still apply. One experienced forum respondent gave Sara some guidelines. First, determine the minimum amount of memory needed for the server operating system, which is 16 MB for NT Server. Next, determine the number of people who will be accessing the system at the same time. For Sara, this is a maximum of 12 users at one time. Finally, determine the average software requests per user and the amount of memory required for the requests. Sara estimates the average user needs 2 MB of memory for programs like Word and Word document files. Sara uses the following calculation:

16 MB for the operating system + (12 users × 2 MB average memory use) = 40 MB of memory

Because there are times when memory use per user might be higher than 2 MB, Sara is implementing 64 MB of memory now and will add more later, if necessary. Also, when purchasing memory, Sara learns it is safest to purchase **error checking and correcting (ECC)** memory chips. This type of chip keeps some memory in reserve for when problems occur. It also makes an automatic correction if a parity error is detected. This prevents the file server from crashing in the event of a memory parity error.

SELECTING A NETWORK INTERFACE CARD

From the forum discussion, Sara learned she can purchase either a 16-bit or a 32-bit network interface card for her file server. She is purchasing a PCI bus computer, and she wants to take advantage of the high-speed 32-bit capability of the bus. However, 16-bit cards are not supported by PCI buses, so Sara believes the best option is to buy a PCI 32-bit NIC. This will offer fast **throughput** for all 12 users in the office, without the need for a second NIC.

Throughput is a general indication of the ability to quickly transfer data from one point to the next.

Sara's forum advisors cautioned her to purchase an NIC made by a well-known vendor such as 3COM, DEC, Hewlett-Packard, IBM, Intel, Novell, or Proteon. They also recommended she consult Microsoft's compatibility list before making the purchase. The NIC is critical because it is the server's link to the network. Both the card and the network drivers provided with the card must be high quality. Some NIC vendors provide regular updates to their drivers to ensure against transmission problems, and many distribute these updates through the Internet. The ability to receive frequent updates from a quick, online source is very important because network drivers are historically problematic.

In Chapter 2, Sara chose a twisted-pair network, which enables her to purchase an NIC with a 10BASET connector. When NICs were first manufactured it was necessary to set "jumpers" or "dip switches" to configure the card for the server. It was recommended to Sara through her NT Server forum that she purchase auto-configuring cards. This means that the card and drivers automatically determine what hardware interrupts and memory locations to use.

Some vendors have NICs that work for both Ethernet (10 Mbps) and fast Ethernet (100 Mbps) networks. This type of NIC is a good investment for those who have plans to upgrade their network for high-speed communications or who have fast Ethernet. Sara decides to purchase one of these NICs because the cost is only $60 more than a standard Ethernet NIC. She decides to install only one NIC in the server, because that is all she needs for an office the size of Nishida and McGuire. If she had a hundred users, then she might need two or more NICs, depending on the use of the server (Figure 2-5 in Chapter 2 shows Ethernet NICs).

CHOOSING A CD-ROM DRIVE

Sara needs to purchase a server that has a CD-ROM drive. The CD-ROM drive is necessary to load the NT Server operating system. Another good reason for having the drive is to run software that is only available on CD-ROM. Ryan Young's employer has a CD-ROM set for legal research that includes treaty and tort law.

According to the forum members, the best choice is a SCSI CD-ROM drive, because these drives generally work well with NT Server. CD-Technology, DEC, NEC, Plextor, Sony, and Toshiba are examples of CD-ROM vendors on Microsoft's hardware compatibility list. CD-ROMs come in various speeds ranging from 2X to 8X. Most server-grade computers will have a 6X or 8X CD-ROM drive. As the firm grows, they will likely want to consider the use of a SCSI-based CD-ROM "jukebox" that can hold multiple CD-ROMs and load any CD-ROM at the request of a user.

TAPE DRIVE

Sara is advised to purchase a tape drive to perform server backups. The tape drive can be mounted inside the server cabinet or it can be an external unit. NT file servers typically use quarter-inch cartridge cassette (QIC), digital audio tape (DAT), or digital linear tape (DLT) backup. Cassette backup systems have the smallest storage capability, in the range of 2 to 4 GB. Use of QIC tapes for backups has decreased over the past several years because the storage capacity is limited.

Much more popular among network administrators is DAT technology, which stores data in the medium gigabyte range. Most administrators have moved from the initial 4mm tape, which holds 2 to 9 GB per tape, to the newer 8mm format, which holds 4 to 25 GB.

Network administrators with high-capacity backup needs are also moving to DLT systems, which store data in the 10 to 40 GB range. Digital linear tapes are more resistant to damage than DAT or QIC tapes and have a longer shelf life, at up to 30 years. DLT systems write information to tape about three times faster than DAT. Sara has decided to purchase an 8mm DAT system because the firm doesn't have a need for the more expensive, "industrial strength" DLT system. The DAT system has sufficient flexibility for her to back up all PCs in the office as well as the server.

Sara decides to purchase a separate SCSI adapter for the tape drive instead of daisy-chaining the DAT drive onto one of the disk drives' SCSI pathways. From the forum discussion, she learned this approach will reduce contention for disk and tape backup resources during backup operations. Data to and from the tape drive will not become congested with the data to a disk drive. The better throughput is cost-effective at a few hundred dollars for the extra adapter.

SETTING UP THE SERVER

Sara orders the new server but is only able to find a system with 32 MB of memory preinstalled. She places a separate order for an additional 32 MB of memory, the DAT tape drive and SCSI controller, and the 32-bit NIC. At the time she placed the order, Sara knew she would need to install the extra memory, the tape controller, and the NIC.

It takes five weeks for all the components to arrive at Nishida and McGuire. When they arrive, Sara unpacks the server and attaches the monitor and keyboard. She lets the computer run for a day before installing any boards. This allows her to see that the components are all functioning properly.

The best way to ensure a successful installation is to take it step by step. Whenever possible, establish the sound operation of a component or installation step before moving to the next one.

Sara is ready to install the extra 32 MB of memory. Like most Intel-based servers, Sara's is designed to use Single Inline Memory Modules (SIMMs). Most Pentium computers use 72-pin SIMMs, where the modules come in megabyte sizes such as 1 MB, 4 MB, 8 MB, 16 MB, 32 MB, and so on. Figure 3-7 shows an example SIMM.

Figure 3-7

A 72-pin SIMM

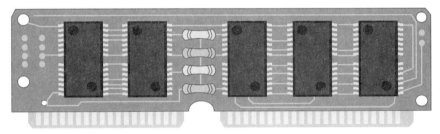

The instructions with the server note that the memory is installed in banks located near the middle of the main circuit board. On this particular server, one bank is composed of two memory slots (open slots for the SIMMs memory). The first bank consists of two SIMMs with 16 MB each. Sara purchased two additional boards with 16 MB each. She purchased two boards so each slot in the second bank will have SIMMs as required by the manufacturer of the server computer. To save money, the manufacturer suggests she install the additional memory herself because she is already familiar with the technique.

The instructions advise Sara to use a wrist grounding strap to prevent electrostatic discharge, as this can damage computer parts such as memory. Sara does not have a wrist strap but is able to borrow one from Ryan. She puts on the wrist strap before removing the modules from their antistatic protective wrapping. She holds the first module at a 45-degree angle over the first available slot and guides the chip into the notches on either side of the slot. Once the module is aligned with the notches, she gently snaps the module into the slot so it is perpendicular with the main board. Sara repeats the procedure to install the second module. Figure 3-8 shows how she guides the modules into the slots.

Figure 3-8

Installing a
SIMM

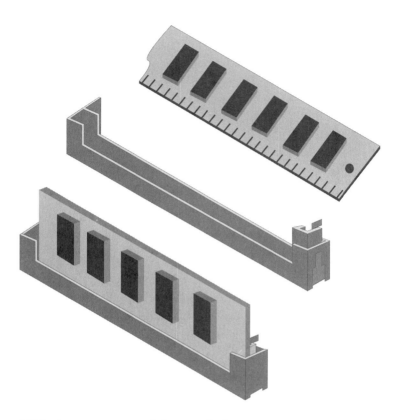

With the memory modules installed, Sara temporarily attaches the monitor, keyboard, and power cord to ensure the computer can detect the memory. Because her computer came with Windows 95, it has Plug-and-Play (PnP) with the operating system. The basic input/output system (BIOS) is also PnP-compatible. PnP means that the computer's BIOS can automatically detect new equipment installations, such as new boards. The boards must have PnP compatibility for the automatic detection to take place. On older computers, Sara would have needed to start the computer and run a setup program in order for the computer to recognize the new boards. Although Sara's computer has a BIOS setup program, she does not have to use it for this installation.

She leaves off the cover and is careful not to touch any electrical circuits when she turns on the computer. The computer performs a memory check, showing the total amount of memory it detects. The check identifies the new memory and reports it is error-free.

 The **BIOS** consists of programs that start the computer and establish communications to computer peripherals, such as the disk drives.

After verifying the memory installation, Sara installs the NIC. She removes the power cord, monitor connection, mouse and keyboard. Because she bought an auto-configuring NIC, there are no switches or jumpers to set on the card before installing it in the server. First, she locates an empty slot for the NIC. The circuit board slots are located at the rear of the main circuit board. At the end of each slot, there is a slot cover on the frame of the server. Sara must remove the slot cover before installing the board. She has two boards to install, so she removes two slot covers. She consults the manual to be certain which are 32-bit and PCI slots, as she has a 32-bit PCI NIC. She does not select two empty slots next to one another because Ryan has advised her to leave space between boards inside the server. This allows better air circulation and reduces the impact of heat generated by the computer. It also helps to prolong the life of the boards.

After removing the slot covers, Sara checks to be sure her wrist grounding strap is on securely. She removes the NIC from its antistatic bag and firmly installs it into a slot (see Figure 3-9). She hears a slight click as the card goes into place against the bottom of the slot.

Figure 3-9

Example installation of a server card

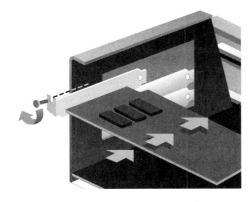

Sara wants to perform a fast test to be certain the NIC is installed properly. She reattaches the monitor, mouse, keyboard, and power cord. Once the computer is on, she runs a test program that came with the NIC. The test program indicates the NIC is installed correctly and ready to be used.

Sara follows the same procedure to install the SCSI adapter for the tape drive, using the second empty slot she selected earlier. She installs the card and again reattaches the monitor and keyboard before turning on the computer. The test program that came with the adapter shows it is functioning perfectly.

The final step is to re-install the outside cover on the server. Sara wears the grounding strap as extra insurance during this procedure. Once the monitor, mouse, keyboard, and power cord are attached, she again starts the computer to be sure it is functioning properly.

SARA'S NEXT ASSIGNMENT

Kristin is pleased with Sara's progress installing the hardware for the server. Together, they decide to explore what's needed and to prepare the workstations for networking. Sara takes on this assignment in the next chapter, where she selects the workstation operating system, installs a workstation drive, and sets up workstation protocols.

KEY CONCEPTS SUMMARY

The server architecture and components in the server have an important influence on the server's performance level. The concepts summarized in this section all impact the server selection process.

basic input/output system (BIOS) This program is on a read-only memory chip within a computer and is used to establish basic communications with components such as the monitor and disk drives.

bus Computers have two main pathways, one for CPU instructions and one for data transfer within the computer. These pathways are buses.

bus mastering This technology enables some processing activities to take place on interface card processors to off-load some of this work from the CPU.

clock speed The speed at which a computer can send information along its internal and external data routes. The clock speed is measured in terms of frequency or megahertz (MHz).

data transfer rate The speed at which data move through the disk controller along the data channel to a disk drive.

disk access time The amount of time it takes for a disk drive to read or write data by moving a read/write head to the location of the data.

disk controller The circuit board used to link one or more disk drives to a computer. The controller sends instructions to a disk to perform certain operations, such as reading or writing data.

error checking and correcting (ECC) memory This type of memory can correct some types of memory problems without causing computer operations to halt.

Extended Industry Standard Architecture (EISA) A computer bus design that incorporates 32-bit communications within the computer. An industry standard used by several computer manufacturers.

Microchannel Architecture (MCA) This bus architecture is used in some IBM Intel-based computers. It provides 32-bit communications within the computer.

multitasking The ability of a single-processor computer to run two or more programs at the same time. Some computers handle several programs by giving each a slice of CPU time and then quickly rotating from time slice to time slice so programs are in effect running simultaneously.

multithreading Involves running several program processes or parts (threads) at the same time.

Peripheral Computer Interface (PCI) A computer bus design that supports 32-bit and 64-bit bus communications for high-speed operations.

reduced instruction set computer (RISC) RISC computers have CPUs that require fewer instructions for common operations. With the instructions compressed into a small set of CPU operation commands, the processor works faster and more efficiently than a processor using a larger instruction set.

redundant array of inexpensive drives (RAID) Techniques used to ensure data are not lost when one or more disk drives fail.

symmetric multiprocessor (SMP) A type of computer with two or more CPUs that share the processing load. These computers are used as file servers because they have the ability to handle high processing loads for network software applications.

throughput A general term that describes how quickly data can be transferred from point to point without impediment.

REVIEW QUESTIONS

1. What type of NIC is best to purchase for a server?
   a. 4-bit
   b. 8-bit
   c. 16-bit
   d. 32-bit

2. What information is transported on a computer's internal bus?
   a. Data
   b. CPU instructions
   c. Clocking data
   d. None of the above

3. SCSI-2 interfaces have speeds up to
   a. 5 Kbytes/sec.
   b. 10 Kbytes/sec.
   c. 5 Mbytes/sec.
   d. 20 Mbytes/sec.

4. RISC computers have a 64-bit bus.
   a. True
   b. False

5. Which of the following technologies uses 4mm tapes?
   a. DAT
   b. DLT
   c. QIC
   d. RVM

6. Which of the following bus architectures offers the fastest data transfer rate?
   a. EISA
   b. PCI
   c. MCA
   d. Both a and b

7. Microsoft provides information about hardware that works with NT Server.
   a. True
   b. False

8. Which of the following affects disk contention?
   a. Disk access time
   b. Disk caching
   c. Number of disk data paths
   d. All of the above

9. Pentium computers have which of the following?
   a. Multithreading
   b. Multitasking
   c. 32-bit bus
   d. All of the above

10. The speed at which data travel to and from the CPU on the computer's bus is called
    a. Clock speed.
    b. Access time.
    c. Transfer rate.
    d. Bus schedule.

11. Only one SCSI interface can be used in a server.
    a. True
    b. False

12. Which type of memory should be purchased for a server?
    a. Nanosecond
    b. 8-byte
    c. ECC
    d. 1 MB chip combinations only

13. The speed of data along a disk pathway or channel is called
    a. Data transfer rate.
    b. Bus rate.
    c. Channel capacity.
    d. Line rate.

14. What is the first address used by a device on a SCSI interface?
    a. 0
    b. 1
    c. 1A
    d. A1

15. 4 MB is sufficient memory for most NT Server installations.
    a. True
    b. False

16. Which of the following bus types is used in IBM computers?
    a. EISA
    b. PCI
    c. MCA
    d. RCA

17. Which of the following tape backup technologies is used less and less due to storage limitations?
    a. QIC
    b. DAT
    c. DLT
    d. 3480

18. A server with four CPUs is an example of a
    a. RISC processor.
    b. Symmetric multiprocessor.
    c. Redundant system processor.
    d. VM turboprocessor.

19. When some processing occurs on an interface card to relieve the load on the CPU, this is called
    a. Time sharing.
    b. Dual processing.
    c. Bus mastering.
    d. Clock reprocessing.

20. A computer that can run a spreadsheet program and a word processing program using one CPU is said to be

    a. Multitasking.

    b. Using flow control.

    c. Application engineered.

    d. Quad-bused.

THE HOLLAND COLLEGE PROJECT: PHASE 3

The Holland College trustees met with President Jackson and Bob Watson in a special session. A grant has been given to the college from its foundation and a local group of physicians. The grant provides money to fully network the Hoyt Administration Building in an effort to provide more efficient business services to the students. Also, in a surprise announcement, the founder of a local company has offered to fund a network for the English and writing lab.

The Hoyt Administration Building will be wired according to the plans you prepared for the president. The president wants all the users in that building to access the same word processing, database, spreadsheet, terminal emulation, and e-mail software. She also wants the administrative users to be able to access the DEC VAX administrative computer and the Sequent computer that houses the academic software. With this knowledge and some research, you have found that the average administrative user will need 4 MB of memory to load these programs.

The English and writing lab is in the Jackson Hall Building on the first floor. The trustees want students to have word processing, desktop publishing, clip art, grammar checking, and banner software in the lab. Also, the professors will have the option to put special assignments for their classes on the server. Your research has shown that the average lab user will require 3 MB of memory to load these programs. Four writing classes will share the lab for a total of 12 hours per week. The lab will be open at other times for students to use for homework and other school-related assignments. Printing for the 35 computers in the lab is shared among two computers on each end of the back row of desks. Computers 1 and 2 are connected by an A/B switch to printer 1 (computer 1 prints with the switch in position A and computer 2 prints with the switch in position B). Computers 3 and 4 are connected by an A/B switch to printer 2. Figure 3-10 is a diagram of the English and writing lab.

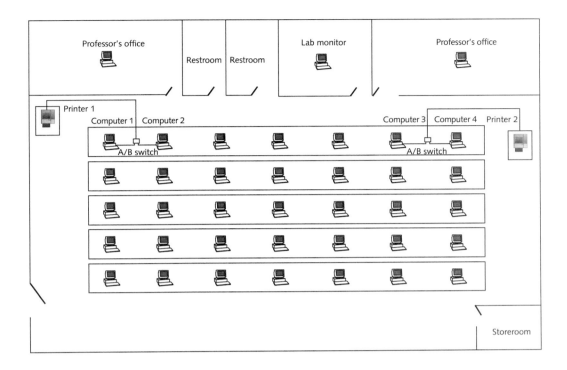

Figure 3-10

The Engligh and writing lab

ASSIGNMENT 3-1

What type of server would you purchase for the network in the Hoyt Administration Building? List each component and tell why you would use this particular component. Use the table given to show how you would choose the components of the server.

Component Description	Reason for Purchasing the Component

ASSIGNMENT 3-2

As you did in Assignment 3-1, complete the specifications for a server to be used in the English and writing lab. Use the following table for these specifications.

Component Description	Reason for Purchasing the Component

ASSIGNMENT 3-3

In the specifications you developed for the Hoyt Building file server, explain how you took into account disk contention, CPU and bus performance, and the need for backups. Then explain how you took these three factors into account for the English and writing lab server.

ASSIGNMENT 3-4

Bob Watson has asked you to determine whether the administration and lab servers could be combined to use one server (assuming a network connection is made between the Hoyt Administration Building and the Jackson Hall lab). What would be the advantages of using one server? What would be the disadvantages? Describe how you would change the component list in Assignment 3-1 to build one server for the campus.

ASSIGNMENT 3-5

Use the Internet to find example prices of the equipment listed in the chart provided.

Equipment	Price
133 MHz or faster Pentium computer with components as close as possible to the following: one 6X CD-ROM drive, one 4 GB hard drive, and 16 MB of memory (specify with the price what computer you selected)	
One SCSI-2 adapter	
One 4 GB hard drive	
One 16 MB SIMM	
One 32 MB SIMM	
One 64 MB SIMM	
One 32-bit NIC	
One 8mm DAT or DLT tape subsystem (specify which subsystem you priced)	
One backup tape for the tape subsystem you priced	

ASSIGNMENT 3-6

In a lab or classroom, practice starting the setup program for the computer's BIOS. List the parameters that can be set. Is the computer PnP-compatible? Look carefully at the setup options for the hard disk. Based on your observations, what problems might occur if you change the hard disk setup options?

Setup Parameters and Description

ASSIGNMENT 3-7

Practice the following procedures in a lab or classroom:

- Remove the cover of a computer to be used as a server.
- Install one or two SIMMs.
- Remove a SIMM.
- Remove a slot cover for an NIC and one for another interface card, such as a SCSI adapter.
- Install the NIC and the second adapter card.
- Replace the cover of the computer.

Was a wrist grounding strap available for your work on the computer? What would you do to ground yourself if a grounding strap was not available?

 ## ASSIGNMENT 3-8

Obtain a copy of the test software that came with the NIC you installed in Assignment 3-7. Run the software to verify the NIC you installed is working. Complete the questions in the accompanying chart to show the information you obtained from the test.

Type of Test	Results
Is the NIC detected by the test?	
What interrupt does the NIC use?	
What I/O port address is used by the NIC?	
What transceiver type(s) is (are) used?	
Can the NIC communicate on the network?	
Does the NIC have a node address? What is it?	
What is the speed of the NIC?	

SERVER CLIENTS

Things rarely proceed perfectly according to schedule in a network installation. Just as Sara is expecting her copy of NT Server to arrive in the mail, she receives a phone call from the software retailer saying the shipment will be delayed by four days due to a clerical error. At first Sara is disappointed, but then she discovers that although some network setup tasks must proceed in a certain order, others can be scheduled more flexibly. In this case, she doesn't have to wait until after the server software installation before preparing her client computers. Although she is changing her original plan, she can still stay more or less on schedule by setting up the clients now while she is waiting for the NT Server software. Sara's research in Chapter 3 on server hardware compatibility, CPU options, disk storage, memory, and NICs will help with the client computer setup.

In this chapter Sara learns how to troubleshoot hardware conflicts and how to set up networking software components such as NIC drivers and network protocols.

Fortunately, Sara was prepared for making the client network upgrades by making sure each computer was already equipped with the necessary operating system and hardware upgrades to properly take advantage of NT Server. Back in Chapter 1, Sara compiled an inventory of the office's computers (see Table 1-1), and based on her recommendation the firm authorized her to make the necessary hardware and software purchases to upgrade the entire office to Windows 95. In the previous weeks, Sara had already upgraded the entire office. Here's how she came to her decisions.

AFTER READING THIS CHAPTER AND COMPLETING THE EXERCISES YOU WILL BE ABLE TO:

- PROVIDE SPECIFICATIONS FOR AN NT SERVER CLIENT.
- SELECT A CLIENT OPERATING SYSTEM.
- INSTALL AN NIC DRIVER.
- RESOLVE A RESOURCE CONFLICT ON A CLIENT.
- SET UP A COMPUTER NAME FOR A CLIENT.
- ADD A PROTOCOL FOR USE BY A CLIENT.
- VERIFY NETWORK PARAMETERS ON A CLIENT.

In her work for Nishida and McGuire, Sara had spent many hours supporting the firm's PCs and had developed much firsthand knowledge of the PC hardware and operating systems. She was well aware of the significant performance differences among PCs and PC operating systems. For example, Windows performs slowly on an 80386 computer, which is why Jason Brown was using DOS instead of Windows on his 386. Sara also knew that computers with Windows 3.1 and 3.11 require regular memory management tuning. They often run out of **conventional memory** during the operation of memory-intensive applications. Windows 95 and Windows NT Workstation do not have this 640 KB limit because they are 32-bit PC operating systems and they use extensive memory swapping to create **virtual memory** from a combination of RAM and disk storage.

Conventional memory is the lower 640 KB of memory on a PC, designated for software applications. Early computers and operating systems reserved memory above 640 KB and below 1 MB for system use.

Virtual memory is a way to extend memory capability by using disk storage or disk "swap" space to complement RAM.

WORKSTATION OPERATING SYSTEMS

Sara learned that many types of client workstation operating systems can connect to NT Server: MS-DOS, Windows 3.1, Windows 3.11 (Windows for Workgroups), Windows 95, and Windows NT Workstation all can be NT Server clients. Some of these operating systems are more compatible with NT Server than others, however. These compatibility issues are discussed in the following sections.

Other operating systems work with NT Server, too, such as OS/2, UNIX, and Macintosh.

MS-DOS

In some cases, it is necessary to have an MS-DOS client to run older, specialized software. One example is a popular address correction program that is used for mass postal mailings. The program is unreliable when run from an MS-DOS window and so must be run using native MS-DOS.

Unfortunately, MS-DOS has many disadvantages for networking, and it is not designed to take advantage of a network operating system like NT Server. For example, an MS-DOS client does not have the facilities for networking features like drive sharing and workgroup participation.

The **workgroup** is an important concept to network operating systems. This concept acknowledges that people work in groups with common job functions. Workgroup computing is intended to provide ways for people to share work information through computers. This is accomplished by sharing files, security access on a file server, or a directory on a hard drive (see Figure 4-1). For example, the supervisor of a business unit may want to share a production schedule on his or her workstation's hard drive. If the supervisor only has MS-DOS, he or she cannot easily share files with some users and restrict files to others.

Figure 4-1

A workgroup sharing data on a member's hard drive

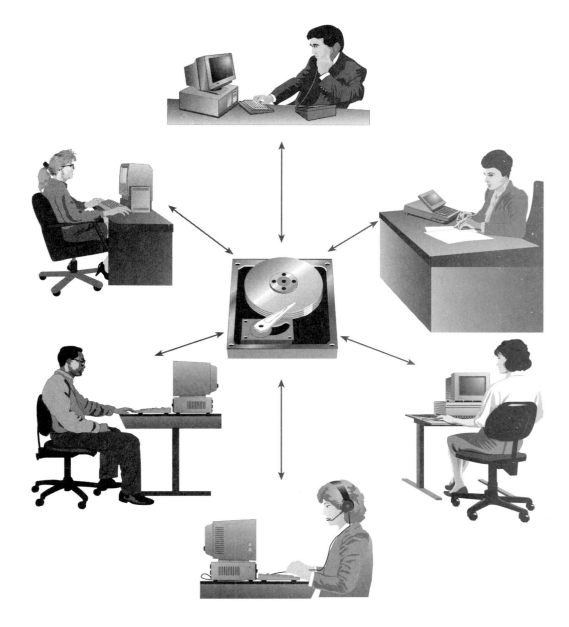

WINDOWS 3.1 AND 3.11

With its GUI interface, Windows 3.1 is a significant step up from MS–DOS, but its networking abilities are almost as limited. With Windows 3.11, Microsoft added significant network capabilities to Windows, such as options to have workgroups. In fact, Windows 3.11 is also referred to as Windows for Workgroups (WFW) and represents Windows' true initiation into networking. WFW is in fact a peer-to-peer network operating system, which means each computer on a network can communicate with other computers on the same network. Peer-to-peer communications open the way for sharing resources such as files and directories. For example, the File Manager application in Windows was upgraded in WFW to include icons to share directories with others.

Although WFW is a network operating system (NOS), it still has several disadvantages compared to a full-fledged NOS like NT Server. As is true for Windows 3.1, WFW is designed to run 16-bit applications and has the same 640 KB conventional memory limitation. Applications from many software vendors are now written for 32-bit operating systems without the 640 KB memory limit. For instance, WFW is not compatible with the full range of Web tools from either Microsoft or Netscape Communications. Also, Microsoft's support for WFW is not as comprehensive as it is for Microsoft's later operating systems. This is particularly important for obtaining specialized software drivers, such as NIC drivers.

WINDOWS 95

Windows 95 is a solid client for NT Server because it has full peer-to-peer communication features. It has an improved capacity for disk sharing, printer sharing, network communications, workgroup activities, and other network operations. Windows 95 introduces an improved GUI interface, with new utilities such as the Windows Explorer.

Because it is a 32-bit operating system, Windows 95 can run both 16-bit and 32-bit software applications. This makes it compatible with Microsoft's 32-bit Web software, such as the 32-bit version of Internet Explorer. It also is compatible with new versions of Microsoft Office, new mail systems, and other new 32-bit software, and it offers improved components to handle e-mail communications for MS Mail and MS Exchange.

Another advantage of Windows 95 is compatibility with Plug and Play (PnP), so that when Sara adds hardware to a computer, the hardware is instantly recognized. This will be handy when she installs NICs in the computers to be networked. Once the NICs are installed, each computer with Windows 95 will detect the presence of the NIC, as long the NIC is designed for Plug-and-Play.

Microsoft also provides stronger technical support for Windows 95 than it does with earlier versions of Windows. Many printer, NIC, and other hardware drivers are available for Windows 95, and if Sara needs a new driver or an enhancement, such as the Dial-Up Scripting Tool for building Netscape or Internet Explorer scripts on dial-up connections, she can download it from Microsoft's Web server.

NT WORKSTATION

Sara also considered upgrading her office to NT Workstation, the client sibling to NT Server. NT Workstation has all the peer-to-peer networking advantages of Windows 95, and with version 4.0, Microsoft equipped NT Workstation to have nearly the same Explorer interface used in Windows 95. An advantage of NT Workstation is that the operating system runs in a protected area that is insulated from "crashes" caused by software applications. This characteristic has given it a reputation as a reliable operating system for business applications. A disadvantage is that some 16-bit software will not run on NT Workstation, which was a concern to Sara because the firm's legal time accounting package was a 16-bit application.

A unique advantage of NT Workstation is that it can act as a small server on a network. Up to 10 computers can access NT Workstation for network file services, such as running software or storing data files. In Sara's office, however, more than 10 users would be accessing the server at the same time, so she would need NT Server for file serving.

SARA'S DECISION

After she completed her research, Sara was invited to speak at a managers meeting to discuss the upgrades that would be necessary to support NT Server. At the meeting, Sara showed the group the inventory in Table 1-1 (in Chapter 1) and recommended that the entire office be upgraded to Windows 95. She explained the importance of taking full advantage of NT Server, a role that Windows 95 would fill. She also suggested that it was much easier (and less expensive) to support a single operating system across the office.

Sara made it clear to the managers, however, that upgrading to Windows 95 would stretch her hardware budget to the limit. She then detailed the various upgrade issues.

CPU REQUIREMENTS

Sara recommended replacing the oldest computers in the office, the two 80486SX computers and the 80386 computer, with three Pentium 133 MHz computers. Sara considered upgrading the CPUs in the 80486 computers used by Sally, Jane, and Beth but found it hard to justify the cost at this time. All three 80486 computers had 66 MHz clock speeds, giving them sufficient computing power for Windows 95.

MEMORY

Having worked with Windows 95, Sara knew it required 8 MB of RAM and ran much faster with 12 MB or 16 MB. For instance, her 90 MHz Pentium was faster than Anne's 100 MHz Pentium because Sara's had 16 MB of RAM compared to Anne's 8 MB.

In addition, many of the new 32-bit software applications such as Microsoft Office 95 require more than 8 MB of memory. For example, Microsoft Access 95 requires at least 12 MB to run efficiently. The legal time accounting and GL accounting packages used by Nishida and McGuire also run best when more memory is available.

Sara told the managers that she planned to upgrade all the office computers to have 16 MB of memory. This would give everyone sufficient performance for Windows 95 and for the software that would be available from the server. Also, this would enable each PC to format print files more quickly for network printing.

DISK STORAGE

Sara planned to equip the three new computers with hard drives of at least 1.2 GB. It was hard to find a Pentium with any less storage than that, and many standard models sported 1.6 GB or more. Sara also decided to replace the hard drives on the 80486 computers used by Sally, Jane, and Beth with 1.2 GB models. Each of these computers had 250 MB or less for disk storage and were nearly out of space.

At first, Sara considered skipping the hard disk upgrades and instead asking these users to store files and applications on the file server. Although this would save money and make backup procedures faster, with fewer files having to be transferred over the network, she finally decided against it. The 486 users had been asking for bigger hard drives for some time and felt uncomfortable with the possible complexity and delays in accessing files from a file server. Although Sara tried to assuage their fears about network file access, in the end she felt a few new hard drives was a small price to pay for the happiness of the users.

CD-ROM DRIVES

Sara's firm had ordered a CD-ROM service to enable the attorneys to research state and federal statutes. Also, the local courts were requiring law firms to provide the forms for jury instructions at trials. But the primary users of these CD-ROMs—Mark Jackson and Jane Randall—did not have CD-ROM drives.

Sara planned to order CD-ROM drives with the three new computers. Because the firm can share directories on the network, Sara recommended purchasing nine licenses for the CD-ROM software. The state and federal statutes software could be loaded in the CD-ROM drive on Jason's new Pentium and the jury instructions software could be loaded in Rick's. All of the attorneys would have the option to access the software through the network with the shared CD-ROM drives.

In the future, Sara planned to research the cost of a CD-ROM array to attach to the file server. This would make it easier to share the CD-ROM software. A CD-ROM array is a networked unit that combines multiple CD-ROM drives. Figure 4-2 shows a CD-ROM array.

Figure 4-2

A CD-ROM server array

NIC REQUIREMENTS

For the same reason she decided to purchase a 32-bit NIC for the file server, Sara recommended purchasing 32-bit NICs for each of the 12 client workstations. The faster throughput of a 32-bit NIC was just as important for each of the clients as for the server. She planned to purchase fourteen 10BaseT NICs so she would have two spares in case any of the NICs malfunctioned. Sara also would make sure the NICs would come with the most up-to-date drivers.

NT WORKSTATION VS. WINDOWS 95

After Sara detailed the upgrade issues, one of the managers suggested that because they were installing NT Server, maybe they should also install NT Workstation on all of the clients instead of Windows 95. Expecting just such a suggestion, Sara showed a chart she had prepared comparing Windows 95 to Windows NT Workstation (Table 4–1). Sara argued that although there were many good reasons to move up to NT Workstation, there were also many more reasons not to do so.

Sara explained that because four people in the office already had Windows 95, it made sense to stay with this system. She pointed out that there might be problems running the 16-bit legal time accounting software on NT Workstation. In addition, Sara calculated that Windows NT Workstation would cost about $100 to $300 more per workstation than Windows 95. (This figure takes into account that NT Workstation is more expensive to license and requires more memory than Windows 95.)

Table 4-1

Windows 95 and Windows NT Workstation 4.0 compared

Windows 95	NT Workstation 4.0
Extensive 16-bit application support	Some 16-bit applications will not work
Limited security	Advanced security
Susceptible to crashes	Virtually crash-proof
Supports one CPU	Supports dual CPUs
No built-in server capability	Can be a server to 10 simultaneous accounts
Has the Explorer interface	Has the Explorer interface
Extensive network compatibility	Extensive network compatibility
32-bit operating system	32-bit operating system
Requires less memory and disk storage	Requires more memory and disk storage

Kristin interjected to say that one copy of NT Workstation should be purchased for Sara's use. Kristin felt it was important for Sara to have a crash-proof computer because Sara would be administering the network and would use software that placed extra demands on a workstation.

After some discussion, the managers approved Sara's upgrade plan and decided to move the entire office to Windows 95. Over the next two weeks Sara implemented the upgrades and installed Windows 95 on each of the new or upgraded computers that did not yet have the operating system.

Microsoft is likely to merge Windows 95 and Windows NT Workstation into one product in the future. For now, Windows 95 is a good choice as a client operating system for those who are starting a network and need backward compatibility to older software. NT Workstation is a good option in situations where there are client/server applications or software applications that require a powerful workstation, as is the case with a network administrator.

NIC SOFTWARE SETUP

After receiving the phone call telling her that the NT Server software would be delayed in arriving, Sara decides to start her client installations by practicing an NIC installation on her own PC. Sara can install the NIC, network drivers, and protocols without having NT Server available on the network. Because the network cabling is still in the process of being installed by the contractor, she can't test the actual communications with the network for a few more days.

Sara installs her workstation NIC using the same procedures as in Chapter 3 for the server NIC. The installation goes flawlessly and the NIC passes the manufacturer's diagnostic tests. With the NIC installed, Sara is now prepared to install the NIC driver. She does this by going to the Windows 95 Start menu and clicking the Settings option. When she clicks the Control Panel, she gets a display like the one in Figure 4-3. Then she clicks the Network icon.

Figure 4-3

Control Panel with the Network icon selected

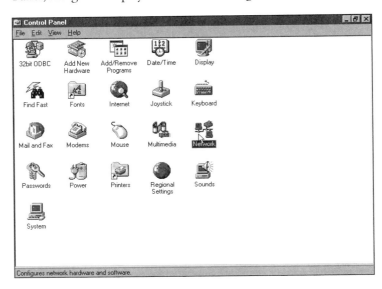

The next screen shows the Network option tabs, like the one in Figure 4-4. This dialog box has three tabs: Configuration, Identification, and Access Control. The Configuration tab is used to set up particular network components, such as an NIC or a protocol. The Identification tab is used for setting up the workstation's network name. The Access Control tab is the section where the workstation owner can specify how others are allowed to access information at his or her workstation, such as password security. Sara selects the Configuration tab and clicks the Add button.

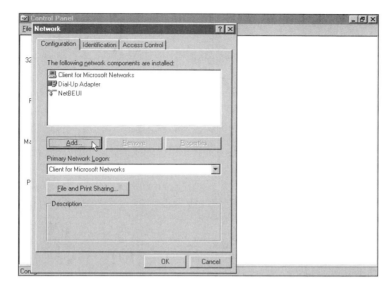

Figure 4-4

The
Configuration
tab in the
Network
dialog box

The next screen shows suggested network components, including Client, Adapter, Protocol, and Service (see Figure 4-5).

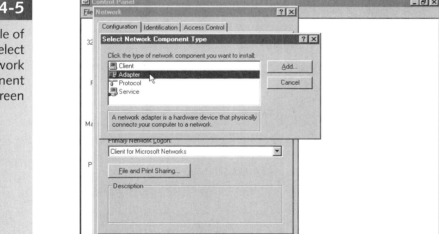

Figure 4-5

An example of
the Select
Network
Component
Type screen

Sara double-clicks Adapter to display the screen shown in Figure 4-6. This screen shows a wide range of network adapter manufacturers on the left, such as 3COM, AST, Cabletron, Compaq, Hewlett-Packard, IBM, and Intel, with their corresponding cards shown in a box on the right. Sara purchased Intel EtherExpress Pro/10 NICs, so she selects this option, as shown in Figure 4-6. On this screen she clicks the Have Disk button to load the drivers from the floppy disk that came with the NIC.

Figure 4-6

Selecting the
network
adapter

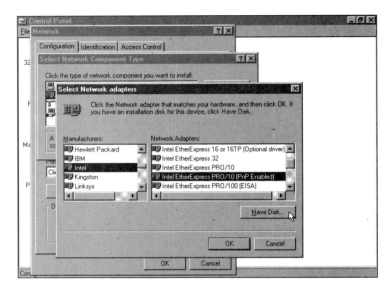

The next screen is where Sara specifies the location of the NIC drivers to be loaded, as shown in Figure 4-7.

Figure 4-7

Installing the
NIC driver
from disk

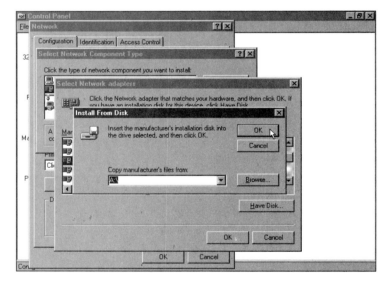

Sara inserts Intel's driver disk into drive A, and then she clicks the Browse button and selects drive A. Because the drivers are in the root directory of her disk, the program can automatically detect them without Sara having to know the name of the install file. Sara clicks the OK button to load the drivers, and once the files are copied, the Network screen appears showing the newly added adapter (see Figure 4-8).

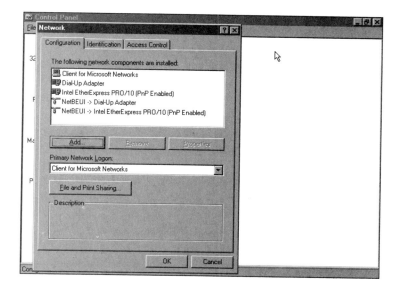

Figure 4-8

Network
screen
showing
Ethernet
adapter is
present

Sara highlights the EtherExpress card selection to activate the Properties button and clicks Properties to check the settings created for the Intel NIC. As Figure 4-9 shows, the Properties screen has four tabs: Driver Type, Bindings, Advanced, and Resources. Because Sara is using a 32-bit NIC, the driver type is compatible with the Enhanced mode, which means it works with 32-bit and 16-bit applications. The Enhanced mode (32 bit and 16 bit) NDIS driver radio button is already selected by default. Only one option can be selected on this screen, and the option already selected provides the full range of support for 32-bit and 16-bit communications, to take advantage of Sara's 32-bit NIC. This selection positions her to use communications for NT, Novell NetWare, TCP/IP, and other network protocols.

The reference on the screen to NDIS in Figure 4-9 is for **Network Device Interface Specification**. NDIS consists of Microsoft's guidelines for communications between NIC drivers and Microsoft networks. This includes specifications for communicating with NT Server's NetBEUI protocol. The options for Real mode (16-bit only) are not selected because this would limit full use of the 32-bit capability of the NIC driver and adapter. The **ODI (Open Datalink Interface)** is used on NetWare networks to combine the transport of several protocols, such as IPX (for Novell NetWare) and TCP/IP (for Internet, UNIX, or other communications). With the default selection shown in Figure 4-9, Sara can use the protocol options supplied with Windows 95 instead of ODI for communicating with Novell or other systems.

Figure 4-9

Driver Type
screen

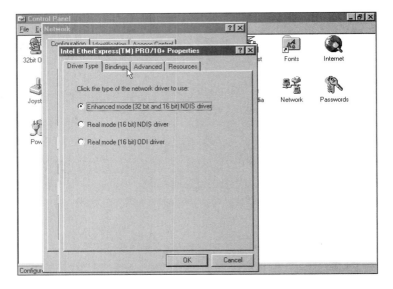

Figure 4-9

Driver Type
screen

Sara clicks the Bindings tab to view the network protocols that will be used by the NIC (see Figure 4-10). Sara selects NetBEUI, which is Microsoft's protocol for NT Server. The IPX/SPX protocols are used by Novell NetWare and are not needed.

Figure 4-10

Network
bindings for
the NIC

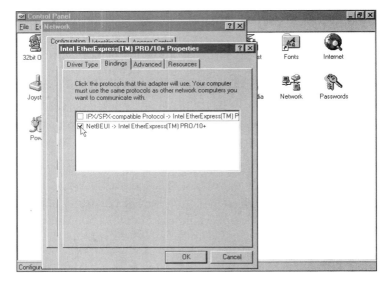

The Advanced tab (Figure 4-11) shows information about the duplex setting, power management, and transceiver type for the NIC. The duplex setting determines whether or not the NIC can send and receive signals at the same time. This should be set to "half duplex," which means the NIC will not send and receive simultaneously, because this is not supported by the firm's network. Duplex network equipment is expensive and is not needed for an installation as small as the firm's.

Power management is the ability to have the NIC automatically shut off when the computer does, if the computer has power management to save electricity. Sara is leaving the NIC's power management turned off, which means the NIC will continue to receive network signals even when the computer is using the power management. If she steps away from her desk and the power management shuts down the monitor and disk drive, she still wants the computer to communicate with the network uninterrupted. As Figure 4-11 shows, the transceiver type is set for auto-connector, which means it will automatically detect the cable type. Another option would be to select twisted-pair, but it is not necessary with the auto-connector capability.

Figure 4-11

Advanced
settings for
the NIC

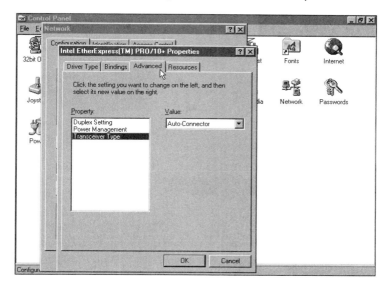

Sara checks the Resources tab to be sure no conflicts are detected with the automatic configuration and PnP detection of the NIC. A hardware conflict is indicated by an asterisk (*) or a pound sign (#) next to one of the settings. A conflict occurs when the NIC uses a resource already allocated to a disk controller, communications port, or other hardware component. As the screen in Figure 4-12 shows, Sara is leaving the settings to use the current configuration selection detected during the installation process. The screen shows there are no conflicts for the hardware resources, IRQ, and I/O address range. The IRQ (Interrupt Request) is a line or channel inside the computer that is used for NIC signals that indicate to the CPU that the NIC has information to send. The I/O address range is a block of memory storage addresses reserved for the exclusive use of the NIC. It is important to be sure the NIC is not using the same resources as another component. If there is a conflict, then neither device will work properly.

Figure 4-12

Resources
used by
the NIC

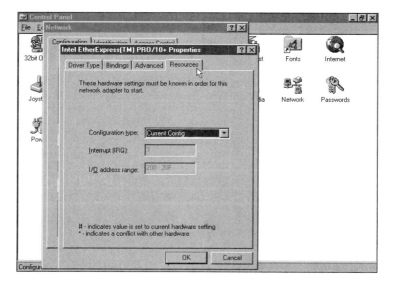

RESOLVING A RESOURCE CONFLICT

If the screen in Figure 4-12 had shown a conflict, Sara would have the option to fix the conflict on that screen. The box with the resource in conflict would not only show a # or *, but also would become active, with up and down arrows to scroll through other resource options. An option without a conflict would be indicated by the absence of the # or *.

Another way to resolve a resource conflict is to start the Control Panel and double-click the System icon. From here, Sara would select the Device Manager tab to view devices (see Figure 4-13).

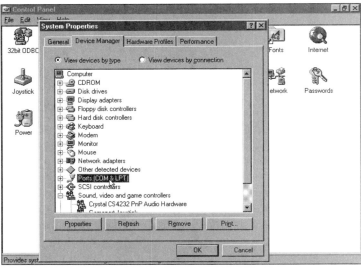

Figure 4-13

System device manager

Details about device components appear when you click a particular component. For example, double-clicking Ports (COM & LPT) would lead to a display of all the communication and printer ports. If Sara's NIC was using IRQ 3 and had a conflict with communications port 4 (COM4), she could disable the communications port because it is not used by her computer.

First, she would double-click the Ports (COM & LPT) icon (Figure 4-13). Next, she would highlight the COM4 icon on the Device Manager screen and click the Properties button. Then the screen in Figure 4-14 would appear.

Figure 4-14

Disabling a device to remove a resource conflict

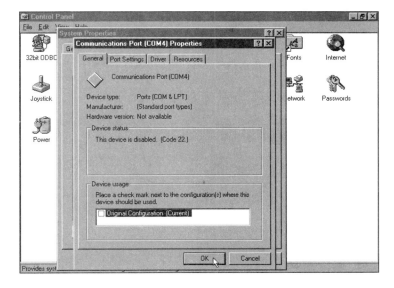

To disable COM4, Sara would need to look at the General tab (default menu setting) and remove the check in the Original Configuration (Current) box under Device usage, and then she would click OK to save the change. She could verify that the device was disabled by returning to the Device Manager screen. Notice the X through the COM4 icon in Figure 4–15.

Figure 4-15

COM4 disabled to solve a resource conflict

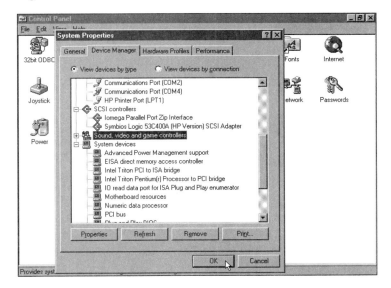

PREPARING WINDOWS 95 FOR THE NETWORK

Because the network is not yet available, Sara can use the Network options in the Windows 95 Control Panel to prepare her workstation. Before starting, Sara knows that she will need to select a computer name to use as identification for the NT Server network. Sara's forum advisors recommended using a name that reflects the user's real name. Some examples for Sara's name would be SMartin, SaraM, S_Martin, Martin, and so on. They cautioned Sara against using names that are hard for others to quickly recognize, such as BigSur or Lawmaster. Sara has decided to use Martin as her computer name.

Also, when the server accounts are created, she will need an account name that is different from her computer name. Sara plans to use SMartin as her account name when she creates accounts in Chapter 7. The computer name identifies her computer to the NT network and the account name identifies Sara for access to specific files and folders on the server.

From the Control Panel, Sara clicks the Network icon. The Network Configuration tab appears. Next she clicks the Add button for the Select Network Component Type screen. On this screen she highlights the Client option and clicks the Add button to add parameters for accessing the NT Server network (see Figure 4-16). In the Manufacturers list box, she selects Microsoft, and in the Network Clients list box, she chooses Client for Microsoft Networks and clicks OK.

Figure 4-16

Adding a client
for a Microsoft
NT Server
network

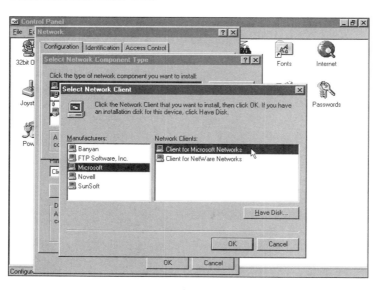

After creating her workstation as a client, Sara wants to specify the properties for the client. This includes entering the name of the domain she will use for Nishida and McGuire on the NT Server. The **domain** is made up of the clients (office members) who will be accessing the server. It is a concept used by NT Server that is similar to a workgroup only with more powerful options, as Sara will explore in Chapter 6.

The name she plans to use for the domain is THE_FIRM. To set up the client properties, Sara clicks the Network icon on the Control Panel. On the Network Configuration screen, she highlights the Client for Microsoft Networks option and clicks the Properties button. The Properties screen appears (see Figure 4-17). Here, Sara places a check in the box for Log on to Windows NT domain. In the empty box for the domain name she types "THE_FIRM." Next she clicks the radio button for Log on and restore network connections, because she wants all the mapped drives to connect at the time she logs onto the network. Figure 4-17 shows the screen she is using to set the client properties. She clicks OK to save the parameters, and the Network screen appears.

Figure 4-17

Client
properties

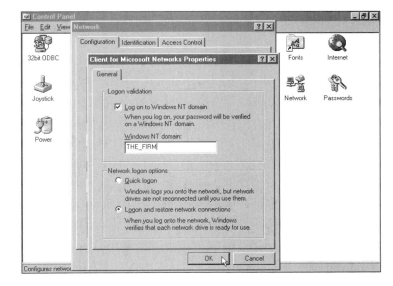

Once she saves the client properties, Sara wants to ensure she can share files on her computer with other network users. On the Network Configuration screen, she clicks the button for file and print sharing (see Figure 4-18). Here, Sara checks the box to share files, but she leaves the printer sharing box unchecked because she does not need to share her dot matrix printer. She clicks OK to save this change.

Figure 4-18

File and printer
sharing on a
client

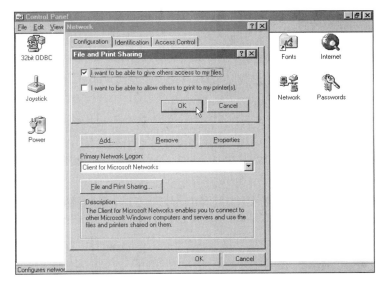

To enter the computer identification, Sara clicks the Identification tab on the Network screen. On the Identification tab, she enters her computer name (Martin), a workgroup name (THE_FIRM), and her full name as the description of her computer workstation. For the present, she uses the domain name as the workgroup name, because she has not defined any workgroups (see Figure 4-19).

Figure 4-19

Sara's computer name

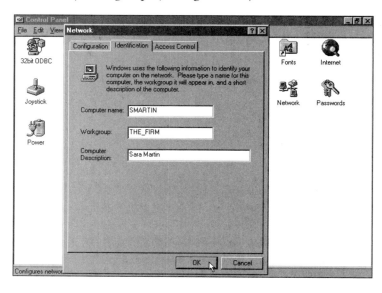

ENTERING NEW PROTOCOLS

Before finishing the client setup, Sara wants to practice entering TCP/IP as a protocol so she will be ready when they decide to install Internet access. As practice, Sara accesses the Control Panel and double-clicks the Network icon. On the Configuration tab, she clicks the Add button. The Select Network Component Type screen appears, where Sara double-clicks the Protocol selection in the list box.

On the Select Network Protocol screen Sara highlights Microsoft under Manufacturers. Four protocol selections then appear in the Network Protocols list box: IPX/SPX-compatible Protocol, Microsoft DLC, NetBEUI, and TCP/IP. Sara selects TCP/IP (see Figure 4-20) and clicks OK.

Figure 4-20

Adding TCP/IP as a network protocol

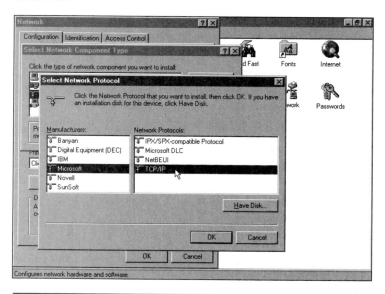

She verifies her selection by displaying the Network Configuration tab and scrolling the list box to see that TCP/IP has been added, as shown in Figure 4-21.

Figure 4-21

Verifying the addition of TCP/IP

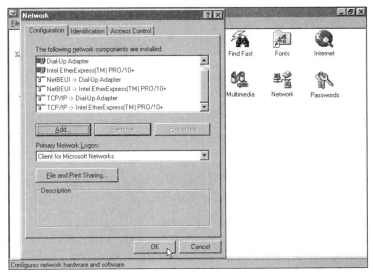

COMPLETING THE INSTALLATION

After having success on her computer, Sara scheduled a time with each person in the office to set up his or her workstation. Prior to the installation, Sara asked each person to decide on a computer name and account name to use for the network. She created a memo to explain her recommendations for selecting these names.

To keep track of the computer and user account names for future reference, Sara created a spreadsheet to share on the network when it is installed. Her spreadsheet is shown in Table 4-2.

Table 4-2

Nishida and McGuire client computer and user account names

Name	Computer Name	User Account Name
Jason Brown	BROWN	JBrown
Rick Kurkowski	KURKOWSKI	RickK
Kent McGuire	MCGUIRE	McGuireK
Joe Candelaria	CANDELARIA	JoeC
Mark Jackson	JACKSON	MarkJ
Sara Martin	MARTIN	SMartin
Sally Morton	MORTON	SMorton
Terry Norton	NORTON	TerryN
Jane Randall	RANDALL	JRandall
Anne Nishida	NISHIDA	ANishida
Beth Stevens	STEVENS	BethS
Kristin Walters	WALTERS	KWalters

SARA'S NEXT ASSIGNMENT

Four days later, Sara is just finishing her last client NIC installation when the NT Server software finally arrives. At the same time, the cabling contractor tells her they have completed the cable installation. It's now time for Sara to inspect the job. Sara has been checking throughout the installation to ensure the cable was run as specified to each office location. She also has been inspecting for poor-quality connectors and bad cable connections. Now it is time to review the test data from the contractor and to view sample connection tests using portable workstations provided by the contractor. All the tests show the cable is ready to use.

With the cable inspection completed, Sara is prepared to tackle the NT Server installation. The server hardware has been running under Windows 95 for the past several days and appears to be solid. Sara's next step is to replace the Windows 95 software with NT Server 4.0, which she does in the next chapter.

Before Sara starts the NT Server installation, Kristin has asked Sara for a schedule of the work to be completed. Sara's schedule allows four weeks to generate the server, finish preliminary administrative tasks, and connect the workstations. The four weeks also will give her time to more fully test the network cabling.

KEY CONCEPTS SUMMARY

The concepts introduced throughout the discussion of NT Server client workstations are reviewed in the following paragraphs.

conventional memory The lower 640 KB of memory on older computers and operating systems reserved for use by application software.

domain A grouping of network clients and resources within NT Server.

Network Device Interface Specification (NDIS) Guidelines developed by Microsoft that specify how NIC drivers and Microsoft networks communicate.

Open Datalink Interface (ODI) This interface, developed by Novell, provides the capability to transport multiple protocols on the same network and is commonly used on NetWare networks.

virtual memory A technique used to extend memory beyond the capacity of RAM by using hard disk space.

workgroup Refers to the capability of a network operating system to allow individual groups in the workplace to share information for specific work purposes, such as sharing a directory on a member's hard drive.

SUMMARY OF WINDOWS FUNCTIONS

The following Control Panel icons and terms were used in this chapter by Sara to set up the client workstations in preparation for connecting to NT Server.

Network Icon in the Control Panel The Network icon is used from the Control Panel to set up network-related options that include the following:

- Adding an NIC
- Installing an NIC driver
- Adding a protocol
- Setting up a Microsoft client
- Creating a computer name
- Specifying a domain or workgroup name
- Enabling file or printer sharing on a network

REVIEW QUESTIONS

1. Which of the following clients can connect to NT Server?
   a. DOS
   b. OS/2
   c. Windows 95
   d. Windows 3.1
   e. All of the above

2. From where is the Control Panel accessed?
   a. My Computer
   b. Windows Explorer
   c. Start menu/Settings option
   d. All of the above

3. Which interface is used to carry more than one protocol?
   a. ODI
   b. NDIS
   c. SPX
   d. All of the above
   e. Both a and b

4. Which of the following does not use a GUI interface?
   a. Windows 95
   b. Windows 3.11
   c. DOS
   d. NT Workstation

5. Which of the following is an example of a resource that might have a conflict on a client?

    a. IRA

    b. IRQ

    c. I/O address

    d. Both b and c

6. Where would you enable printer sharing on a Windows 95 client?

    a. From the Printer icon

    b. From the Network icon

    c. From the client printer

    d. From the NIC

7. Which of the following is also known as Windows for Workgroups?

    a. Windows 95

    b. Windows 3.1

    c. Windows 3.11

    d. Windows 2.1

8. Which of the following is designed for peer-to-peer communications?

    a. Windows 95

    b. Windows 3.1

    c. NT Workstation

    d. Both a and c

9. From where would you set a client's computer name in Windows 95?

    a. The Configuration tab in the Network icon

    b. The NIC driver setup

    c. The Identification tab in the Network icon

    d. The computer name cannot be set from Windows 95

10. The protocol used by a Windows 95 client cannot be set up from within Windows 95.

    a. True

    b. False

11. From where is a new protocol added for networking on a Windows 95 client?

    a. From the Protocol icon in the Control Panel

    b. From the Network icon in the Control Panel

    c. From the File option in My Computer

    d. From the Protocol option in the Start menu

12. Which type of NIC is most desirable for a Pentium client?

    a. A 32-bit NIC

    b. A 16-bit NIC

    c. An 8-bit NIC

    d. A NIC with dip switches

13. When a computer can automatically detect a new adapter, this is called
    a. Auto-circuit.
    b. Plug-and-Play.
    c. NPN.
    d. Power management.
14. Ten computers can use which of the following as a server?
    a. Windows 95
    b. NT Workstation
    c. Windows for Workgroups
    d. None of the above
15. Which protocol is used on a Novell NetWare network?
    a. IPX/SPX
    b. NPX
    c. TCP/IP
    d. RTS
16. COM4 is another name for
    a. Communications port 4.
    b. Network printer 4.
    c. The modem port.
    d. A communications protocol.
17. Which of the following are guidelines used for communications between NIC drivers and Microsoft networks?
    a. ODI
    b. NDIS
    c. ODBC
    d. IEEE
18. What is the best source of an NIC driver?
    a. The NIC manufacturer
    b. A newsgroup on the Internet
    c. A friend who manages a network
    d. Through the UNIX bulletin board service
19. An X through a device's icon on the Device Manager screen means
    a. The device does not need client resources.
    b. The device is disabled.
    c. The device needs to be upgraded.
    d. None of the above.
20. Which of the following means that data signals cannot be sent and received at the same time?
    a. Full duplex
    b. Half duplex
    c. Triplex
    d. Singplex

THE HOLLAND COLLEGE PROJECT: PHASE 4

Bob Watson is interested in preparing the administrative users and the English and writing lab for networking. He wants you to coordinate this process by investigating the need for NICs and upgrades to workstation operating systems. Bob is interested in cost estimates and any other relevant information that would be of help.

Because the president and trustees are anxious to see the process move along, Bob also wants you to prepare in advance for the tasks required to set up the client workstations.

ASSIGNMENT 4-1

Contact your local computer supplier or dealer to find out prices of 32-bit NICs. Find prices from four or five vendors. Once you have the prices, complete the following spreadsheet:

NIC Vendor	Price per NIC	Number of NICS (Administration Building and English/Writing Lab)	Total Cost

ASSIGNMENT 4-2

Review your information about client operating systems on campus, noting that both labs are using Windows 3.1. Next contact a local computer dealer or use the Internet to find out the cost of upgrading from Windows 3.1 to Windows 95 or Windows NT Workstation and the cost of upgrading from Windows 95 to Windows NT Worksatation.

- Would you upgrade any client operating systems used in the Hoyt Administration Building? Which ones would you upgrade? What would you upgrade them to, and why would you upgrade them? What would be the cost of the upgrade, including the cost to upgrade any hardware? (*Hint:* Use the hardware pricing you obtained in Assignment 3-5.)

- Would you upgrade any client operating systems used in the English and writing lab? Which ones would you upgrade? What would you upgrade them to, and why would you upgrade them? What would be the cost of the upgrade, including the cost to upgrade hardware?

ASSIGNMENT 4-3

Review your information about the hardware used on campus.

- Would you upgrade any hardware in the Hoyt Administration Building? If so, why would you upgrade the hardware? What would you upgrade it to?

- Would you upgrade any hardware in the English and writing lab? If so, why would you upgrade the hardware? What would you upgrade it to?

ASSIGNMENT 4-4

In a lab that your instructor has provided:

- Install an NIC in a client workstation for NT Server
- Install the NIC driver
- Bind the NIC to NetBEUI and TCP/IP
- Experiment with changing the duplex, power management, and other advanced settings for the NIC
- Verify the NIC setup
- Run the test program that accompanies the NIC
- Try connecting to a campus server using the NIC

ASSIGNMENT 4-5

Set up a client to run the IPX/SPX protocol. Next, set up the client to run TCP/IP.

 ## ASSIGNMENT 4-6

Access the Device Manager for the client you used in Assignment 4-4. Create a conflict with the resources used by LPT1. After creating the conflict, write down how the devices appear in the Device Manager. Next, fix the conflict you created.

 ## ASSIGNMENT 4-7

Set up a Microsoft client on a Windows 95 workstation by doing the following:

- Enter a domain name
- Enter a computer name
- Enter a description of the computer
- Enable file sharing
- Enable printer sharing

ASSIGNMENT 4-8

Prepare a memo for Bob Watson to describe your recommendations for creating client computer names for the Hoyt Administration network users.

In your memo, also include recommendations on guidelines for creating client computer names for computers or users of the English and writing lab. An example memo format is provided here.

HOLLAND COLLEGE INTEROFFICE MEMO

TO: BOB WATSON

FROM:

SUBJECT: GUIDELINES FOR ESTABLISHING COMPUTER NAMES

            AND PASSWORDS

CC:

 ASSIGNMENT 4-9

Assume that Jackie Herrera has forgotten her computer name. Where would she look to view it?

ASSIGNMENT 4-10

Assume you have just installed an NIC in your client workstation. When you attempt to access the network, the NIC does not seem to be able to communicate. Further, your Network Neighborhood screen does not show any domain members (see Figure 4-22). Describe the steps you would take to troubleshoot this problem.

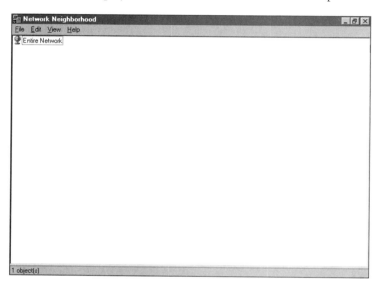

SERVER INSTALLATION

Sara arrived at the office this morning feeling anticipation mixed with a little apprehension. Today she starts work on installing Microsoft Windows NT Server. She knows she is well prepared. The server hardware is ready and functioning well. The workstations are set up with NICs, drivers, and the NetBEUI protocol. Thanks to her work over the past few days, she knows more about Windows software installation for networking than she did before.

AFTER READING THIS CHAPTER AND COMPLETING THE EXERCISES YOU WILL BE ABLE TO:

- PLAN FOR THE NT SERVER INSTALLATION.
- EXPLAIN THE DIFFERENCES BETWEEN FILE SYSTEMS USED BY MICROSOFT OPERATING SYSTEMS.
- PARTITION AND FORMAT A DISK FOR NT SERVER.
- SELECT THE SERVER TYPE FOR NT SERVER SETUP.
- RUN THE NT SERVER SETUP AND SETUP WIZARD TO CREATE AN NT SERVER.

ADVANCED PREPARATIONS

In this chapter, Sara performs all of the tasks necessary to install the NT Server operating system. At first, she prepares by gathering the information she will need during the installation, which includes decisions about partitioning drives, what file system to use, and what naming conventions to set. Next, Sara starts the installation which is in two parts, one to verify server components and the second to configure the operating system. When the installation is finished, Sara performs a quick test to ensure the operating system is installed.

Sara has an appointment with Ryan to review in advance the information she needs for the NT Server setup. Ryan describes the overall setup process and how Sara needs to prepare for each step. Together they create a spreadsheet listing the preparation steps along with an empty column for Sara's decisions about each step. As they build the spreadsheet, Sara realizes there are a number of decisions to make. These include server hardware information, where to install the NT files, what file system to use, what type of server to set up, what to name the server, what to name the domain, and whether to create an Emergency Repair Disk. The spreadsheet Sara and Ryan compose is shown in Table 5-1.

Table 5-1

Preparation task list for NT Server installation

Installation Preparation Task	Decision Step
Prepare a list of hardware components	
Hardware configuration information (BIOS setup parameters)	
NT Server system requirements check	
What partition to use—C or D?	
What file system should be installed?	
Name of the NT directory	
Name for the server	
Administrator account password	
Type of server	
Install the Internet Information Server?	
Protocol selection	
Name for the domain	
Create an Emergency Repair Disk?	

When Sara and Ryan finish, Sara thanks Ryan for his help and returns to her office to work. Kristin stops in to ask how the last client installation went. Sara explains that all went well and says she is moving on to preparations for the server software installation. Kristin wishes her luck and promises to check back later with some fudge for encouragement. Sara returns to her spreadsheet, starting with the server hardware components. Her goal is to have the spreadsheet completed by early afternoon, barring any office computer emergencies.

SERVER HARDWARE COMPONENTS

Sara puts together a list of hardware components such as computer type, monitor adapter, SCSI adapters, keyboard type, hard disk drive capacity, CD-ROM controller, and NIC type. Although she may not need all this information, she wants to have it available in case a question arises during installation. Sara's list of server components is the following:

- 166 MHz Pentium computer
- SVGA monitor using an S3 Trio adapter
- PCI bus type
- 64 MB of memory
- 2 SCSI adapters for hard disk drives (Adaptec AHA-2920 adapters)
- 2 formatted hard drives with 4.3 GB each
- 1 1.44/1.25 MB 3.5-inch floppy disk drive
- 101/102 keyboard
- Intel EtherExpress Pro 10 network adapter
- 1 Sony CDU-561 CD-ROM drive with SCSI adapter

Ryan suggests that, in addition to making the hardware list, Sara record the BIOS configuration settings in case a problem arises and a setting is lost. Sara makes a list of the BIOS settings by pressing F1 as the computer boots to enter the BIOS setup program (see Figure 5-1). The BIOS setup menus include information about the BIOS version and manufacturer, hardware components, which drive to boot from first, drive statistics such as the size and number of cylinders per disk, floppy drive type, and so on.

Figure 5-1

The BIOS
setup screen

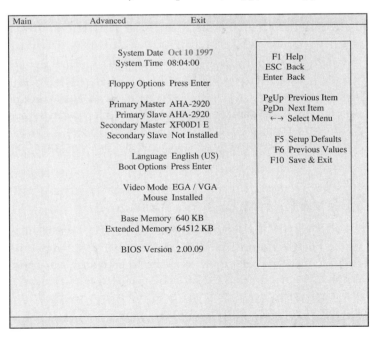

NT SERVER REQUIREMENTS CHECK

Next, Sara checks Microsoft's published requirements for an NT Server computer, shown in Table 5-2. Sara purchased a server that meets or exceeds all the minimums, based on the needs of the firm.

Table 5-2

Minimum hardware requirements for an NT Server

Minimum NT Server Hardware Requirements
32-bit bus computer with an 80486 25 MHz (or faster) processor
VGA or better resolution monitor
High density 3.5-inch floppy disk drive
CD-ROM drive
16 MB or more memory
One or more hard disks with 148 MB
Network interface card (needed for network communications)

DISK PARTITION SELECTION

Sara purchased the server with two pre-installed hard drives connected to separate SCSI controllers. Each hard drive came partitioned for DOS and preformatted. **Partitioning** is a process in which a section or a complete drive is set up for use by an operating system. A disk can be formatted after it is partitioned. **Formatting** is an operation that divides a disk into small sections called sectors for storage of files.

The disk drives on Sara's computer, drives C and D, are partitioned for DOS. The fact that the disk drives are already partitioned is not a problem for NT Server. At the time of installation, NT Server can create its own partition. Sara plans to install the NT Server files on the C disk drive, because the BIOS is set to boot from drive C before drive D.

The BIOS setup program usually has an option to specify the boot drive order. This is the order in which the computer checks drives for an operating system boot sector. Most network administrators have the BIOS check drives in the order of the drive letters: A, B, C, D, and so on. This provides the option to boot first from a floppy drive, in case there is a need to use a floppy setup or diagnostic disk. If the floppy drives are empty, the computer boots from drive C.

NT SERVER FILE SYSTEMS

The NT Server file system options available to Sara are: the Windows NT File System (NTFS) or the File Allocation Table (FAT) system. NTFS is a modern file system designed for the needs of a network server environment. In particular, Microsoft designed NT security to pass the U.S. government's C2 security specifications. C2 security refers to high-level standards for data protection, system auditing, and system access that are required by some government agencies. By comparison, the FAT system was originally developed for DOS-based computers and does not have the security a file server needs for network operations. Once the NTFS system is installed, many options are available to the network administrator including security, large file capability, and file activity tracking.

SECURITY

NTFS security accomplishes several purposes. One is to create permission for the network administrator to access directories and files owned by a user. The permission enables the network administrator to access these user files for backups and other maintenance work. In addition, NTFS enables you to set up specified directories as shared directories, so designated users can access them and share files and programs. These are called "trust and privilege relationships" and can be established in many ways to share and also to protect information. For example, a protected directory and its contents can be set up so there is no access beyond that of the owner. Another directory might be set up so users can read and share the contents but cannot change information or write new files to that directory. Or a directory can be set up so anyone in a specified group can add, change, or delete files.

The FAT directory system does not have the comprehensive security of NTFS. If Sara selected this file type for the firm's server, there would be very limited ways to protect certain files from being read or changed. The firm's server will hold many confidential documents, some involving privilege between only one attorney and his or her client. For this reason Sara plans to use the NTFS file option when she installs the NT Server software.

FILE COMPRESSION

In their meeting earlier, Ryan mentioned the file compression capability of NTFS. File compression is a process that significantly reduces the size of a file by techniques such as removing unused space within a file. Some files can be compressed by more than 40%, saving important disk space for other storage needs. This is particularly useful for files that are accessed infrequently. NTFS provides the ability to compress files as needed. FAT does not come with a file compression facility, although compression is possible through third-party products.

 File compression can be used on specified files after the server is generated. A disadvantage is that compressed files take longer to access because they must be decompressed when retrieved.

FILE SIZE

Although it doesn't affect the firm presently, NTFS can be scaled to accommodate very large files, particularly for database applications. A Microsoft SQL Server database file might be 20 GB or larger. This means, one day, the firm could store images of contracts and legal documents in a database for fast retrieval. The NTFS system can support files up to 64 GB, which makes imaging a very real possibility as the firm grows. The FAT file system only supports file sizes to 4 GB.

FILE ACTIVITY INFORMATION

The NTFS system keeps a log or journal of file system activity. This is a critical process should there be a power outage or hard disk failure. Important information can be retrieved and restored in these situations. FAT does not have this capability.

FILE RECOGNITION

Sara is not planning to partition the server for another operating system, such as MS-DOS or Windows 95. She learned through her forum group that it is not desirable to have the server acting as a workstation, too. It is best to strictly dedicate the computer to providing network services to its clients.

In some instances, a network administrator may need to have two systems on the server due to a shortage of workstations or a special application. In this situation, he or she may need to share files between the operating systems. A limitation of NTFS is that it cannot recognize other file types on a computer running two systems. For example, if Sara needed to have a partition on the server for Windows 95 and one for NT Server, NTFS would not permit NT Server to recognize the FAT-based Windows 95 files. If she set up NT server for the FAT system, then the server system would be able to access or share the Windows 95 files.

 The NT Server installation can convert existing FAT file systems to NTFS, but NTFS file systems cannot be converted to FAT. Do not convert a FAT system to NTFS unless you are sure you do not need to run operating systems other than Windows NT on a server.

FILE LOCATION AND NT DIRECTORY NAME

Next on Sara's planning list is to decide where to place the NT Server system files and what to name the directory. A small complication is that some computers come preloaded with Windows 95 or Windows NT Workstation. NT Server can coexist with one of these operating systems, but it is important that you do not put the NT Server system files in the same directory. If you do, it is difficult to determine which files belong with which operating system. This can be a problem later if you need to remove one of the operating systems. Also, when NTFS is selected as the file system, files cannot be shared or migrated between NT Server and Windows 95 when running Windows 95.

Sara's computer came with Windows 95 preloaded. She plans to format the hard drives to avoid having dual operating systems. However, before she does this, she is making a Windows 95 boot disk, for two reasons. One is that she can use it to format the hard drives. Another is to have a fall-back position in case something goes wrong during the installation. She can use the disk to boot the server from drive A as a means to diagnose problems. She makes the boot disk by going to the Control Panel. From the Control Panel she selects the Add/Remove Programs icon (see Figure 5-2).

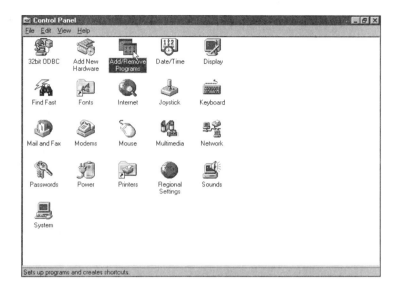

Figure 5-2

The Control Panel with Add/Remove Programs highlighted

The Add/Remove Programs Properties screen has three tabs: Install/Uninstall, Windows Setup, and Startup Disk. Sara selects Startup Disk (see Figure 5-3). She places a labeled and formatted 3.5-inch floppy disk in the computer and clicks the Create Disk button. After the startup disk is created, she reboots the computer from that disk. The computer boots from drive A because earlier Sara had set the BIOS to check drive A first. Next she runs MS-DOS and types "format C:" at the MS-DOS command prompt. When drive C is formatted, she repeats the procedure for drive D.

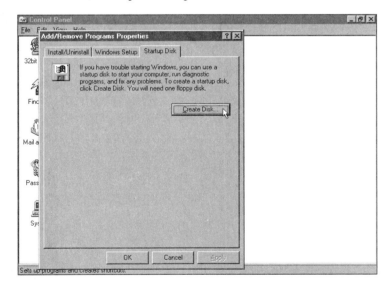

Figure 5-3

Creating a Windows 95 startup disk from the Add/Remove Programs Properties dialog box

As she waits for the drives to format, Sara considers a name for the NT directory. Ryan has advised Sara to use names that are easy for people to remember and to type. The directory containing the NT files is most easily remembered if "NT" is part of the directory name. The default name provided by Microsoft during the installation process is WINNT. Sara plans to use this directory name and to make it a directory under the main (root) directory on the C disk volume.

SERVER NAME

Because the server name affects the entire office, last week Sara asked Kristin for input from the management team. Sara learned in her forum discussions that it is wise to bring others into the process of naming the server. This helps ensure their support of the project, and it ensures an appropriate name is selected. At their Monday morning meeting, the managers decided on the name LAWYER. This is a relatively short name and it is descriptive of the server's function. With this step decided, Sara enters LAWYER on her spreadsheet.

Make the server name easy to remember and use; and ensure it is not already taken by another network computer or domain

ADMINISTRATOR ACCOUNT

At the time of installation, NT Server creates a master account called the Administrator account. This account has access to all areas of the server, including security administration, file administration, and control of user accounts. Entry into the Administrator account is controlled by a password that is established at the time the server is created. The password can be changed later, but it saves time to have a password ready before starting the installation.

Ryan advised Sara to have a password in mind before she got started. He suggested that she write down the password and store it in a safe place for later reference. Passwords must be 14 characters or less. Sara uses a 10-character password.

INTERNET INFORMATION SERVER

The Internet Information Server (IIS) is Web server software that Microsoft includes with NT Server. When installed and connected to the Internet, this software will enable the firm to make Web pages about their legal services available to others. IIS also provides the capability for Internet users to exchange files with the server.

IIS also supports intranet services, where an organization creates an Internet-like network for sharing reports and other information within that organization. For example, on a university campus where administrators are spread throughout several buildings, an intranet service allows them to access a common set of reports.

Sara is interested in exploring how the firm can take advantage of IIS, but for the present her primary objective is to make basic NT Server services available to the office. With this goal in mind, Sara decides not to install IIS at this time.

PROTOCOL SELECTION

Sara learned in Chapter 2 that protocols establish rules for communications on networks. NT Server is compatible with several protocols. Ryan told Sara that for now she only needs to implement NetBEUI because it is native to Windows 95 applications. NetBEUI is appropriate for small networks with 50 or fewer users and no other network operating systems, such as Novell NetWare. As the network grows or when Sara connects to the Internet, she can easily set up TCP/IP as practiced in Chapter 4. TCP/IP is popularly used on large networks throughout the world. For now, she records NetBEUI in her decision spreadsheet.

SERVER DOMAINS

Microsoft employs the concept of the domain to identify belonging to a group. Sara thinks of a domain as similar to membership in her health club, The Athletic Center. A domain, like the health club, has a name to give it an identity. Sara decides to call the server's domain THE_FIRM.

When people join the health club, they become members and receive privileges to use the club's resources. Some people pay a fee that allows them to use only the swimming pool. Others pay for gym and pool privileges. Each person has an identification card that gives her or him access to the entitled services. The identification card has the member's name and a picture for security validation.

As with the health club, each user in a domain is identified by his or her account name. Sara's account name is SMartin. When she sets up the domain, SMartin will be known as a member of the domain with specific assigned privileges. Her account name is like the health-club membership card. Just as her card picture serves as a security validation, Sara's account password is the domain validation.

The domain is intended to simplify server management. It makes it possible for accounts, privilege levels, and user information to be managed from one place. A network can have more than one domain, as a means to divide users into different network groups, particularly on a WAN. Although Sara is not considering more than one domain, at present, it will be handy to have additional domains when the law firm opens two new branches in the future.

Another option is when two or more servers are on a network. Each server can be in the same domain or might have a different domain. For instance, if the law firm's network is joined in the future with an accounting network in the same building, each of their servers would likely have a separate domain. However, if Sara's firm eventually has two servers, one for software applications and one for databases, then both could be in the same domain.

SERVER TYPES

Sara is starting with one server, but she has read about configuring the network for more. Also, Ryan advised that when Sara installs the server software, she needs to define the server's relationship to the domain. One type of server is called the **primary domain controller (PDC)**. The PDC acts as the main domain for administration of members and for security management. The PDC is home to the **security accounts database** and keeps track of security information on each user.

Another type of server is the **backup domain controller (BDC)**. The BDC has a copy of the security accounts database and can be pressed into service should the PDC server experience a problem. A BDC server can be designated only when there are two or more NT servers and one has already been assigned as the PDC.

A third server type is called a **standalone server**. This type of server does not handle logon or security validations. The most typical case is a client/server operation where one server holds the database information for the network. The database server does not need to handle logon checking because the information it houses is accessed indirectly through software applications on a PDC or BDC server that checks the logon permissions. Another type of standalone server is one devoted to handling print, CD-ROM, or fax services.

Client/server is a technique used to develop modern application systems where software functions are performed at the most efficient location. GUI functions occur at the workstation, applications run from an application server, and database functions run from a database server. Access to the database is often controlled by the applications on the application server, relieving the database server from extra work.

Because every NT Server network must have a PDC and because there is currently only one server on the network, Sara decides to designate the server as the PDC.

SELECTING A DOMAIN NAME

The domain name Sara selected is THE_FIRM. This name provides a good description of the purpose of the domain and is easy for everyone to remember. To avoid confusion, the domain name should not be the same as the server name. Also, each domain must have a unique name.

If NT Server is installed on a computer that is not connected to the network, it cannot check for duplicate domain names. Sara's server is not connected to the network, but typically this is not a problem with small networks where one person coordinates the naming.

CREATING AN EMERGENCY REPAIR DISK

At the end of the installation, NT Server provides the opportunity to create an Emergency Repair Disk. Sara plans to have a high-density 1.44 MB 3.5-inch floppy disk ready for this step. Microsoft highly recommends creating the disk, as it can be used to repair and troubleshoot problems if they occur. The Emergency Repair Disk is used to fix problems with drivers, the NTFS file system, and the NT Server operating system. Ryan told Sara to create a new Emergency Repair Disk whenever she makes a change to NT Server, such as installing new adapters or a new NIC, restructuring a partition, or upgrading the operating system.

Sara now completes her checklist of tasks, with an entry for each decision step. Her pre-installation decisions are shown in Table 5-3.

	Installation Preparation Task	Decision Step
Table 5-3	Prepare a list of hardware components	Completed and available for the installation
Sara's completed pre-installation checklist	Hardware configuration information (BIOS setup parameters)	Completed and available for the installation
	NT Server system requirements check	Requirements have been reviewed and are met
	What partition to use: C or D?	Will use the partition on C
	What file system should be installed?	NTFS
	Name of the NT directory	WINNT
	Name of the server	LAWYER
	Administrator account password	One has been selected
	Type of server	Primary domain controller
	Install the Internet Information Server?	Not at this time
	Protocol selection	NetBEUI
	Name for the domain	THE_FIRM
	Create an Emergency Repair Disk?	Yes: have a formatted 3.5-inch floppy disk ready and labeled

THE INSTALLATION: PART 1

With her advance preparations completed, Sara is ready to begin installing NT Server. The software comes with three floppy disks and one CD-ROM. She boots the computer from the floppy labeled Windows NT Server Setup Disk #1. Another option is to boot directly from a CD-ROM for computers with a BIOS supporting the El Torito Bootable CD-ROM format. Sara checks the documentation to find her computer does not support the bootable CD-ROM format, so her first steps are:

1. Turn off the computer.

2. Place Setup Disk #1 in drive A.

3. Turn on the computer, which boots from Setup Disk #1.

 Be certain to have all the Windows NT Server floppy disks and the CD-ROM handy for the installation. Also, keep the CD-ROM case available because it has the identification key printed on a sticker.

SETUP CHECKS THE SYSTEM CONFIGURATION

When Sara boots the computer, a screen shows NT Server Setup checking the computer's system configuration. When it finishes the check, a message appears at the bottom of the screen showing Setup loading files. The next screen, shown in Figure 5-4, is a request to insert Setup Disk #2 into drive A and press [Enter] (the mouse doesn't work on these initial setup screens).

Figure 5-4

Request for
Setup Disk #2

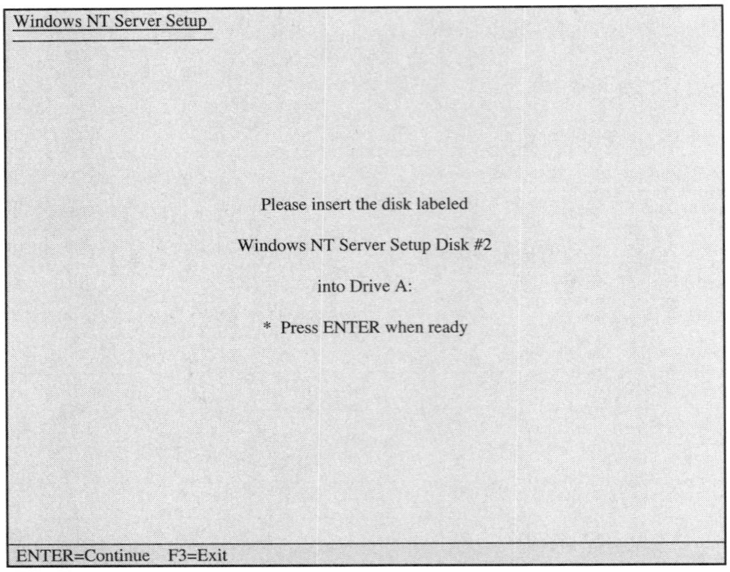

```
┌─────────────────────────────────────────────────────────┐
│ Windows NT Server Setup                                   │
├─────────────────────────────────────────────────────────┤
│                                                           │
│                                                           │
│                                                           │
│                                                           │
│                                                           │
│                   Please insert the disk labeled          │
│                                                           │
│              Windows NT Server Setup Disk #2              │
│                                                           │
│                        into Drive A:                      │
│                                                           │
│                 *  Press ENTER when ready                 │
│                                                           │
│                                                           │
│                                                           │
│                                                           │
│                                                           │
│                                                           │
│                                                           │
├─────────────────────────────────────────────────────────┤
│ ENTER=Continue    F3=Exit                                 │
└─────────────────────────────────────────────────────────┘
```

SETUP INTRODUCTION

Next, the four NT Server Setup options appear as shown in Figure 5-5: learn more about NT Setup, continue with setup, repair a previously installed version, or quit. Sara presses [Enter] to continue the installation.

Figure 5-5

Introduction to
NT Server
Setup

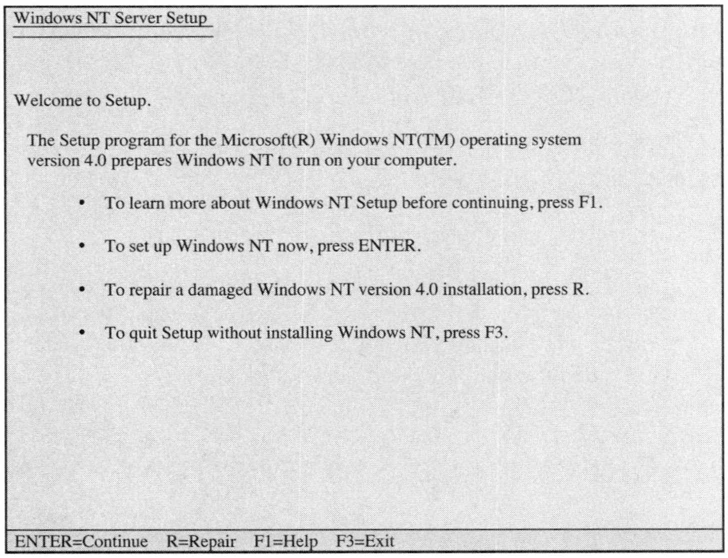

```
┌─────────────────────────────────────────────────────────┐
│ Windows NT Server Setup                                   │
├─────────────────────────────────────────────────────────┤
│                                                           │
│ Welcome to Setup.                                         │
│                                                           │
│   The Setup program for the Microsoft(R) Windows NT(TM) operating system │
│   version 4.0 prepares Windows NT to run on your computer.│
│                                                           │
│       •  To learn more about Windows NT Setup before continuing, press F1. │
│                                                           │
│       •  To set up Windows NT now, press ENTER.          │
│                                                           │
│       •  To repair a damaged Windows NT version 4.0 installation, press R. │
│                                                           │
│       •  To quit Setup without installing Windows NT, press F3. │
│                                                           │
│                                                           │
│                                                           │
│                                                           │
│                                                           │
├─────────────────────────────────────────────────────────┤
│ ENTER=Continue    R=Repair    F1=Help    F3=Exit          │
└─────────────────────────────────────────────────────────┘
```

MASS STORAGE DETECTION

As shown in Figure 5-6, Setup now attempts to automatically detect mass storage device controllers, such as ESDI, IDE, and SCSI. Sara presses [Enter] to continue.

Figure 5-6

The Setup warning screen for mass storage device detection

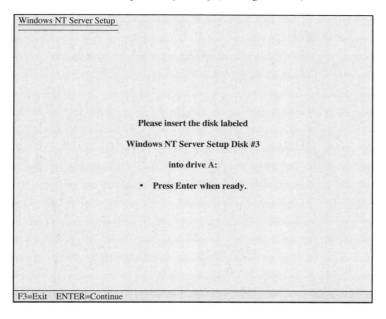

```
Windows NT Server Setup

Setup automatically detects floppy disk controllers and standard
ESDI/IDE hard disks without user intervention. However, on some
computers detection of certain other mass storage devices, such as
SCSI adapters and CD-ROM drives, can cause the computer to become
unresponsive or to malfunction temporarily.

For this reason, you can bypass Setup's mass storage device detection
and manually select SCSI adapters, CD-ROM drives, and special disk
controllers (such as drive arrays) for installation.


      •   To continue, Press Enter.
          Setup will attempt to detect mass storage devices in your computer.

      •   To skip mass storage device detection, press S.
          Setup will allow you to manually select SCSI adapters,
          CD-ROM drives, and special disk controllers for installation.




F3=Exit    ENTER=Continue    S=Skip Detection
```

The mass storage detection process requires Setup to load a large number of device drivers from many hardware vendors. Setup Disk #3 contains the device drivers. As requested, Sara inserts Disk #3 and presses [Enter] (see Figure 5-7).

Figure 5-7

Instruction to insert Setup Disk #3

```
Windows NT Server Setup




                    Please insert the disk labeled

                    Windows NT Server Setup Disk #3

                            into drive A:

                    •   Press Enter when ready.







F3=Exit    ENTER=Continue
```

Sometimes Setup has problems detecting SCSI adapters for hard drives and CD-ROM drives. Or you might need a supplementary disk from the manufacturer to install drivers for certain SCSI adapters. Fortunately, Sara followed the advice of her NT Server forum advisors and purchased well-supported, name-brand components from the hardware compatibility list.

Once the device drivers were loaded, the program correctly detects all of Sara's mass storage devices, as shown in Figure 5-8. (If the information had not been correct, Sara would have been given the option to type S and manually select additional devices.)

Figure 5-8

Setup screen showing attached SCSI adapters

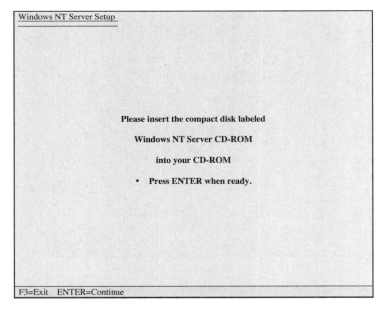

```
Windows NT Server Setup

  Setup has recognized the following mass storage devices in your computer:

    SCSI CD-ROM PCI SCSI Controller
    SCSI Adaptec AHA-2920 SCSI Controller
    SCSI Adaptec AHA-2920 SCSI Controller

      •  To specify additional SCSI adapters, CD-ROM drives, or special
         disk controllers for use with Windows NT, including those for which
         you have a device support disk from a mass storage device
         manufacturer, press S.

      •  If you do not have any device support disks from a mass storage
         device manufacturer, or do not want to specify additional
         mass storage devices for use with Windows NT, press ENTER.

S=Specify Additional Device    ENTER=Continue    F3=Exit
```

Sara presses [Enter] to continue the installation and is prompted to insert the CD-ROM labeled Windows NT Server CD-ROM and press [Enter] (see Figure 5-9).

Figure 5-9

Instruction to insert the NT Server CD-ROM

```
Windows NT Server Setup




                    Please insert the compact disk labeled

                       Windows NT Server CD-ROM

                          into your CD-ROM

                     •  Press ENTER when ready.




F3=Exit    ENTER=Continue
```

Setup loads the Microsoft license agreement, as shown in Figure 5-10. The agreement is in English and French. Sara uses the Page Up and Page Down keys to move through the document. When she reaches the end, she agrees to the terms of the license by pressing F8.

Figure 5-10

NT Server
Licensing
Agreement
screen

Windows NT Licensing Agreement

Windows NT Server
MICROSOFT LICENSE AGREEMENT
SERVER LICENSE FOR MICROSOFT SERVER PRODUCTS

IMPORTANT READ CAREFULLY: This Microsoft End-User License Agreement
("EULA") is a legal agreement between you (either an individual or
a single entity) and Microsoft Corporation for the Microsoft software
product identified above, which includes computer software and
associated media and printed materials, and may include "online'
or electronic media documentation ("SOFTWARE PRODUCT" or "SOFTWARE").
By installing, copying, or otherwise using the SOFTWARE PRODUCT,
you agree to be bounded by the terms of the EULA. If ;you do not
agree to the terms of the EULA, promptly return the unused
SOFTWARE PRODUCT to the place from which you obtained it for
a full refund.

MICROSOFT SOFTWARE LICENSE
the SOFTWARE PRODUCT is protected by copyright laws and
international copyright treaties, as well as other intellectual
property laws and treaties. The SOFTWARE PRODUCT is licensed, not sold.

1. GRANT OF LICENSE. this Microsoft product contains some or all of
the following types of software: "Server Software" that provides
services on a computer called a server and "Client Software" that
allows a computer or workstation to access or utilize the servers
provided by the Server Software. Microsoft grants to you the
following rights to the Server Software and the Client Software

Page Down=Next Page

UPGRADE OPTION

If Sara had a version of Windows NT loaded on her server, she would have seen an upgrade offer like the one shown in Figure 5-11 on the following page. This screen did not appear for Sara because she hadn't previously loaded any versions of NT. Had she installed an earlier version of NT Server, it would have made sense to press [Enter] to upgrade. However, as Ryan advised, she should not upgrade from an old version of NT Workstation, such as NT Workstation 3.51, to Windows NT version 4.0 because her new version of NT Server would be limited as a standalone server, not a full-fledged PDC or BDC. To avoid this, she could choose to skip the upgrade or press N to install a new version of NT Workstation from a separate licensed copy.

 If the Setup program detects a copy of NT on the computer, only use the upgrade option for a previously installed Windows NT Server version and not for Windows NT Workstation.

Figure 5-11

Setup detects
previous
versions of NT

```
┌─────────────────────────────────────────────────────────────┐
│ Windows NT Server Setup                                       │
│ ══════════════════════                                        │
│                                                               │
│ Setup has found Windows NT on your hard disk in the directory │
│ shown below:                                                  │
│                                                               │
│     C:\WINNT "Windows NT Workstation Version 3.51"            │
│                                                               │
│ Setup recommends upgrading this Windows NT installation to    │
│ Microsoft Windows NT version 4.0.  Upgrading will preserve    │
│ user account and security information, user preferences,      │
│ and other configuration information.                          │
│                                                               │
│     •  To upgrade Windows NT in the directory shown above,    │
│        press ENTER.                                           │
│                                                               │
│     •  To cancel upgrade and install a fresh copy of Windows  │
│        NT, press N.                                           │
│                                                               │
│                                                               │
│                                                               │
│                                                               │
│                                                               │
│ F3=Exit   ENTER=Upgrade   N=New Version                       │
└─────────────────────────────────────────────────────────────┘
```

COMPUTER VERIFICATION

The next screen verifies information about the core computer parts, such as the type of PC, the display type, the keyboard, the keyboard type (English or a foreign language), and the pointing device. This screen is shown in Figure 5-12.

Figure 5-12

Setup screen
showing
computer
components

```
┌─────────────────────────────────────────────────────────────┐
│ Windows NT Server Setup                                       │
│ ══════════════════════                                        │
│                                                               │
│                                                               │
│ Setup has determined that your computer contains the following│
│ hardware and software components.                             │
│                                                               │
│                                                               │
│          Computer: Standard PC                                │
│           Display: Auto Detect                                │
│          Keyboard: XT, AT, or Enhanced Keyboard (83-104 keys) │
│   Keyboard Layout: US                                         │
│    Pointing Device: Microsoft Mouse Port Mouse (includes      │
│                     BallPoint)                                │
│                                                               │
│     No Changes: The above list matches my computer.           │
│                                                               │
│ If you want to change any item in the list, press the UP or   │
│ DOWN ARROW key to move the highlight to the item you want to  │
│ change. Then press ENTER to see alternatives for that item.   │
│                                                               │
│ When all the items in the list are correct, move the highlight│
│ to "The above list matches my computer" and press ENTER.      │
│                                                               │
│                                                               │
│ ENTER=Select   F3=Exit                                        │
└─────────────────────────────────────────────────────────────┘
```

If Sara needs to make a change, she can use the [up arrow] key to highlight the selection and press [Enter] to view the list of alternatives. For example, if Sara had a dual-processor computer, she would use the [up arrow] key to highlight "Computer," and a screen showing the possible selections would appear. The information on the screen in Figure 5-12 is correct, so Sara highlights the line "No Changes: The above list matches my computer." She presses [Enter] to move to the next screen.

DISK DRIVES AND DISK PARTITIONING

The next screen shows the detected disk drives on the computer. As Figure 5-13 shows, two partitioned disks are detected as drives C and D. The partitioned portion of drive C (the volume already partitioned by the vendor, using the FAT file structure) is highlighted as the default by the Setup program. Sara leaves the drive highlighted so it will be home to the NT Server system files, as she planned in advance on her checklist. She presses [Enter] to accept the choice and advance to the next screen.

Sara could also choose to press D to delete the FAT partition and later repartition the drive for NTFS. This would be an extra step, because Setup provides an opportunity to convert the partition to NTFS on the next screen, as shown in Figure 5-14. This screen confirms the drive location for the NT Server partition and lists the following choices:

- Format the partition using the FAT file system.

- Format the partition using the NTFS file system.

- Convert the partition to NTFS.

- Leave the current file system intact (no changes).

Figure 5-13

Selecting a disk volume for the partition to house NT Server files

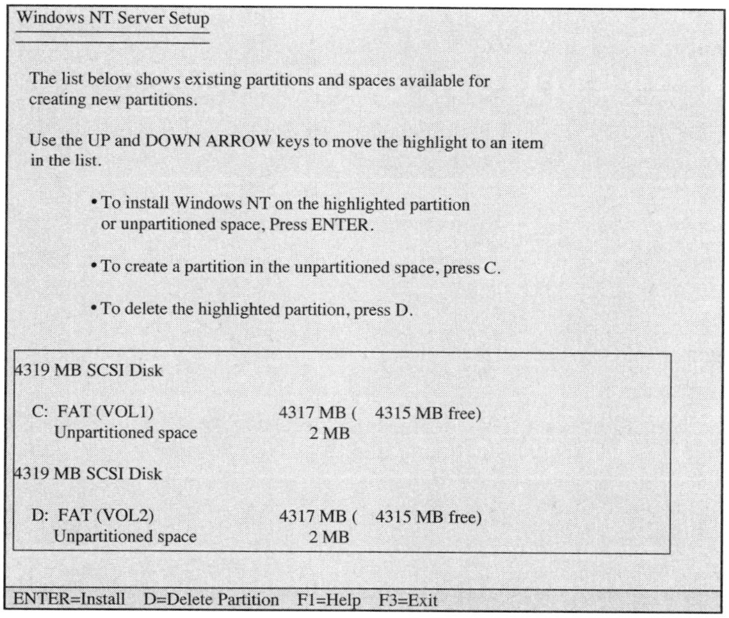

```
Windows NT Server Setup
─────────────────────────

   The list below shows existing partitions and spaces available for
   creating new partitions.

   Use the UP and DOWN ARROW keys to move the highlight to an item
   in the list.

            • To install Windows NT on the highlighted partition
              or unpartitioned space, Press ENTER.

            • To create a partition in the unpartitioned space, press C.

            • To delete the highlighted partition, press D.

  ┌─────────────────────────────────────────────────────────────────┐
  │ 4319 MB SCSI Disk                                                 │
  │                                                                   │
  │   C: FAT (VOL1)              4317 MB (   4315 MB free)            │
  │      Unpartitioned space        2 MB                             │
  │                                                                   │
  │ 4319 MB SCSI Disk                                                 │
  │                                                                   │
  │   D: FAT (VOL2)              4317 MB (   4315 MB free)            │
  │      Unpartitioned space        2 MB                             │
  └─────────────────────────────────────────────────────────────────┘

  ENTER=Install   D=Delete Partition   F1=Help   F3=Exit
```

Figure 5-14

NT Server
Setup file
system
selection

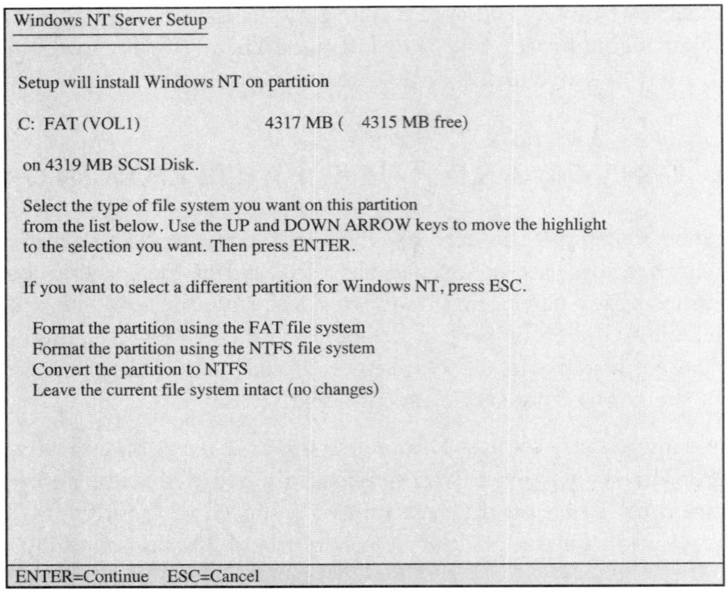

```
Windows NT Server Setup
_____

Setup will install Windows NT on partition

C:  FAT (VOL1)                    4317 MB (    4315 MB free)

on 4319 MB SCSI Disk.

Select the type of file system you want on this partition
from the list below. Use the UP and DOWN ARROW keys to move the highlight
to the selection you want. Then press ENTER.

If you want to select a different partition for Windows NT, press ESC.

    Format the partition using the FAT file system
    Format the partition using the NTFS file system
    Convert the partition to NTFS
    Leave the current file system intact (no changes)




ENTER=Continue    ESC=Cancel
```

During advance preparations, Sara decided she wanted to use NTFS instead of FAT. Viewing
Figure 5-14, she can choose to either format the partition for NTFS or convert the partition. Either choice is appropriate; however, because the partition is already formatted for
FAT, Sara decides to convert it to NTFS. This is faster than partitioning the drives again. Sara
highlights her selection and presses [Enter]. A confirmation screen appears so Sara can be certain the correct drive is selected (see Figure 5-15). Sara presses F to continue.

Figure 5-15

Confirming the
decision to
format

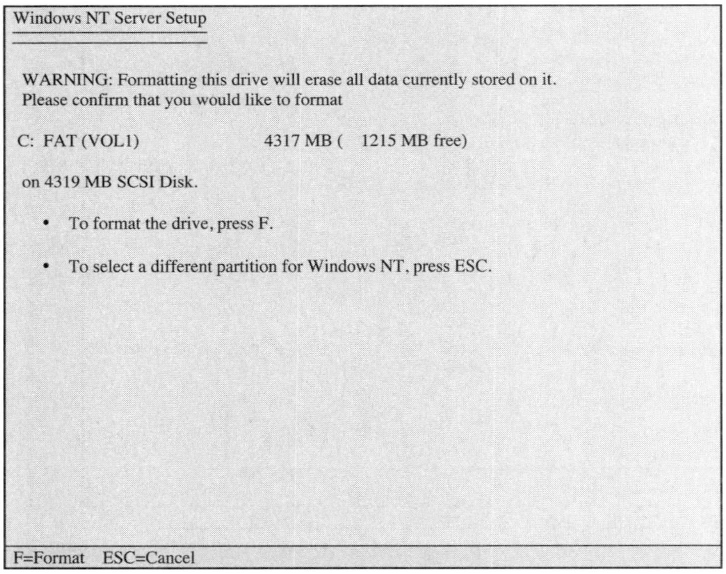

```
Windows NT Server Setup
_____

    WARNING: Formatting this drive will erase all data currently stored on it.
    Please confirm that you would like to format

C:  FAT (VOL1)                    4317 MB (    1215 MB free)

on 4319 MB SCSI Disk.

    •  To format the drive, press F.

    •  To select a different partition for Windows NT, press ESC.






F=Format    ESC=Cancel
```

DIRECTORY PATH AND SERVER NAME

The next screen, Figure 5-16, allows Sara to designate a directory path and name for the NT Server files on drive C. The screen shows the default option, \WINNT, for the directory name and path. As Sara planned earlier, she accepts the default by pressing [Enter].

Figure 5-16

Specifying the directory name and path in Setup

```
Windows NT Server Setup

Setup installs Windows NT files onto your hard disk. Choose the locations
where you want these files to be installed:

 \WINNT

To change the suggested location, press the BACKSPACE key
to delete characters and then type the directory where you want
Windows NT installed.




ENTER=Continue   F3=Exit
```

Before the files are written to disk, Sara is given the option to perform a thorough test of the hard disk storage. Ryan told Sara this is advisable, so she presses [Enter] to perform the basic and exhaustive examinations (see Figure 5-17). The test takes about 15 minutes, and upon completion a message appears that shows the files are being copied to the hard disk.

Figure 5-17

Setup option to perform basic and exhaustive tests of the disk storage

```
Windows NT Server Setup

Setup will now examine your hard disk(s) for corruption.

In addition to a basic examination, Setup can perform a more exhaustive
secondary examination on some drives.  This can be a time consuming
operation, especially on large or very full drives.

     •  To allow Setup to perform an exhaustive secondary examination of
        your hard disk(s), press ENTER.

     •  To skip the exhaustive examination, press ESC.




ENTER=Continue    ESC=Skip Operation
```

Next, Sara is instructed to remove all media from the floppy and CD-ROM drives (see Figure 5-18). Sara removes the setup disk from drive A and the CD from the CD-ROM drive and presses [Enter] to reboot.

Figure 5-18

Notice to remove disks and restart the computer

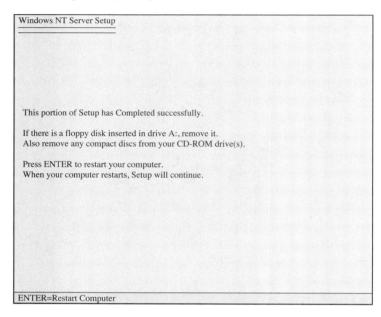

The INSTALLATION: PART 2

When the computer reboots, Sara is prompted to load the NT Server CD-ROM and click OK (see Figure 5-19). (From this part of the installation forward you can use the mouse.) When the CD-ROM is loaded, a message appears saying that the computer is loading files. Then the NT Server Setup Wizard starts.

Figure 5-19

Instruction to load Windows NT Server CD-ROM

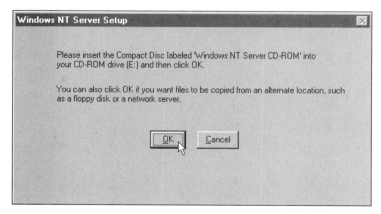

Figure 5-20 shows the Setup Wizard screen with instructions for the next three parts of Setup: 1) gathering information about the computer, 2) installation of NT networking, and 3) the wrap-up steps to complete the installation. From this screen, Sara can select Back to retrace previous installation steps or Next to continue with the installation. She clicks Next.

Figure 5-20

Collecting information about the computer

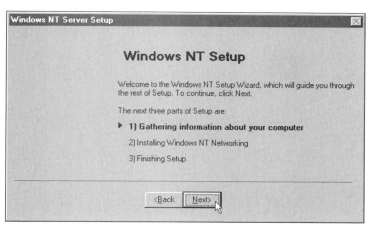

SOFTWARE PROTECTION AND LICENSING

A brief on-screen message indicates Setup is preparing for the installation. Then Sara is prompted to enter her name and the firm's name (see Figure 5-21). This information is used to identify the owner of the software licenses and to customize selected screens. After entering the information, Sara clicks Next to continue.

Figure 5-21

Entry screen for name and organization

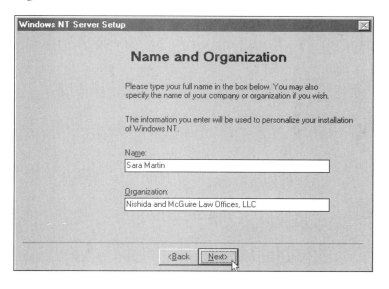

Like many software programs, NT Server is protected from unauthorized use by a key code unique to the license holder. The next screen requests a 10-digit key code, or CD Key, as shown in Figure 5-22. Sara copies the key code from the sticker on the back of the NT Server CD-ROM case and clicks Next to proceed.

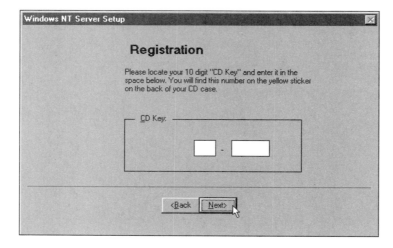

There are two ways to license NT Server: Purchase a specific number of licenses per server, or purchase separate "seat" licenses for each workstation. In larger settings, such as a company or university, where there are many servers, it may be more cost-effective to purchase a license for each workstation. This way, the licensed workstation is billed only for access to those servers where it has security authorization. However, in most smaller office settings such as the firm's, where there is only one server, a server license with a set number of workstations makes more sense. Sara used this option when she purchased NT Server to obtain a license for 20 concurrent users, so she selects the Per Server option and types "20" in the box (see Figure 5-23). When she finishes, she clicks Next.

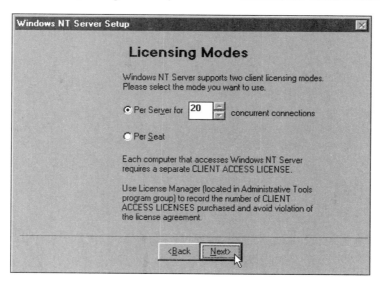

SERVER NAME AND TYPE

Sara next is prompted to enter the name of the server, as shown in Figure 5-24.

Figure 5-24

Entering the server name

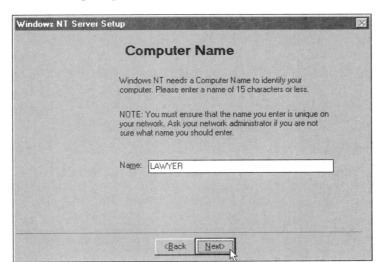

Sara enters "LAWYER" and clicks Next to proceed. The next screen is a request to select the server type. Sara is prepared with her response. She clicks the Primary Domain Controller radio button and then clicks Next (Figure 5-25).

Figure 5-25

Entering the server domain type

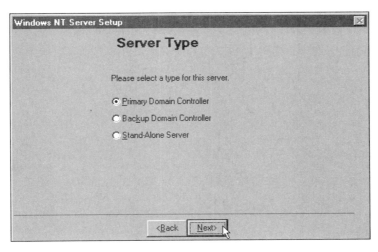

ADMINISTRATOR FUNCTIONS

On the next screen, Sara is prompted to enter her Administrator account password in the first empty box (Figure 5-26).

Figure 5-26

Entering the Administrator account password

She types it again in the second box and moves on by clicking Next. The screen shown in Figure 5-27 is where Sara can choose to create an Emergency Repair Disk. Sara already decided she would create the disk, so she clicks the Yes radio button and then clicks Next.

Figure 5-27

Choosing Yes to create an Emergency Repair Disk

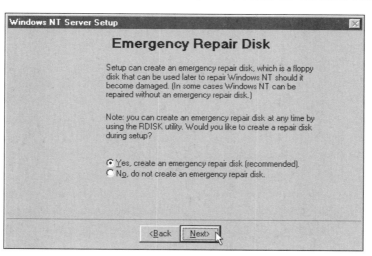

If the No radio button is clicked for the Emergency Repair Disk, the disk can be created later by running the RDISK program in NT Server.

SOFTWARE COMPONENTS

NT Server comes with a number of software components that can be added at the time of installation or later. The Setup Wizard automatically marks the most commonly used components for installation during setup. Ryan discussed this step with Sara in advance, recommending the default selections (see Figure 5-28).

Figure 5-28

Selecting components to install

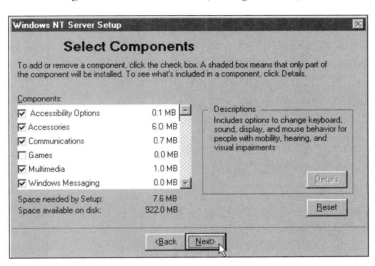

- Accessibility Options: These options enable the server to be set up for people with hearing, movement, or visual disabilities.

- Accessories: NT Server comes with accessory programs such as the Wordpad word processor, a calculator, the Paint program for creating graphics, a tips and tour guide to NT Server, and a range of Internet tools.

- Communications Software: This includes software to dial up the Internet, to connect to mainframe computers, to send files over the Internet, and so on.

- Games: This includes games that can be loaded from the server. Some network administrators load games as a way to test the network. There are better ways to monitor the network, such as by using tools bundled with NT and by purchasing software designed for this purpose.

- Multimedia: This is software to control the speaker volume, to record sound, to record visual images, and to enable the CD-ROM drive to play music.

- Windows Messaging: This sets up Microsoft messaging services.

Start with the software components already selected by Setup. This keeps your initial installation simple and reduces problems. Other components can be added later as you need them.

Sara accepts the defaults by clicking Next and successfully completes the first part of the Setup Wizard. Now it is time to start the second part, making the server network ready. Viewing the screen in Figure 5-29, Sara clicks Next to continue with the Setup Wizard.

Figure 5-29

Setting up
Windows NT
networking

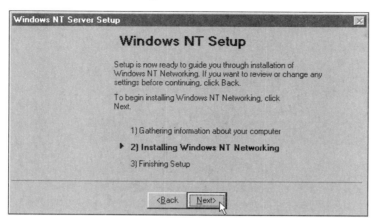

PREPARING THE NETWORKING OPTIONS

As shown in Figure 5-30, Sara needs to indicate whether the server is directly connected to a network, used for dial-up access, or both. In Chapter 3, Sara installed an Intel EtherExpress PRO 10 NIC to connect to the LAN. Because the firm's main goal is to use the server on the local network, Sara clicks the box labeled "Wired to the network." She leaves the remote access option blank. This option is for dial-up modem access to enable users to work from home or while traveling by using a workstation modem. Ryan advised her to leave this blank and set up remote networking capability at a later time. This keeps the initial installation simple, with less to troubleshoot if there should be a problem.

Figure 5-30

Setting up the
type of
network
installation

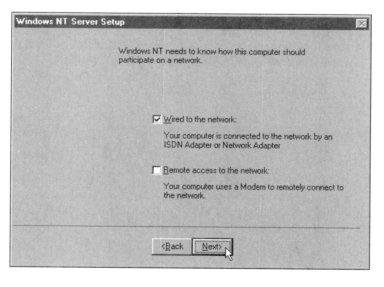

Part of the network installation is the option to install Microsoft's Internet Information Server software. Sara leaves this option box blank because she is not ready to install a Web server at this time, and then clicks Next (see Figure 5-31).

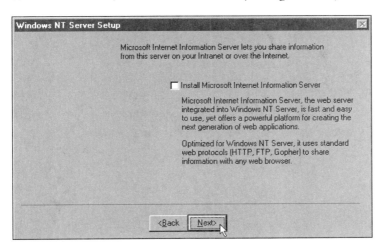

SETUP FOR THE NIC

At this point, the Setup Wizard is ready to search for network interface cards. The screen in Figure 5-32 gives Sara an opportunity to begin the search.

Figure 5-32

Searching for network adapter cards

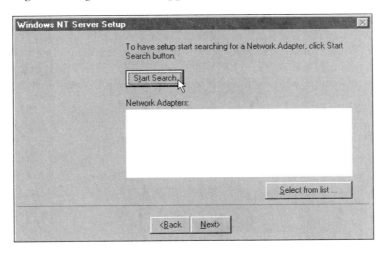

Sara clicks the Start Search button. The presence of the Intel EtherExpress PRO 10 NIC is verified and the name is displayed. Sara clicks Next to display a screen listing network protocols (Figure 5-33). As Sara earlier planned, she selects NetBEUI only and clicks Next to continue.

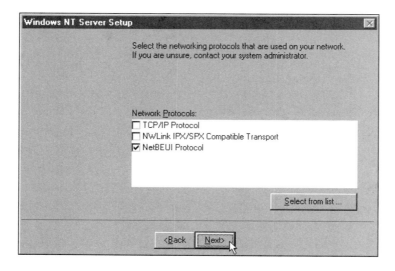

Figure 5-33

Selecting network protocols

NETWORK SERVICES

The next screen shows a list of services to install, as shown in Figure 5-34. Sara selects NetBIOS to provide compatibility for older DOS-based applications still used in the office. She also checks the boxes to install server and workstation services. These network services enable connectivity between the server and the workstation clients. Postponing her Web server installation, she leaves the IIS box blank. She also skips the RPC (remote process connection) configuration, which is used to remotely run jobs on UNIX or other large systems.

Figure 5-34

Selecting network services

INSTALLING THE NETWORK COMPONENTS

With these steps completed, Sara is ready to use Setup to install the network components she chose earlier. The screen in Figure 5–35 gives her the choices to continue or to backtrack and change her selections.

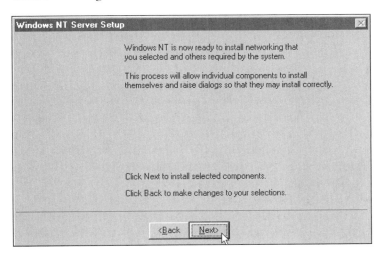

Figure 5-35

Installing the network components

Sara clicks Next to continue. The Setup Wizard starts the installation by automatically detecting the system settings for the Intel Ethernet card, with one exception. It detects the transceiver type as coaxial instead of twisted-pair. Because she installed a twisted-pair NIC, Sara clicks to make this box active and selects twisted-pair in the list of options. She stays with the other settings, because it is better to let the program determine these choices (see Figure 5–36). Sara clicks Continue and sees a brief message indicating Setup is installing the network components.

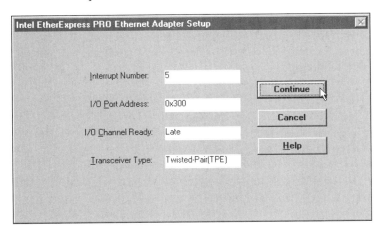

Figure 5-36

NIC configuration settings

After the components are installed, Sara views the network bindings screen shown in Figure 5–37. **Network bindings** are part of the NT Server system used to coordinate the software communications among the NIC, the network protocols, and network services. Bindings ensure that communications are established to optimize performance of the hardware and software. Setup automatically configures the bindings for highest performance.

This screen gives Sara the opportunity to disable the preselected bindings and to set them manually. Ryan advised Sara to leave the bindings as created by Setup, because this ensures the best performance on the firm's network. The plus signs (see Figure 5-37) next to NetBIOS Interface, Server, and Workstation indicate that the bindings have been enabled. Sara clicks Next to accept the automatic selections made by Setup.

Use the default bindings selected by Setup, unless otherwise directed by an expert source, such as an NIC manufacturer.

Figure 5-37

Enabling the network bindings

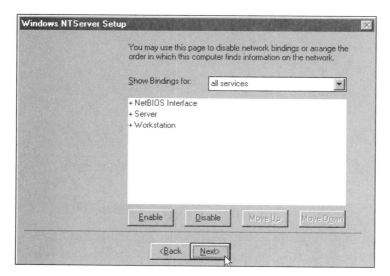

STARTING NETWORK COMMUNICATIONS

Setup is ready to start network communications and complete the installation. Sara checks to ensure the server is connected to the network and clicks Next on the screen shown in Figure 5-38 to proceed.

Figure 5-38

Starting the network to complete the installation

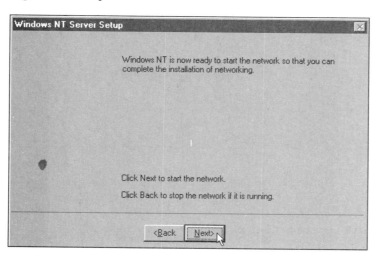

The next screen is a prompt to enter the domain name in a box under the computer name. Sara types "THE_FIRM" in this box, as shown in Figure 5-39. With the network started, Setup can check for any identical domain names. Although it is not applicable to Sara's network, this step is important where more than one NT server is in use. Sara notices that the box with the computer name LAWYER is disabled so that she cannot reenter the name on this screen. However, the computer name can be changed through NT Server's administration tools after the installation is finished.

Figure 5-39

Entering the
domain name

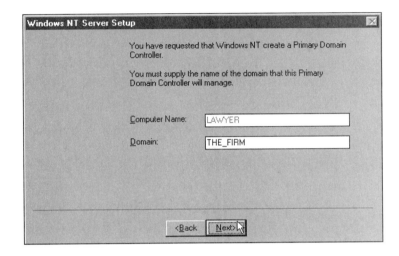

CONFIGURING THE SERVER

As Figure 5-40 shows, Setup is nearly finished.

Figure 5-40

Setup is almost
finished

When Sara clicks Finish, a short message informs her that the software is configuring the server. Next the Date/Time Properties screen appears, enabling Sara to adjust the date, time, and time zone. The system date and time are important on a server because this information is used to put a creation time on files and data. Sara clicks the Date & Time tab and enters the current date and the current time. Then she clicks the Time Zone tab and uses the scroll box (the down arrow) to select the time zone.

On the screen in Figure 5-41, she notices that the time zone is highlighted on the world map.

Figure 5-41

Adjusting the date, time, and time zone settings

Setup additionally needs to verify the display settings for the video monitor attached to the server. On the screen in Figure 5-42, Sara clicks the Test button to check that the color and resolution are accurate.

Figure 5-42

Video testing

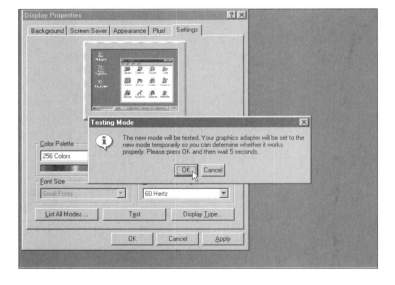

The test completes successfully in a few seconds and Sara clicks OK to proceed. From this point, several short messages indicate that Setup is installing program shortcuts, security, and messaging services.

The time, date, and video settings can be reset from the Control Panel once NT Server is running.

When these tasks are finished, a message appears asking that the blank disk for the Emergency Repair Disk be inserted into drive A, as shown in Figure 5-43. Sara inserts the disk and clicks OK.

Figure 5-43

Creating the emergency repair disk

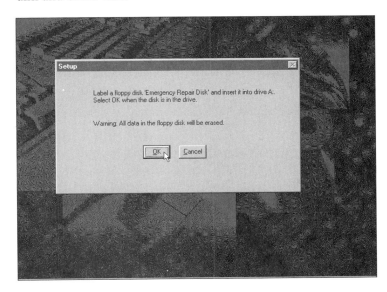

Finally, Setup is successfully completed. As requested on the screen in Figure 5-44, Sara removes all disks and clicks the Restart Computer button.

Figure 5-44

Restarting the computer

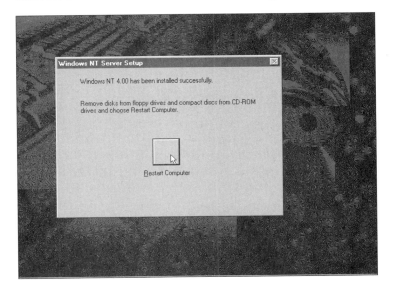

TESTING THE NEW SERVER

When the new server restarts, a logon screen appears with a message to press [Ctrl]+[Alt]+[Del] keys at the same time. When NT Server boots, the [Crl]+[Alt]+[Del] combination is used to start the logon screen and does not reboot the server. Sara presses the keys and is asked to provide an account name and password. She logs on using the Administrator account and the password specified to the Setup Wizard in Figure 5-26.

The logon is a success and Sara sees a screen similar to the Windows 95 screen she uses on her workstation (see Figure 5-45). To celebrate her success, Sara calls Ryan to treat him to coffee and a donut.

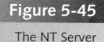

Figure 5-45

The NT Server screen

SARA'S NEXT ASSIGNMENT

Now that she has a working server, Sara's next project is to prepare it for use by the other members in the office. This involves refining the domain setup, creating security, establishing file structures and user accounts, setting up print services, and performing regular server maintenance. In the next chapter, Sara gets a start by working with the domain and with security.

KEY CONCEPTS SUMMARY

The concepts introduced in this chapter relate to installing a Windows NT Server. The following is a review of these concepts.

backup domain controller (BDC) This NT server acts as a backup to the primary domain controller server. It can be used to administer server accounts and security information should the primary domain controller fail.

domain Windows NT uses groupings of workstations and file servers to help perform common administrative functions such as security and user account management.

format This process makes a disk ready for storing data. It magnetically creates storage areas, or sectors, with header and footer information so data are stored and retrieved within each area.

network binding Server and workstation NICs, protocols, and communication software activities are coordinated by means of binding.

partition This software process prepares a section of a disk for a particular operating system, such as DOS or Windows NT.

primary domain controller (PDC) This type of NT server is the master administrator when there are two or more servers on the same network.

security accounts database This database stores account and security information on NT Server users.

standalone server This type of NT server usually is not for direct user access and does not need account management functions for groups of users.

SUMMARY OF WINDOWS FUNCTIONS

The NT Server installation process is performed in two stages: character-based screens and the Windows-based Setup Wizard. Each process is summarized in this section.

Character-Based Setup Activities This portion of the installation process detects hardware components such as disk controllers, SCSI adapters, CD–ROM drives, and other hardware information that is used by Setup. Also, it is used to partition and format drives for Windows NT Server. Once the disk drives are prepared, the NT Server files are copied to the computer.

Setup Wizard The Setup Wizard performs the majority of software setup functions. These include the following:

- Specifying the licensing mode
- Specifying the computer and domain names
- Designating the server type
- Establishing the administrator account and password
- Creating the emergency repair disk
- Installing the server components
- Installing network services and connectivity
- Establishing network protocols and bindings
- Verifying the server's network interface card
- Verifying the time, date, and video settings

REVIEW QUESTIONS

1. Which of the following file systems is used by Windows 95?
    a. FAT
    b. NTFS
    c. OSF
    d. RPG

2. Which of the following file systems conforms to the U.S. government's C2 security specifications?
    a. FAT
    b. NTFS
    c. CPC
    d. RPG

3. NT Server requires a minimum of 148 MB of hard disk space for installation.
    a. True
    b. False

4. NT Server requires a minimum of 4 MB to run on a computer.
    a. True
    b. False

5. Which file system has the capability to re-create lost information after a power failure?
    a. FAT
    b. NTFS
    c. RPG
    d. Both a and b

6. The FAT file system supports file sizes to which of the following?
    a. 4 GB
    b. 10 GB
    c. 16 GB
    d. 64 GB

7. NT Server can be set up to use the FAT file system.
    a. True
    b. False

8. An NT Server computer name can be how long?

    a.   8 characters or fewer

    b.   10 characters or fewer

    c.   15 characters or fewer

    d.   There is no length limit

9. The first NT server installed on a network is designated as which of the following?

    a.   Primary domain controller

    b.   Backup domain controller

    c.   Secondary domain controller

    d.   None of the above

10. An Internet Information Server can be used for which of the following communications?

    a.   Internet communications

    b.   Intranet communications

    c.   File transfers

    d.   All of the above

11. During installation is the only time an Emergency Repair Disk can be created for NT Server.

    a.   True

    b.   False

12. Which type of account has access to all areas of an NT server?

    a.   Administrator

    b.   Guest

    c.   Anonymous

    d.   Supervisor_One

13. NIC settings can be changed from the Setup Wizard.

    a.   True

    b.   False

14. When might a server be designated as standalone?

    a.   When it houses large databases used by software applications

    b.   When it maintains account and security administration information

    c.   When it is the only one in the machine room

    d.   All of the above

15. Which of the following are software components that can be loaded from the Setup Wizard?

    a. Multimedia software

    b. Communications software

    c. Accessory software

    d. All of the above

    e. Software components are not loaded from the Setup Wizard

16. _____ provide coordination among NICs, protocols, and network communications software.

    a. Network bindings

    b. Network Wizards

    c. I/O memory locations

    d. CPU time slices

17. Which of the following are licensing methods used by NT Server?

    a. Licenses per server

    b. Licenses per seat

    c. Licenses per directory

    d. Both a and b

18. Windows NT Server Setup can automatically detect which type of controller or adapter?

    a. IDE

    b. SCSI

    c. ESDI

    d. All of the above

19. Windows NT Server Setup can detect the type of CPU and video adapter in a computer.

    a. True

    b. False

20. How many times can one domain name be used on the same NT network?

    a. One

    b. Two

    c. Four

    d. Unlimited times

THE HOLLAND COLLEGE PROJECT: PHASE 5

President Jackson funded Bob Watson for two servers, one in the administration building and one for the English and writing lab. Bob purchased the two servers based on recommendations you developed in Assignments 3-1 and 3-2. He now wants you to purchase the Windows NT Server software.

When the software arrives, Bob wants you to set it up on both servers. Most of the network cabling is already installed in the Hoyt Administration Building, so you will be able to test the servers on that network. In preparation, you have already installed network interface cards and the other components purchased for the servers. You verified that the NICs are operational by running the test software, as in Assignment 3-8. The servers both came with Windows 95 pre-installed.

ASSIGNMENT 5-1

Using the following table, determine how many Windows NT Server client access licenses will be needed for the Hoyt Administration Building server and the English and writing lab server. Show the licensing mode you would use for each server.

Server	Number of Licenses	License Mode

ASSIGNMENT 5-2

List the tasks you would perform before installing the NT Server software on the Hoyt Administration and the English and writing lab servers. Use the worksheets provided for each server. After your lists are complete, please answer the following questions:

- What parts of the installation do you anticipate will be the same for both servers?

- What parts will be different?

- Does the presence of the Windows 95 operating system present a problem for these installations?

- Do you recommend leaving Windows 95 on one or both of the servers? Why or why not?

Hoyt Administration Building NT Server Setup	
Installation Preparation Task	**Decision Step**

English and Writing Lab NT Server Setup	
Installation Preparation Task	**Decision Step**

ASSIGNMENT 5-3

If a training server is available to you, record hardware information about that computer to have ready for an NT Server installation. Use the form provided here to record the information.

Hardware Information to Prepare for an NT Server Installation

ASSIGNMENT 5-4

Describe the similarities and differences of the NTFS and FAT file systems. Which of these file systems is used by the following:

- Windows 3.1
- MS-DOS
- Windows 3.11
- Windows 95
- Windows NT Workstation
- Windows NT Server

When you generate the servers for Holland College, what file system(s) will you use for each server? Explain why you would make each choice.

ASSIGNMENT 5-5

Because you have Windows 95 on both computers that will be the Holland College servers, practice making a Windows 95 boot disk. Once the disk is made, boot a Windows 95 computer to be certain the disk works. Briefly explain how you made the boot disk. Also, explain the steps you took to boot the computer with the disk. Did the computer boot successfully? Why would it be handy to have this disk?

 ASSIGNMENT 5-6

Explain the difference between a primary domain controller and a backup domain controller. What would you make the server in the Hoyt Administration Building? Why? What would you make the server in the English and writing lab? Why? Base your answers on the fact that the Hoyt Administration Building and the lab networks are joined into one network.

 ASSIGNMENT 5-7

One way to set the time, date, and time zone is through the Windows NT Control Panel. Go to the Control Panel and click the Date/Time icon. Practice setting the date and time. Also practice setting the time zone. Explain why it is important to keep this information current on a server. As the Holland College network administrator, how often would you update the time and date information on the servers?

 ASSIGNMENT 5-8

On an NT Server or NT Workstation computer, practice testing the video settings. Describe where you go to adjust these settings. What happens when you click the Test button? What properties can be set for the video display?

 ASSIGNMENT 5-9

Practice an installation of Windows NT Server and answer the following questions about your installation:

- How did you initially boot the computer to start the installation?
- What mass storage devices did Setup detect?
- Did you need to specify additional mass storage devices that were not detected?

- What hardware and software components were identified by Setup? Did it identify all components successfully?

- Did you install NT Server on an existing partition or did you create a new one?

- How much disk space is available for the installation?

- Did the examination of the hard drives find any problems? If so, what were the problems?

- Did you make the server a primary or backup domain controller or a stand-alone server? Why?

- What software components did you install? Why? How much disk space did they require?

- Did Setup correctly identify the NIC and NIC settings?

- What protocols did you select? Why?

- What network services did you select? Why?

- What bindings were selected?

- Did you choose to make an Emergency Repair Disk? At what point did Setup make the disk?

- Did the server boot successfully after the installation? If it didn't, why not?

 ASSIGNMENT 5-10

In a lab, try generating an NT Server without an NIC installed or without a live connection to the network. Record and describe the results. Are there any circumstances where you might wish to do this, if possible?

SERVER MANAGEMENT: DOMAINS

Sara felt a sense of accomplishment because the installation of NT Server went flawlessly. Her preplanning for the hardware requirements, disk partitioning, file system, server type, protocols, and domain name was well worth the effort. It's satisfying to log on to the server and see a functional system ready for the finishing touches.

At the coffee shop, Ryan congratulated Sara, and asked to hear a short recap of the installation. Sara described the initial process of the hardware detection and confirmation. She explained how she partitioned the server drives and loaded the software and described how she used the Setup Wizard, the automated step-by-step process to configure the NT software. She said the system was performing without a hitch.

AFTER READING THIS CHAPTER AND COMPLETING THE EXERCISES YOU WILL BE ABLE TO:

- DETERMINE WHEN TO SET UP A NETWORK FOR WORKGROUPS OR DOMAINS.
- DETERMINE WHEN TO USE SINGLE OR MULTIPLE DOMAINS.
- DISTINGUISH BETWEEN DIFFERENT TRUST RELATIONSHIPS.
- SET UP TRUST RELATIONSHIPS IN A DOMAIN.
- SET UP MASTER DOMAIN MODELS.
- ADD A COMPUTER TO A DOMAIN.
- SELECT A DOMAIN ON WHICH TO WORK.
- SYNCHRONIZE SECURITY ACCOUNTS MANAGER DATABASES ACROSS A DOMAIN.

Ryan inquired about Sara's plans for the remainder of the server setup. What were her thoughts on domain setup, creating user accounts, and network printing? Because Sara likes advance planning, she provided Ryan with a verbal outline of what comes next and asked for his feedback. Her list of server projects follows:

- Domain setup and management
- Create user groups and accounts
- Set up network printing capabilities
- Create directories
- Load the application software
- Set up system monitoring
- Take measures to protect the system

Ryan inquired whether Sara had made any backup provisions, because it wasn't mentioned in her list. Sara said she ordered a DAT backup system and is presently reading the documentation and setup procedures. (Tape backup, tape management, and alternative backup techniques are covered in depth in Chapter 11.) However, she did have many questions on domains and workgroups. She wanted to discuss these concepts with Ryan before moving ahead. This chapter reflects their conversation, which covered workgroups, domains, domain security, trust relationships, and domain management. Later, Sara returns to her office and takes a first run at domain management.

WORKGROUPS

An NT network can be set up to use either a workgroup structure or a domain structure. The peer-to-peer networking services in a Microsoft Windows 95 and NT Server network provide the capability to have computer users work in groups, as mentioned in Chapter 4. One way for the firm to do this would be to create a decentralized **workgroup** environment for each workstation on the server. This would be done by establishing specific groups from each network station that share access to directories or printers.

For example, Terry Norton could create an accounting software workgroup consisting of himself, Kristin, and the managing partners. Mark Jackson could create a workgroup to share wills and bankruptcy forms. Sara could set up a group of all members in the office who will share access to applications on the same drive. The first group would be managed by Terry, the second by Mark, and the third by Sara (see Figure 6-1). Each of the three would share one or more directories and maintain a list of who could access a given directory. The list of people would have access restrictions, such as read and write or read-only capability.

Figure 6-1

Decentralized structure using workgroups created by multiple users

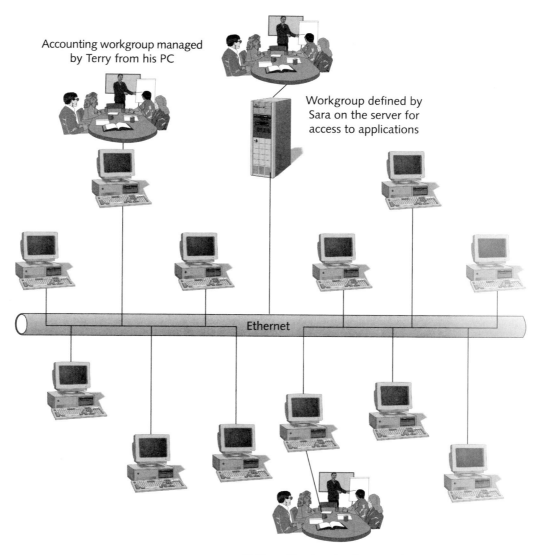

Accounting workgroup managed by Terry from his PC

Workgroup defined by Sara on the server for access to applications

Ethernet

Wills and bankruptcy forms workgroup managed by Mark from his PC

The basic workgroup concept is effective for sharing information, but it has serious limitations. Most serious is that no centralized management or set of rules governs who can access what. If Terry is ill for three days, who would make changes to the workgroup he created? If Mark is unavailable, who would manage access to wills and bankruptcy forms? In a small setting like the firm, these are not difficult problems to address, but they might become difficult when new branch offices are added. These questions are greatly magnified where there are multiple servers and workstations in a large organization. For these reasons, Ryan advises Sara to avoid using workgroups and recommends the domain concept as a better alternative.

Avoid using the workgroup structure in an NT Server environment. A workgroup configuration not created within the domain robs the network administrator of the ability to control and manage workgroup properties effectively. Also, when workgroups are created on individual stations, users cannot share drives and directories with other domains. Workgroups can be an administrative nightmare because there is no central coordination of how they're set up. Conversely, a domain structure incorporates work groupings organized into a central point of administration.

DOMAINS

An NT **domain** is a collection of resources and of users who have access to the resources. Resources are servers, printers, CD-ROM arrays, and other equipment. A single domain can have one or more servers as members. Some servers may have generalized functions, such as providing logon services and serving files. Others may be specialized, such as print servers, database servers, or CD-ROM servers. And some, such as the firm's, incorporate several functions into one server. Figure 6–2 shows an example of two domains, A and B.

Figure 6-2

Example domains

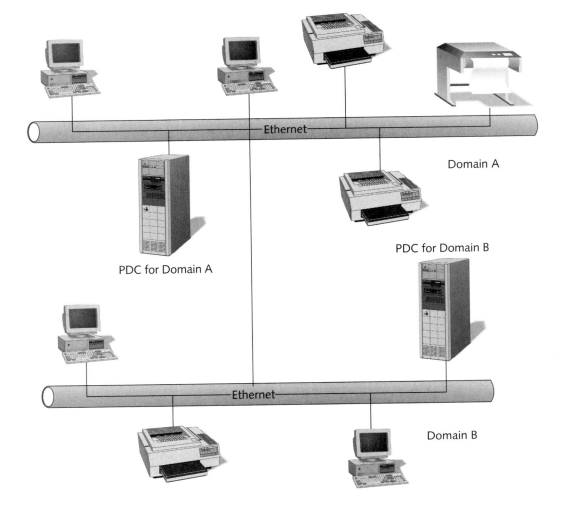

When file servers were first introduced, users logged on to each network server individually. One user might have to log on to three servers: one for word processing and spreadsheet applications, one for CAD applications, and one for accounting data. He or she would have an account on each server. Access rights and other services for that user would have to be set on each server, with every server having its own record of the user's privileges. When networks were small, having a few servers was manageable, but time-consuming. As networks have grown, individual server management is not productive for administrators or users.

The domain on an NT server allows the network administrator to manage resources and users as one unit. When the user needs resources, he or she logs on to the domain instead of several file servers. The user needs only to log on to the domain one time with one password. The domain has a record of the resources the user is allowed to access and makes these available at logon.

Domains consist of clients and resources used by the clients. User accounts and user groups compose the client side. File servers, print servers, and other network services are the resources.

One or more groups can be defined to the domain, with a user having membership in any or all groups. The concept of the domain preserves the idea of work groupings, without the headaches of managing them individually from multiple workstations and file servers. For example, the firm is interested in creating a management group with access to the accounting, legal time, and billing software. The group can be created to include all five managing partners as well as the business administrator, Terry Norton. If an attorney is promoted into the management group, Sara, as network administrator, can easily add him or her to the management group, with all privileges belonging to that group. Another group might be printer operators, consisting of Mark Jackson, Jane Randall, and Sara. Members of this group would have privileges to control any print jobs to the laser printers.

The domain concept will save time for Sara as she sets up users, privileges, and groups. It also will save time when the two branch offices are established. At some point, each branch office will have its own network and file server. Each office can have its own domain or be a part of the main office domain. The advantage of having separate domains is that server management can be centralized under Sara, decentralized at each office, or a combination of both. Networks can be spread over great distances and still use the domain concept through Ethernet, dial-up, satellite, and other communication methods.

For many office situations, Microsoft recommends one domain, because a single domain can have 26,000 users and 250 groups. Multiple domains would be in order on a college campus, where administrative and academic computing are separated, or for a business with branches in different cities or states. Multiple domains also work well for organizations with foreign and domestic locations.

With network administration centralized at the domain, only one database is needed to store information on all users and their security privileges. Microsoft calls this the **Security Accounts Manager (SAM)** database or, more recently, the directory services database. This database tracks user names, passwords, account privilege information, and account policies. Sara's research in Chapter 5 showed that the database is maintained on the primary domain controller (PDC). When there is more than one NT server on a network, the database is backed up on each server designated as a backup domain controller (BDC) (see Figure 6-3). The SAM is regularly backed up or **synchronized** at intervals established in the NT Server operating system. If there is more than one BDC, the SAMs are synchronized in a staggered order to reduce network traffic.

Figure 6-3

Domain
controllers
with SAMs

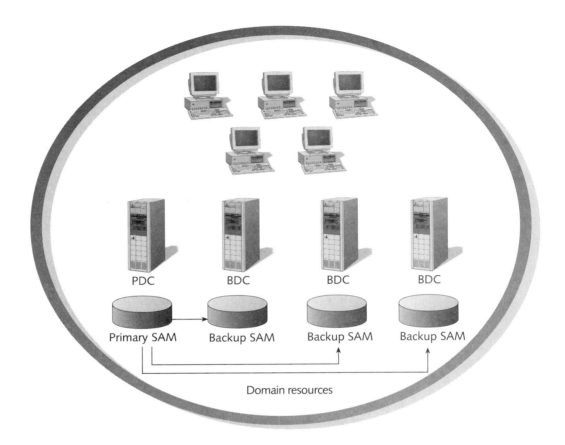

The Security Accounts Manager (SAM) database tracks information about user accounts such as user name, password, access privileges to files and directories, and group memberships. One SAM can hold a maximum of about 26,000 accounts or can be up to 40 MB in size.

Synchronization is an NT Server process used to back up the PDC SAM to all BDCs in the same domain.

Should the PDC malfunction or go offline, the network administrator "promotes" one of the BDCs to become the PDC. Both PDCs and BDCs validate a user's logon, depending on which resource is accessed. However, an update to the database, such as a changed password, is always performed on the PDC.

TRUST RELATIONSHIPS

In situations where there are two or more domains, users can access domains other than their own through trust relationships set up by the network administrator. Each trust relationship has two parties, the "trusted" domain and the "trusting" domain. The **trusted domain** is the one that is granted access to resources, whereas the **trusting domain** is the one granting the access. For example, assume a manufacturing business has a main office and branch offices in five states, each with its own NT file server and domain. The main-office domain needs access to all five branch-office domains, which is granted. In this scenario, the main office is the trusted domain and the branch offices are the trusting domains. There are several combinations of trust relationships, but three are most common: one-way trust, two-way trust, and universal trust relationships.

A trusting domain is one that allows another domain security access to its resources, such as file servers.

A trusted domain is one that has been granted security access to resources in another domain.

ONE-WAY TRUST

In a one-way trust, the trust relationship is not reciprocated. One domain is the trusted party and the other is trusting. This might be the case on a small college campus where one domain is for administrative computing and another is intended for academic computing. In this case, members of the administrative domain may need to use resources on the academic side, such as statistics software, or to design Web pages for the Internet. Access to the administrative side from the academic domain must be kept locked due to auditors' requirements preventing students from accessing transcripts or tuition billings. Members of the administrative domain can access resources and belong to groups in the academic domain. However, users in the academic domain have no access to files, groups, or resources in the administrative domain. Figure 6-4 on the next page illustrates a one-way trust as signified by the arrow going from the trusting to the trusted domain.

TWO-WAY TRUST

The trusting relationship is reciprocated in a two-way trust. For example, a chemical company might have its business office downtown and a production plant in an industrial park across town. Two separate domains might be established for the sake of routing e-mail and other electronic communications. However, members of each domain need to access resources in the other domain. A two-way trust enables full sharing of resources between domains (see Figure 6-5). Also, members of one domain can belong to groups in the other domain. The PDC and BDC servers in each domain check logon privileges by means of their SAM databases, to ensure users are authorized to access resources.

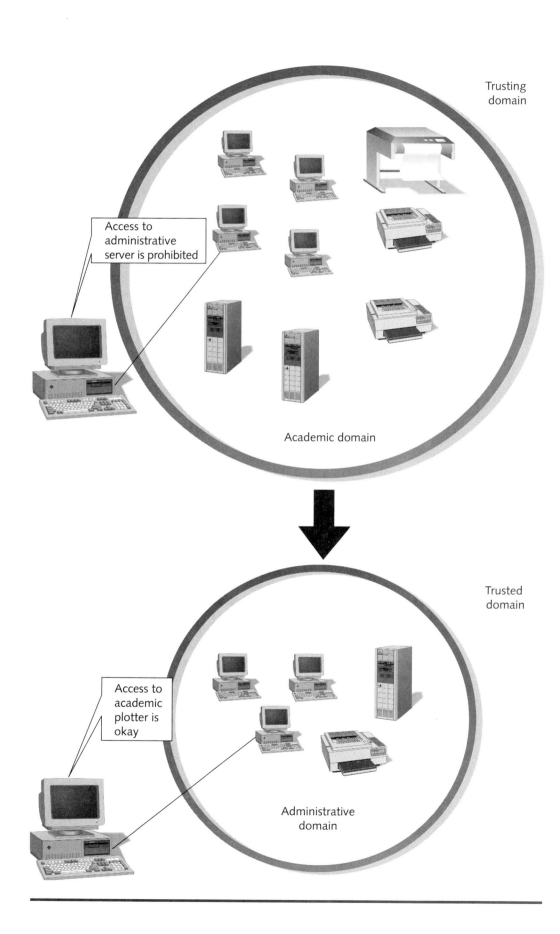

Access to
administrative
server is prohibited

Trusting
domain

Academic domain

Trusted
domain

Access to
academic
plotter is
okay

Administrative
domain

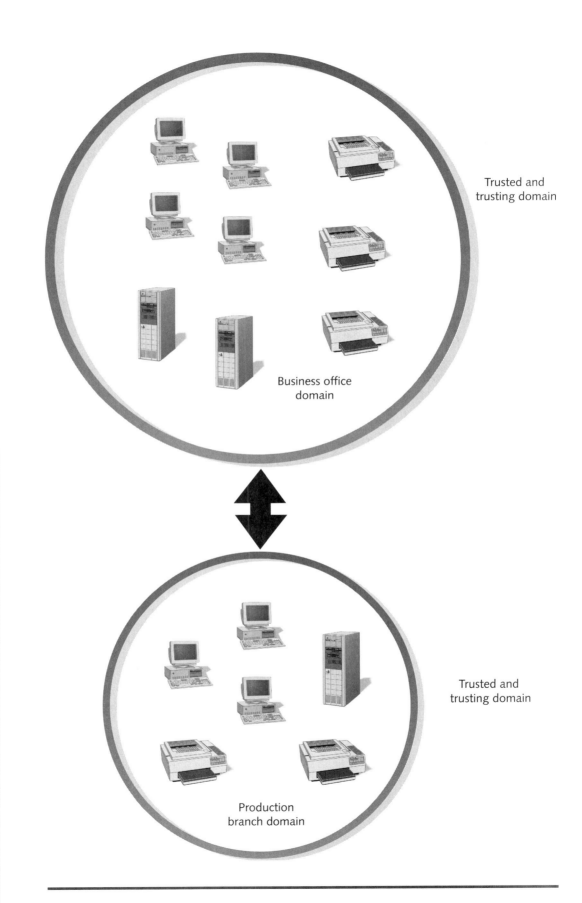

Figure 6-5

Two-way trust

Trusted and
trusting domain

Business office
domain

Trusted and
trusting domain

Production
branch domain

UNIVERSAL TRUST

Sara is interested in the universal trust, where several domains equally share resources. Each domain is trusted and trusting. When the firm adds two new branches, each branch could have its own domain for the sake of e-mail communications. As members at one branch become partners, they could be added to the management group in the domain at the main office. Figure 6-6 shows this as a hypothetical scenario for Nishida and McGuire with the possible domain names EASTLAW and WESTLAW. These are names that they might use for the branch offices when they are established, but they are not established yet.

Figure 6-6

Universal trust

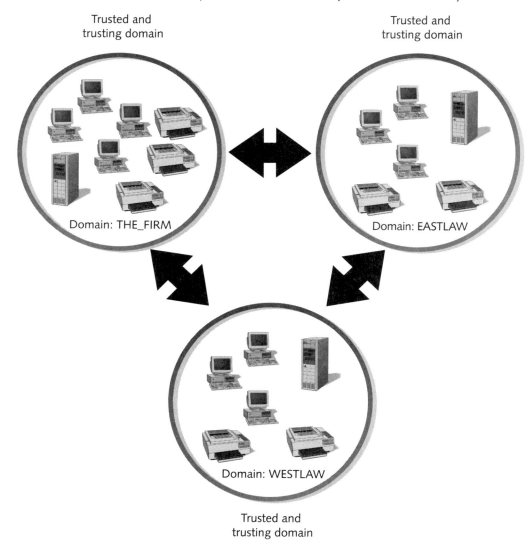

Trusted and
trusting domain

Domain: THE_FIRM

Trusted and
trusting domain

Domain: EASTLAW

Domain: WESTLAW

Trusted and
trusting domain

SINGLE MASTER DOMAIN MODEL

Ryan points out to Sara that the drawback to the universal trust model is extra administration of resources and accounts. A universal trust with three domains equals three SAMs to maintain because each domain would have user accounts. He recommends Sara consider a single master domain model built on one-way trust relationships. Each branch office could have a domain, but it would be administered from the main-office domain, THE_FIRM, using one-way trust relationships (see Figure 6-7). THE_FIRM would be the trusted domain with both EASTLAW and WESTLAW as trusting domains. EASTLAW and WESTLAW would each have resources, such as servers and printers, but no user accounts. THE_FIRM would be home to all user accounts at the three offices, making it the master domain.

Figure 6-7

Single master domain

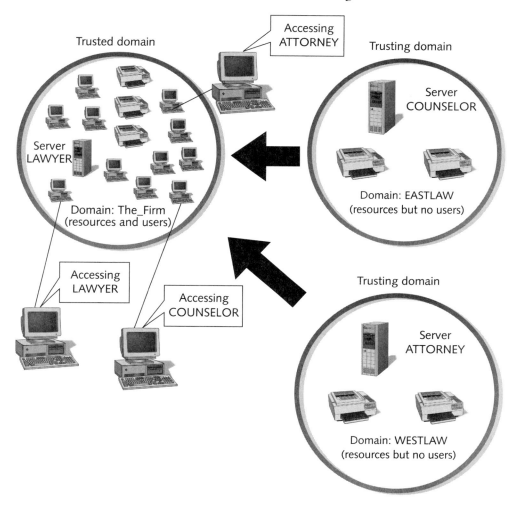

The advantage of the single master domain is that all users could access resources in all the domains. Sara's job would be easier because she could administer user accounts and groups from one domain.

This model works particularly well for small organizations where several hundred users are spread across several branches or business units. The advantages are the following:

- Accounts and groups are centrally managed.
- Resources are available to all users (as determined by the network administrator).
- One consistent security policy applies across the organization.
- Groups can be tailored across organizational unit boundaries.
- The SAM data are easy to maintain and keep synchronized.

MULTIPLE MASTER DOMAIN MODEL

Sara and Ryan discuss how an organization with thousands of users might be set up for easy administration using a method called multiple master domains. This domain model consists of multiple single master domains connected through two-way trust relationships. For example, an international foods company might have single master domains established at company sites in the United States, Brazil, and Norway. The master domains at each site are linked in two-way trust relationships, as shown in Figure 6-8. In this instance, the Brazil master domain has a one-way trust with its two local domains. It has a two-way trust with the United States and Norway master domains. Because users are defined in the master domains in each country, all users have access to the resources of each domain. Administration of this system can be centralized in one domain or decentralized to each master domain. The advantages of this model for a large organization are the following:

- Administration can be centralized or decentralized.
- Thousands of users can share resources across the country or around the world.
- Groups can be formed to span domains.
- Security policies can be standardized for thousands of users and resources.

Figure 6-8

Multiple master domain model

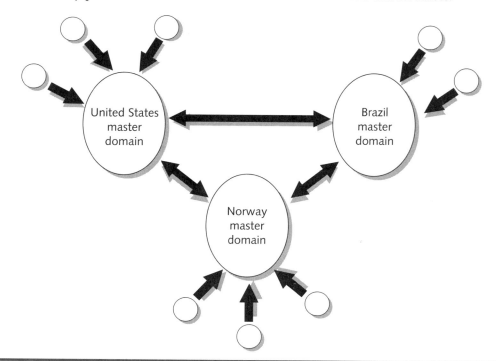

Companies use networking capabilities such as domains to enhance business practices to make them more competitive. Watch for new ways to use trust and master domain relationships as business strategies in management, sales, and production.

INTRODUCTION TO ADMINISTRATIVE TOOLS

Sara is anxious to begin work on the administrative tasks that need to be completed on the firm's server. To start, Sara wants to review the screens affecting domain administration. She begins by logging on to the server on the Administrator account. The Administrator account has authorization from NT Server to manage the server's domain. From the Start menu, Sara clicks the Programs option and then highlights the Administrative Tools (Common) option. This yields the following menu of administrative options (see Figure 6-9 on the next page):

- Administrative Wizards for automated procedures to add programs, manage groups and users, manage file access, administer clients, and set up printers

- Backup tools to back up the server

- Disk Administrator for managing server disk volumes

- Event Viewer to view server events such as logons, error conditions, and other server activities

- License Manager to set and administer the number of authorized NT Server software and client access licenses

- Migration Tool for Netware to move users, groups, and files from NetWare servers to NT servers

- Network Client Administrator for assistance in startup tasks for workstation clients

- Performance Monitor to track information on server operations such as CPU use

- Remote Access Admin to control off-site access of NT Server through dial-up communications

- Server Manager for managing functions such as shutdown, sending messages to users, adding servers to the domain, and sharing server directories

- System Policy Editor to modify files that establish system policies, such as user access

- User Manager for Domains for managing domain functions such as creating trust relationships, accounts, and groups

- Windows NT Diagnostics to report information on the server components for troubleshooting problems

Figure 6-9

The Administrative Tools menu

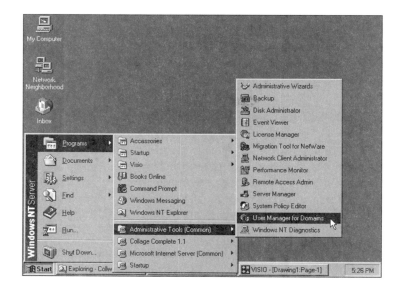

In this chapter Sara examines two options on the Administrative Tools menu that affect domain management: User Manager for Domains and Server Manager. She explores the remaining options in later chapters. From the menu in Figure 6-9, she selects User Manager for Domains. The next screen (see Figure 6-10) shows a list of users and of groups automatically created by NT Server during installation: the Administrator account, the Guest account, and an Internet guest account (for when Sara implements Internet services). The bottom of the screen shows a default list of groups that NT Server provides as a starting point to help you generate the actual groups. The user accounts and groups compose the non-resource portion of the domain. Notice the domain name is at the top of the screen.

Figure 6-10

The User Manager screen

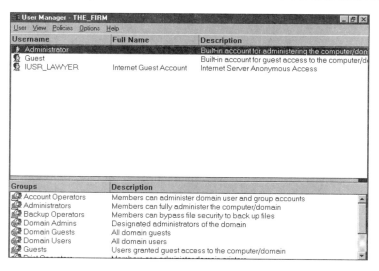

CREATING TRUSTS

Next, Sara clicks the Policies menu because she wants to view how trust relationships are established in a domain. She selects the Trust Relationships option, as shown in Figure 6-11.

Figure 6-11

The Policies menu

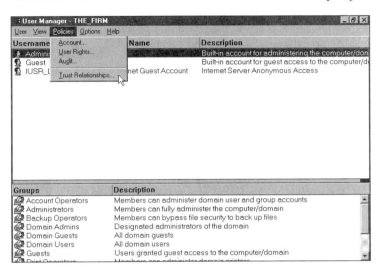

The next screen shows where Sara can designate domains as trusted or trusting (see Figure 6-12).

Figure 6-12

Designating trust relationships

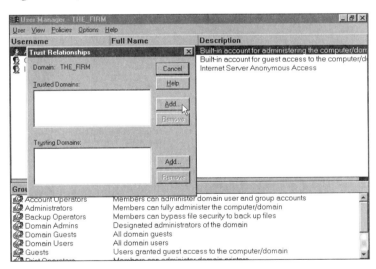

There are two empty list boxes because Sara has not specified any domains as trusted or trusting. The following steps explain how Sara would establish trust relationships in the hypothetical model using EASTLAW and WESTLAW, with NT servers administered remotely by Sara at each location.

STEP 1: CREATING ACCOUNTS

Several steps must occur to set up trust relationships. First, the appropriate accounts should be created in each domain. For example, if Sara chooses the universal trust model, she would need to create accounts in each domain. Users at the main office would have accounts in THE_FIRM, and users at the branch offices would have accounts in each branch office domain. If she chooses the master domain model, Sara would need to create all accounts in THE_FIRM. Account creation and management are discussed in Chapter 7.

STEP 2: DESIGNATING TRUSTING DOMAINS

The second step is to designate the trusting domains. In the universal trust model, THE_FIRM, EASTLAW, and WESTLAW would be trusting domains, giving each domain access to their resources. Trusting domains are set up from the screen shown in Figure 6-12 for the domain THE_FIRM. On this screen Sara would click the bottom Add button. On the next screen, Sara would start by entering EASTLAW as trusting (see Figure 6-13), plus a password for THE_FIRM to use as access to EASTLAW. The password is confirmed by typing it again. Passwords are protected from view by asterisks in the password box. On the screen in Figure 6-13, Sara would click OK to save the information, and EastLaw would appear in the Trusting Domains list box in Figure 6-11. Sara would repeat the same procedure to add WESTLAW as trusting.

Figure 6-13

Adding a
trusting
domain

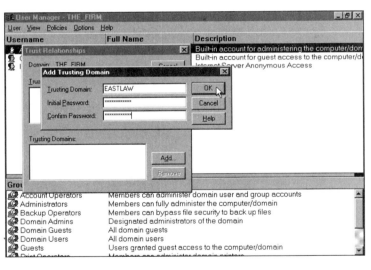

After completing the trusting relationships on THE_FIRM, Sara would log on to EASTLAW and use the screen in Figure 6-13 to make THE_FIRM and WESTLAW trusting. She would do the same on WESTLAW to make THE_FIRM and EASTLAW trusting.

If she uses the single master domain model, Sara would only make EASTLAW and WESTLAW trusting in THE_FIRM. Therefore, she would not log on to EASTLAW or WESTLAW to establish trusting relationships. However, she could change domain models at any time by shifting accounts between domains and changing the domain trust relationships.

STEP 3: ESTABLISHING TRUSTED RELATIONSHIPS

The third step is to create the trusted relationships. Sara would do this no matter what model she chooses. Trust relationships are created using the Administrator account or an account with the same system-wide privileges. Sara would use the Trust Relationships dialog box shown in Figure 6-12 to designate THE_FIRM as the trusted domain. For the universal trust model, she would make each domain trust every other domain: THE_FIRM, EASTLAW, and WESTLAW.

For instance, using the Administrator account on THE_FIRM, she would designate EASTLAW and WESTLAW as trusted. First, she would click the top Add button shown in Figure 6-12. Starting with EASTLAW, she would enter the domain name and the password of that domain, as in Figure 6-14. Next, she would click OK to save the information, and EASTLAW would appear in the Trusted Domains list box. She would repeat the same steps to make WESTLAW a trusted domain. Once Sara completed this on THE_FIRM domain, she would log on to the Administrator account on EASTLAW to make THE_FIRM and WESTLAW trusted; then she would do the same on WESTLAW, to make THE_FIRM and EASTLAW trusted.

For the single master domain model, only THE_FIRM would be set up as trusted. Sara would log on to the EastLaw domain in the Administrator account and use the screen in Figure 6-14 to make THE_FIRM trusted. Next, she would make THE_FIRM trusted by logging on to the WESTLAW domain and following the same procedure. The screen shown previously in Figure 6-12 can be used to remove trust relationships as well as to add them. To remove a relationship, Sara would highlight the domain to be removed from either list box and then click Remove. Once she was finished working with the trust relationships, she would click Cancel to return to the User Manager screen shown previously in Figure 6-10.

Figure 6-14

Adding a trusted domain

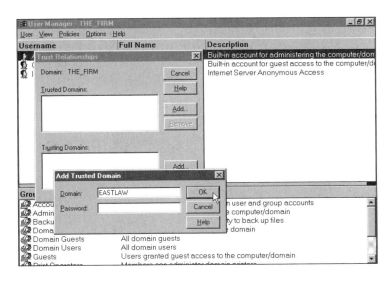

INTRODUCTION TO THE SERVER MANAGER FOR DOMAIN TASKS

After reviewing the trust relationships screens, Sara tries the Server Manager option from the Administrative Tools menu. The Server Manager screen is shown in Figure 6-15. This screen has a list of the NT servers in THE_FIRM domain. Because there is just one server, LAWYER, it is the only one listed. The Type column indicates whether a server is a PDC, BDC, or stand-alone computer.

Figure 6-15

The Server Manager screen

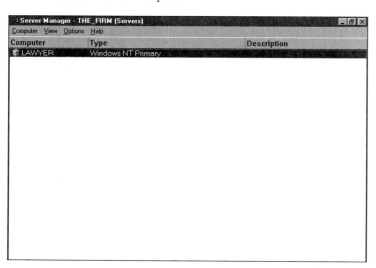

ADDING A DOMAIN COMPUTER

If THE_FIRM adds a second server to the network, the server can be added to the domain as a resource from the Server Manager screen. Sara wants to see how to add a server, so she clicks the Computer menu. Next, she clicks Add to Domain, as shown in Figure 6-16.

Figure 6-16

The Computer menu

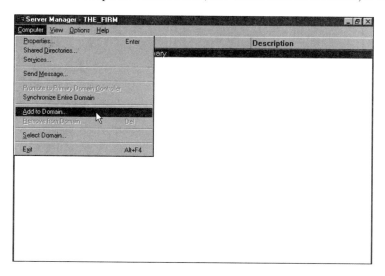

The next screen has two options: 1) to add an NT workstation or an NT stand-alone server or 2) to add a BDC server. These options are shown in Figure 6-17.

Figure 6-17

Adding a
computer to
the domain

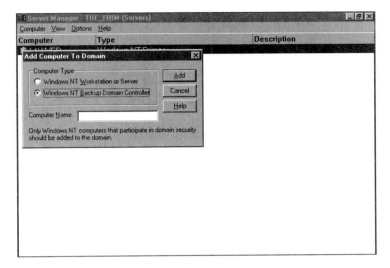

The first option is to add an NT workstation as a resource for sharing files or as a limited server with 10 licenses. Or it can be used to add a standalone server for specialized applications, such as a database or print server. The second option is to add a BDC server as a resource. For example, if Sara had another BDC server, she would add it by clicking the bottom radio button and then entering the server's name. Next, she would click the Add button to add the server to the domain. The server would then appear in the list of servers on the Server Manager screen in Figure 6-15.

SELECTING A DOMAIN

If there is more than one domain, such as in the master domain model, the other domains can be accessed from the Server Manager by using the Computer menu (see Figure 6-16). Sara displays the Computer menu and clicks the Select Domain option. The next screen shows a list of available domains in the list box labeled Select Domain (see Figure 6-18). Sara's screen shows only one domain, THE_FIRM. If there were other domains, she would have two options to access them. One option would allow her to double-click the domain in the list box. The other would let her type the name of the domain in the text box labeled Domain and then click OK.

This screen will be valuable for Sara when the branch offices are established with their own domains. She will be able to access any of the domains by selecting one from the screen in Figure 6-18. When a domain is selected, she will have access to the Administrator account in that domain for working on trust relationships, accounts, and other management activity.

Figure 6-18

Selecting a domain

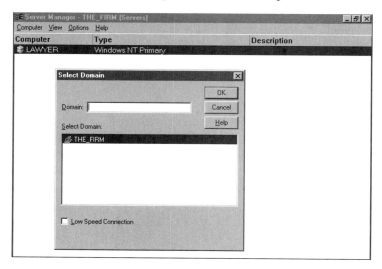

SYNCHRONIZING DOMAINS

It's nearly 5:20 P.M., and Kent McGuire just passed by, wondering whether Sara is planning to go home. Sara wants to check one more task related to domains before leaving for the day. The SAM databases on BDC servers are backed up automatically, but they can be backed up manually as well. This is an important feature if the network administrator believes one or more BDC databases are out of sync with the PDC, something that can happen if many accounts have been added or modified. After working on a range of accounts, the network administrator may want to back up his or her work. Sara notices there is an option to synchronize the entire domain on the Computer menu (Figure 6-16). She clicks Help and finds that this option will synchronize all the BDCs at her command. All she needs to do is click this option on the Computer menu.

If only one BDC is out of sync because it has been temporarily disconnected for repair, Sara can synchronize it alone by returning to the Server Manager screen and highlighting that server from a list. Then, on the Computer menu, under the Synchronize option, she will be given the opportunity to synchronize only that BDC.

SARA'S NEXT ASSIGNMENT

Sara has only one domain, so it is not much work for her at this point. When the branch offices are added, there will be more administrative work. At that time she will have to decide whether to have more domains and what type of trust relationships to create if there are multiple domains. The single master domain model is appealing to Sara because of the ease of administration.

The real work of administering the server begins in the next chapter, when Sara creates user accounts and user groups. A significant part of this task will be to establish account policies within NT Server and to achieve agreement about the account policies among the firm's management. Account policies determine requirements for passwords, general security access, and other information about how account holders can access specific resources in their trusted domain.

Sara is still concerned about fully testing the network cabling to ensure all connections work. Once the user accounts are created, Sara can begin to fully test the cable installation for any problems.

KEY CONCEPTS SUMMARY

Many of the concepts discussed in this chapter relate to domain security access and to directory services, as summarized below.

domain A domain within NT Server consists of computer resources and user accounts that have access to those resources, all of which can be managed from one or more servers.

promote This procedure is used to select a BDC to become the PDC when the original PDC is not available.

Security Accounts Manager (SAM) database This database is kept on the PDC and replicated on all BDC computers within a domain. It stores information about user accounts and groups.

synchronize the domain The SAM is regularly backed up from the PDC to all BDCs on an NT Server network by a process called synchronization.

trusted This is one domain in a trust relationship that has access to the resources in another domain.

trusting This domain in a trust relationship makes its resources available to another domain.

workgroup In a Windows environment, a workgroup consists of users who share drive and printer resources in an independent peer-to-peer relationship outside of a centralized domain.

SUMMARY OF WINDOWS FUNCTIONS

Several NT Server tools are introduced in this chapter. These are summarized in the following paragraphs.

Administrative Tools Menu The Administrative Tools menu offers a central source of programs to manage NT servers and server domains. The following is a list of options available in the Administrative Tools menu:

- Administrative Wizards
- Backup
- Disk Administrator
- Event Viewer
- License Manager

- Migration Tool for Netware
- Network Client Administrator
- Performance Monitor
- Remote Access Admin
- Server Manager
- System Policy Editor
- User Manager for Domains
- Windows NT Diagnostics

Server Manager This tool manages server resources on the network. It is used to add a computer to the domain resources, to synchronize SAM databases, and to select a domain on which to work.

User Manager This tool contains the user accounts and groups created within a domain. For domain services, it is used to create trust relationships and master domain models. In multiple domain networks, it can be used to select a domain for access. The User Manager is accessed from the Administrator account or an account with similar privileges.

REVIEW QUESTIONS

1. File servers, print servers, and database servers are resources within a given domain.

    a. True
    b. False

2. A one-way trust has which of the following?

    a. A trusted domain
    b. A trusting domain
    c. A trustworthy domain
    d. Both a and b

3. For a network with an NT server, it works best to set it up as

    a. Domain-based.
    b. Workgroup-based.
    c. Server-based.
    d. None of the above.

4. A single domain can have _____ users.

    a. 1,000
    b. 5,000
    c. 10,000
    d. 26,000

5. A trusted domain is one that
   a. Has given access to its resources to another domain.
   b. Has access to the resources in another domain.
   c. Has only PDC computers.
   d. None of the above.

6. A single master domain model has how many trusted domains?
   a. One
   b. Two
   c. Three
   d. Multiple trusted domains

7. In a universal trust relationship, how many trusts are two-way?
   a. One
   b. Two
   c. Three
   d. All

8. On a network with multiple NT servers, where is the information immediately changed when a user changes his or her password?
   a. On a BDC
   b. On a PDC
   c. In an Excel spreadsheet
   d. At the network hub

9. In a two-way trust relationship
   a. Both domains are trusted and trusting.
   b. One domain is trusted and trusting and the other is only trusting.
   c. One domain is trusted and trusting and the other is only trusted.
   d. Both domains are only trusting.

10. In the workgroup model
    a. There is a limit of 24 workgroups.
    b. Each workstation keeps track of workgroups and user information.
    c. The hub station is the first to be connected.
    d. All of the above.

11. Which of the following are advantages of the master domain models?
    a. The ability to standardize security policy
    b. The option to have centralized domain administration
    c. Groups can span domain boundaries
    d. All of the above

12. What is the maximum size of a SAM?
    a. 10 MB
    b. 20 MB
    c. 30 MB
    d. 40 MB

13.   Synchronization on an NT network refers to which of the following?

    a.   Synchronizing the time at each workstation

    b.   Synchronizing the software at each workstation

    c.   Using the PDC SAM to synchronize the BDC SAMs

    d.   Using the BDC SAMs to synchronize the PDC SAM

14.   An NT Workstation can be a resource on an NT Server-based network.

    a.   True

    b.   False

15.   Which of the following is not a domain resource?

    a.   A BDC server

    b.   A standalone server

    c.   A user's PC

    d.   Both a and b

    e.   All of the above

16.   What would you use to create a trust relationship on an NT domain?

    a.   The User Manager

    b.   The Server Manager

    c.   The Network Manager

    d.   The Start Manager

17.   What would you use to synchronize SAMs in a domain?

    a.   The User Manager

    b.   The Server Manager

    c.   The Network Manager

    d.   The Start Manager

18.   Which menu option on the Server Manager screen permits you to select domains?

    a.   Computer

    b.   View

    c.   Options

    d.   None of the above

19.   Where do you begin when creating trust relationships?

    a.   Designate the trusted domain(s) first

    b.   Designate the trusting domain(s) first

    c.   Create the users first

    d.   None of the above

20.   From where would you access the User Manager?

    a.   Directly from the Start menu

    b.   In the Startup group

    c.   From Administrative Tools on the Start menu

    d.   From Domain Tools on the Start menu

21.   Groups can span domains in a one-way trust.
   a.   True
   b.   False

THE HOLLAND COLLEGE PROJECT: PHASE 6

Just as for Sara, your server installation has gone well thus far. Bob Watson has scheduled a meeting with you to review the progress and to go over what work comes next. He has asked you to bring this information to the meeting so you both can create a rough schedule. At the meeting, you plan to discuss the concepts of domains and trust relationships with Bob. You want him to have a general understanding of these so he can advise you about setting up the administrative and lab servers.

In the assignments that follow, you will create a list of administrative work to be completed on the servers and prepare background information on domain management to share with Bob. Also, you will have an opportunity to practice domain administration.

ASSIGNMENT 6-1

In the following table, record the NT Server activities you will discuss with Bob. List the activities in the order you anticipate working on them. Put a check in the appropriate column(s) to show whether the activity will be for the administrative server, the lab server, or both.

Server Task	Admin. Server	Lab Server

ASSIGNMENT 6-2

Create a description of trust relationships and master domain models for Bob Watson. Describe the following in your report to Bob:

- One-way trust
- Two-way trust
- Universal trust
- Single master domain model
- Multiple master domain model

 ASSIGNMENT 6-3

Assume that the campus network joins the administrative and lab servers. How many domains would you create? What domain model would you recommend? What trust relationships would exist?

 ASSIGNMENT 6-4

Access the Administrative Tools menu and review the available options. What option would you use to remove a computer from the domain? What option would you use to select a domain? From where would you port NetWare users and accounts to NT Server? Briefly tour the following options and prepare a summary of each:

- Server Manager
- User Manager
- Event Viewer
- License Manager
- Windows NT Diagnostics

 ASSIGNMENT 6-5

In a lab provided by your instructor, access the User Manager and review the screens used for creating trust relationships. Create the following:

- A one-way trust
- A two-way trust
- A single master domain model

Explain how you created each of these. Which trusts require a password and why? What appears in the password box(es)?

ASSIGNMENT 6-6

From where on the Administrative Tools menu would you synchronize servers? In a lab provided by your instructor, select this option and synchronize the servers on the network. Describe the steps you took. Also, describe what circumstances would cause a network administrator to manually synchronize the servers.

ASSIGNMENT 6-7

Assume that you need to add the Holland College lab server to the administrative server domain. Use the Administrative Tools menu to add a server to an existing domain. Next, remove the server from the domain. Describe the steps and menu options you used to add and to remove the server.

ASSIGNMENT 6-8

In a lab provided by your instructor, practice the following and use the accompanying table to record a log of the steps you took:

- Turn a two-way trust into a one-way trust.
- Turn a master domain model into a universal trust.
- Turn a one-way trust into a two-way trust.
- Remove all trust relationships.

Practice Activity	Description of the Steps

CHAPTER SEVEN

SERVER MANAGEMENT: USER ACCOUNTS, GROUPS, AND RIGHTS

After completing and verifying the domain setup as she did in Chapter 6, Sara is preparing to set up user accounts and groups in the domain. Each user needs his or her own account as an individual doorway into the domain resources. Accounts are known to the domain by unique IDs and passwords. By setting up groupings of users with similar access requirements, Sara is simplifying server maintenance work.

Her review of the existing domain, THE_FIRM, shows it is ready for use. LAWYER is correctly set as the domain's PDC and as a domain resource. The Administrator account has full system privileges in the domain to access the User Manager and the Server Manager from the Administrative Tools menu. And Sara has practiced where to set up trusted and trusting relationships when the branch offices are established.

AFTER READING THIS CHAPTER AND COMPLETING THE EXERCISES YOU WILL BE ABLE TO:

- ESTABLISH USER ACCOUNT POLICIES.
- CREATE NEW ACCOUNTS.
- EXPLAIN THE DIFFERENCE BETWEEN LOCAL AND GLOBAL GROUPS.
- CREATE NEW GROUPS.
- EXPLAIN THE DIFFERENCE BETWEEN RIGHTS AND PERMISSIONS.
- ESTABLISH USER RIGHTS POLICIES.
- CREATE ACCOUNTS AND GROUPS BY USING THE ADMINISTRATIVE WIZARDS.

Sara is anxious to set up the user accounts and groups, but first she needs management's approval on several of the following key issues:

- User account policies
- Use of the server for home directories
- Group members
- Group policies
- Hours for the server to be available

Sara earlier discussed the issues with Kristin, who is scheduling a presentation to the managers. The following sections in this chapter explain the issues Sara covers in her presentation. At the end of the chapter, Sara incorporates their decisions as she creates user accounts and groups.

USER ACCOUNT POLICIES

NT Server enables Sara to establish general password and logon security stipulations for some or all user accounts. The account policy options are the following:

- Password expiration
- Password length
- Password history
- Account lockout
- User home directories

There is no requirement to implement the security options, but most network administrators choose to use them. Many organizations like to have some guidelines to help computer users take advantage of computer security features so as to protect company information from people inside or outside the organization who could misuse it. Security features also protect the domain from malicious vandalism.

PASSWORD SECURITY

The first line of defense for NT Server is password security, but it's only effective if users are taught to use it properly. Many users are careless about security, viewing it as an impediment to their work. They may tape passwords inside a desk drawer or use easily guessed passwords, such as the first name of a family member. Some users keep the same password for months or years, even though it may be known to several other people through past conversations. Systems like NT Server have built-in capabilities to help users become more conscious of maintaining passwords. One option is to set a password expiration period, requiring users to change passwords at regular intervals. Sara encourages the managers to use this feature and recommends that users change their passwords every 45 to 90 days. The managers agree and decide each user should change his or her password every 60 days.

Some organizations require that all passwords have a minimum length, such as six or seven characters. This requirement makes passwords more difficult to guess. Another option is to have the operating system "remember" passwords that have been used previously. For example, the system might be set to recall the last five passwords, preventing a user from repeating one of these. Password recollection forces the user to change to a different password instead of re-using the same one. The managers ask Sara to set the minimum password length at six characters and to have the system recall the five most recently used passwords, so they cannot be repeated.

NT Server is capable of monitoring unsuccessful logon attempts, in case an intruder attempts to break into an account by trying various password combinations. The operating system can lock out an account after a number of unsuccessful tries. **Account lockout** means no one is allowed to access the account, including the true account owner using his or her password. The lockout can be set to release after a specified period of time or by intervention from the network administrator. Anne Nishida knew of a law firm where a member of the custodial service attempted to access server information by trying different passwords from a workstation. The managers agree with Anne's concern and ask Sara to use the lockout feature, with lockout set to go into effect after five unsuccessful logon attempts. They also decide to have lockout release after 30 minutes. The 30 minutes would create enough delay to discourage intruders, while giving some leeway to an attorney who might have forgotten a recently changed password.

USER HOME DIRECTORIES

Sara tells the managers she wants to make directory space available on the server for each user. This will enable them to easily share files or other information with the rest of the office. Each office member would have his or her own directory, called a **home directory**, in which to store files. Sara presents an example of the directory structure, as shown in Figure 7-1.

 A **home directory** is a dedicated location on a file server or a workstation for a specific account holder to store files.

Figure 7-1

Home directory structure

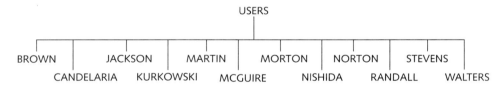

As Figure 7-1 shows, each user's home directory is a subdirectory of the main directory, USERS, which has no directory levels above it. Every account holder can place information in his or her directory, such as a letter to a client or notes for a trial. Sara will closely monitor the size of the home directories to ensure they do not grow beyond the capacity of the server disks. She'll also take into account the tasks and file sizes required by each user, as well as the space available on the user's local hard disk. Those users with overcrowded hard disks will be encouraged to make full use of the user directories, whereas the users with lots of disk space will be discouraged unless a file needs to be shared. All users will be encouraged to regularly delete unused files in their home directories. Sara works further on the directory design in Chapter 8.

NT Server 4.0 does not have a built-in utility to limit the amount of disk space allocated to a particular user. If home directories are used on the server, the network administrator must closely watch to ensure they do not grow too large. Another approach is to purchase software to limit disk space allocated to home directories.

Organizations larger than Nishida and McGuire create more elaborate directory structures to reflect the composition of units, divisions, or departments. For example, a company with accounting, sales, research, and production divisions might have a USERS directory with these four divisions as subdirectories, with the user home directories under each division subdirectory.

The managers accept Sara's recommendation for home directories. They also approve the directory structure she designed. Kent McGuire asks Sara to keep them informed about disk space needs as they arise.

GROUP POLICIES

In the presentation, Sara explains there are three ways domain resources can be managed: by individual user, by group, or by resource. Managing by individual user is the most labor-intensive method. This requires setting up security access customized for each user account. At Nishida and McGuire there are 12 accounts to set up individually, with more to come as the branch offices are added. Sara needs to keep track of what access is allowed per each user, in case accesses need to be rebuilt after a disk failure. This is not unmanageable on a small network, but it becomes unmanageable as the network grows. Also, setting up accounts for several people with identical access is repetitive and inefficient.

Another way to manage network access is by the resource. Assume the resources on a network are two file servers and one print server. One file server is for business applications and one is for scientific research applications. The business unit in the organization would have access to the business applications server and the print server. Scientists would have access to the server with science-related applications. Some managerial people would have access to all three resources. The problem with this security model is that access management is still labor-intensive because it is customized by user and by resource.

The group management concept saves time by eliminating repetitive steps in managing user and resource access. This is based on the idea that users can belong to one or more groups having the same access needs. NT Server has two types of groups: local and global. Local groups are particularly useful for managing access to resources within a domain. Global groups have user accounts as members and enable resource sharing across domains.

LOCAL GROUPS

Local groups are most closely identified with a home server or a domain. In Sara's situation, local groups will be applied to the resources and users of the domain THE_FIRM. The only resource at this time is the server, LAWYER. Future resources might be Sara's NT workstation, print services, fax services, a database server, and other services. The characteristics of local groups are the following:

- They are used to help manage rights and permissions on a server within a domain.
- User accounts can be members of local groups.

- Domain resources can be assigned to local groups.

- Global groups can belong to local groups.

- Local groups can be used to make domain resources accessible to trusted domains, such as in the master domain models.

Rights enable an account or group to perform predefined tasks in the domain. The most basic right is to have privilege to access a server. More advanced rights give privileges to create accounts, manage server functions, and even modify the operating system. **Permissions** are associated with directories and files, controlling the way an account or group accesses information. For example, access can range from no permission to view files in a directory to full permission for adding or changing any files in the directory. Rights are a higher level of access than permissions. If Sara gives Joe Candelaria permission to access all software application files on the server but forgets to give him rights to access the server, he cannot access the applications.

 Company and organization auditors are receiving advanced training in the setup of security privileges on network systems and expect to find good security practices.

NT Server comes with several predefined local groups. These are groups common to most network applications, such as an administrator group to manage server functions, a user group for server users, and various operator groups to perform specific functions such as server backups. Table 7-1 shows the predefined local groups with a description of their purpose.

Table 7-1

Predefined local groups

Local Group	Description
Account operators	This group of users has rights to create, delete, and manage accounts on a server or domain.
Administrators	This group has access to all server and administrative functions.
Backup operators	These operators have rights to back up all files on a server or within a domain.
Guests	This group has limited access to a server or domain, such as for temporary employees, part-time help, or Internet visitors.
Print operators	This group can manage designated print services such as holding or deleting print jobs.
Replicator	This is a unique group for automating the replication of files, such as databases. For example, some application systems use two identical databases, one for updating data and one for reporting on data. The update database is regularly copied to the reporting database so they remain in sync.
Server operators	This group has privileges to manage specific server functions, such as dismounting disk volumes or shutting down servers.
Users	These are the regular users on a server or domain who access server files and applications.

GLOBAL GROUPS

Global groups are intended as a means to provide links between domains in a multiple domain environment. Their purpose is to easily manage access rights among domains. Because global groups have access to trusting domains, they are a way to provide users access across domains. The access is made possible by adding a global group with trusting domain rights to a local group where users need access to the trusting domain. The characteristics of global groups are the following:

- They provide rights access across domains by linking rights from trusting domains to groups in trusted domains.

- Global groups can have domain user accounts as members but not local groups, to avoid circular group relationships.

- Global groups can be members of local groups.

- Global groups cannot have resources as members. They gain rights to resources through belonging to a local group.

Three global groups come predefined with NT Server: one administrator group and two user groups. These are described in Table 7-2.

<table>
<tr><td>Table 7-2</td><td colspan="2"></td></tr>
</table>

Global Group	Description
Domain Administrators	This group enables network administrators to have administrative rights across domains. Domain Administrators is pre-established as a member of the Administrators group in the home domain.
Domain Users	This group is used to manage user access rights across multiple domains. The group is pre-established as a member of the Users group on the home domain. All new users are automatically added to the group to ensure domain access.
Domain Guests	This group enables network administrators to manage guest account access across multiple domains. The group is pre-established as a member of the Guest group in the home domain.

Predefined NT Server global groups

When there are multiple domains, the process for managing rights is to first assign users and resources to a local group. Next, you assign users who need cross-domain access to the global group in their domain. Access rights between domains are enabled by adding the global group of a trusted domain to the local group in the trusting domain. For example, let's use the hypothetical situation from Chapter 6 where Sara would manage three domains, THE_FIRM, EASTLAW, and WESTLAW. Also, assume that Kristin is her backup as network administrator. Sara or Kristin can access all three domains as administrators by following the order of these steps:

1. Add Sara and Kristin to the local Administrators group for THE_FIRM.

2. Check to be certain the EASTLAW Domain Administrators group is already a member of the EASTLAW Administrators group, which should be set up by default.

3. Check to be certain the WESTLAW Domain Administrators group is already a member of the WESTLAW Administrators group.

4. Add the THE_FIRM Domain Administrators to the Administrators group for EASTLAW.

5. Add the THE_FIRM Domain Administrators to the Administrators group for EASTLAW.

Step 1 gives administrator rights and permissions to Sara and Kristin. Steps 2 and 3 ensure administrator rights and permissions are already given to domain administrators on EASTLAW and WESTLAW. Finally, steps 4 and 5 bring administrator rights and permissions from EASTLAW and WESTLAW to Sara and Kristin (see Figure 7-2).

Figure 7-2

Managing administrator groups in multiple domains

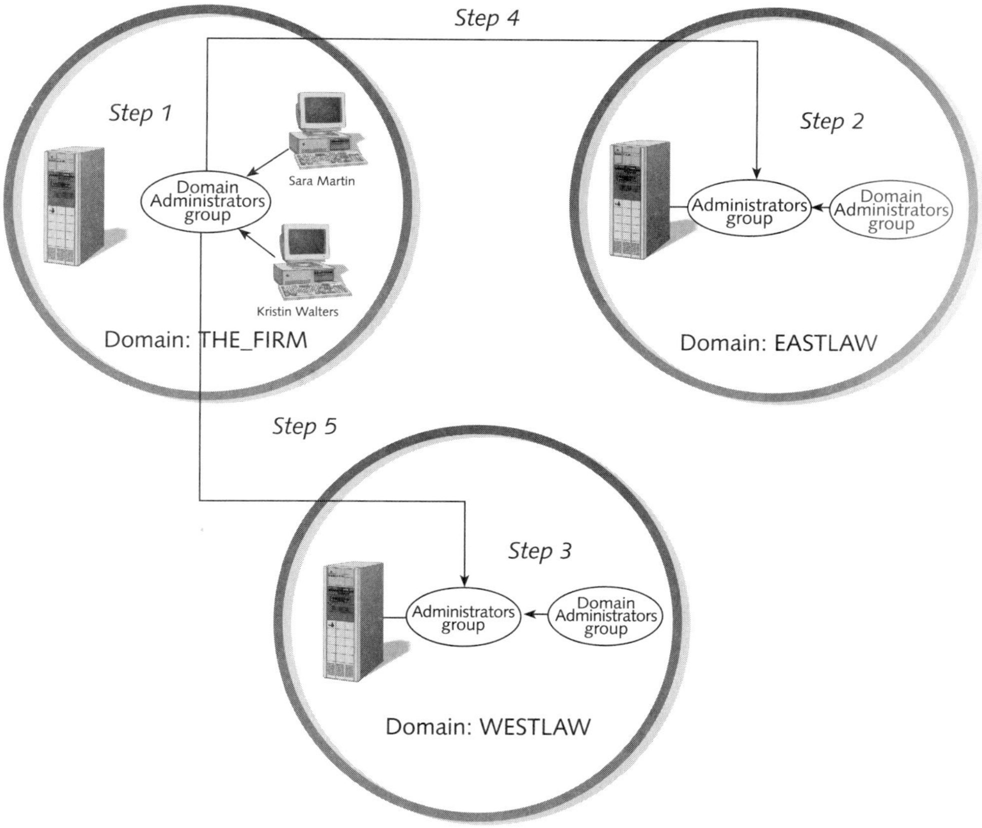

Building groups represents some work initially, but it saves work once all the groups are set up. Many individual account management tasks are reduced by lumping them into fewer group management tasks. For example, if Kristin leaves and Terry is promoted into Kristin's job, only two steps are required to make the change as administrator. Kristin is removed from the local Administrators group on THE_FIRM and Terry is added. Otherwise, without the local and global group setup, these two steps would be repeated for the local Administrators groups on EASTLAW and WESTLAW, adding four extra steps. Although this is a small savings in the present example, the savings are greatly multiplied when working with many users and large networks.

SARA'S RECOMMENDATIONS

Sara provides a brief summary of groups to the managers and recommends Kristin act as the backup administrator for those times when Sara is out of the office. Because the printer services would initially use the two laser printers near Mark and Jane, Sara recommends making them print operators, along with the administrators who have print services rights by default. Sara recommends Mark and Jane be designated as backup operators so they can fill in for server backups should one or both of the administrators be gone. She suggests using the local guest group for consultants hired by the firm to do special research or act as expert court witnesses.

Sara recommends adding two additional local groups: a managers group and a business group. The managers group would consist of the five managing partners for the firm. This group would share management reports, minutes from the management meetings, human resources information, and financial data. The other group would be for business services and would include all members of the management group plus Terry and Kristin (see Figure 7-3). Table 7-3 shows the groups Sara recommends as a starting point. The managers accept the recommendations for groups.

Business group

Figure 7-3

Business group composition

Table 7-3

Group membership for Nishida and McGuire

Group	Membership
Administrators	Sara Martin, Kristin Walters, Domain Administrators group
Print operators	Mark Jackson, Jane Randall, Domain Administrators group
Backup operators	Mark Jackson, Jane Randall, Domain Administrators group
Domain users	All office members added by default
Users	All office members, Domain Users group
Domain guests	Visiting consultants and retained expert witnesses
Guests	Visiting consultants and retained expert witnesses
Managers	Anne Nishida, Kent McGuire, Beth Stevens, Rick Kurkowski, Jason Brown
Business	Managers group, Kristin Walters, Terry Norton

Plan in advance the groups you will implement, so you are not performing extra administrative tasks for groups you don't need.

SERVER AVAILABILITY

Sara explains she has the option to make the server unavailable to all but the administrators for periods when system work is required and also to keep it safe from intruders when the regular office members are away. Sara asks to reserve system time for work on the server every Wednesday night from 8:00 to 10:00 P.M. Kent McGuire mentions he often comes in to work on Wednesday evenings because his wife is chair of the City Development Board, which meets on that night. Sara offers to move the system time to Thursday nights barring any other conflicts. The managers agree to her request but prefer to leave the server accessible at all other times.

From the start, plan to have domain servers unavailable at designated hours for system time activities such as installing software, adding drivers, and changing or adding hardware.

SETTING ACCOUNT POLICIES

Sara is relieved that her presentation to the managers is over and wastes no time logging on to the server from the Administrator account. The first task she wants to accomplish is to set up the account polices. Once she logs on, Sara goes to the Administrative Tools menu and clicks User Manager for Domains. From the User Manager, she highlights the Policies menu and selects Account, as shown in Figure 7-4.

Figure 7-4

Policies menu in the User Manager with Account selected

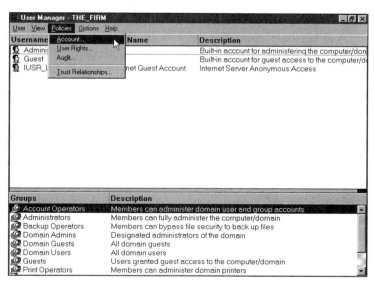

The next screen is where Sara can invoke the account policies established by the managers (see Figure 7–5). In the area called Maximum Password Age, Sara clicks the radio button for Expires in ____ Days and enters "60" in the text box. Because the text box has Up and Down Arrows to increment values, she could choose to use the Up Arrow to increment to 60 instead of typing it in the box. This parameter forces users to change their passwords every 60 days. For Minimum Password Age, she clicks the radio button labeled Allow Changes Immediately, so passwords can be changed at any time and used immediately. As Sara shows in Chapter 11, the network administrator can assign new passwords should a user become forgetful.

Figure 7-5

Account Policy screen

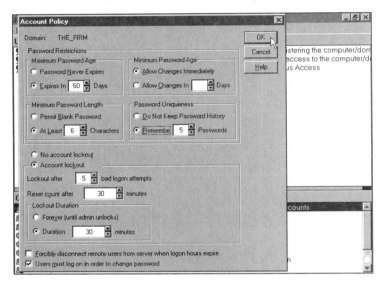

Under Minimum Password Length, Sara clicks the radio button for At Least ____ Characters and enters "6" in the text box. Her response to Password Uniqueness is to click the radio button for Remember ____ Passwords. Then she enters "5" in the text box.

In the middle of the screen, Sara clicks the radio button for Account lockout, which activates the area below it for Sara to input the lockout parameters. She enters "5" to limit to that number of bad logon attempts. Next, she enters 30 minutes as the time the system waits before resetting the number back to zero. Under Lockout Duration, Sara clicks the radio button for Duration ____ minutes and enters "30", which enables the system to keep an account locked for this amount of time.

Sara leaves the second to last parameter blank because the server is not set up for remote access. Also, when there are remote users, she does not want to force them to log off during system time, because a user might lose work that has not been saved. However, Sara wants users to be connected to the server when they change passwords so the SAM is immediately updated with the new information. She places a check in the last box on the screen and clicks OK to save the changes.

CREATING ACCOUNTS

With the account policies set, Sara is ready to create accounts for all the firm's users, starting with her own. The account policies will automatically apply to each account she creates, although they can be overridden for individual cases. There are two ways to set up accounts: through the User Manager or through the New Account Setup Wizard. Sara is comfortable with the User Manager and prefers to learn it thoroughly because it is the central location for managing user accounts after they are created.

NT Server has a Setup Wizard for creating new accounts that can be used as an alternative. The advantage of the Setup Wizard is that it guides new administrators through account setup step by step. The disadvantage is that it does not offer the same full control of account setup as is available through the User Manager. Sara plans to later use the Setup Wizard for one account to give it a try, but first she goes to the User Manager to create her own account. Back on the main User Manager screen, Sara clicks the User menu at the top of the screen and clicks New User, as shown in Figure 7-6.

Figure 7-6

User menu with New User selected

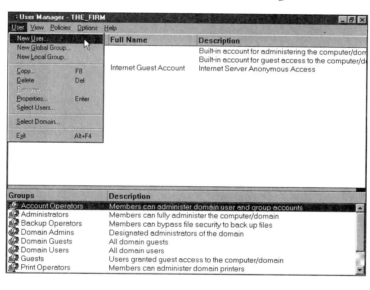

The next screen enables her to enter information for her new account (see Figure 7-7). To begin, Sara enters her user name, SMartin, on the first line. Below that she enters her full name, Sara Martin, which is helpful information when it is difficult to tell the user's name from the abbreviated account name. On the description line she enters her office title, Network Administrator. Next, she enters a password and verifies she has entered it correctly on the Confirm Password line.

Figure 7-7

New User screen with Sara's account information

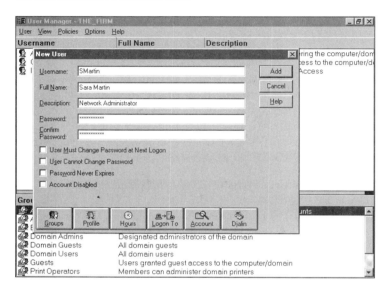

The next four parameters enable her to control the account further. For her account, she leaves unchecked the option labeled User Must Change Password at Next Logon. On all other accounts she plans to check this box. It is common practice for the network administrator to create an account, notify the user the account has been created, and have the user change the password immediately.

The account policies are set up to require that passwords change after 60 days, so Sara does not check Password Never Expires. This option is used in situations where an automated programming process requires a special account from which to run. Passwords on this type of account should not expire without intervention from the network administrator to ensure the process does not fail unexpectedly, such as when an automated data update is running.

The bottom check box on the screen enables the network administrator to disable an account. This option is used, for example, when a professor is on a sabbatical and will need access renewed when he or she returns. Figure 7-7 shows the New User screen with Sara's information entered.

THE GROUPS BUTTON

Sara moves on to the options at the bottom of the screen and clicks the Groups button first. NT Server has already added Sara to the Domain Users group by default. She highlights the Administrators group on the right side of the screen and clicks the Add button to place herself in this group, as shown in Figure 7-8. The Administrators label moves to the left side of the screen, into the Member of box. The deactivated Set button at the bottom of the screen is to set Sara's primary group. Domain Users is automatically set as the primary group. A primary group must always be a global group. Sara clicks OK to save the changes, bringing her back to the New User screen.

Figure 7-8

Group Memberships screen in the New User section

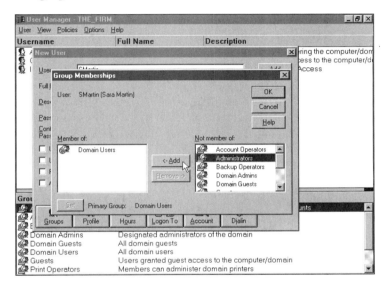

Primary groups are used exclusively by Macintosh or POSIX workstations that access NT Server. NT Server requires that these systems be members of a global group.

THE PROFILE BUTTON

Next, Sara clicks the Profile button, producing a screen where she can link each user account with a user profile, a logon script, a home directory, and a home drive to connect to the server (see Figure 7-9). She begins with the home drive information, as that is all she wants to enter on this screen. Logon scripts and user profiles can develop into lots of maintenance work. They may require large-scale changes when servers are added or when a group of users gets new computers. Users and workstation operating systems are more advanced than in the past, creating less need for user scripts and profiles.

Sara plans to standardize the home drives of all users to drive H, which is common practice among network administrators. She does this by selecting the Connect radio button on the bottom of the screen.

She enters "H" in the first box and specifies the home drive path of \USERS\MARTIN in the right box (see Figure 7-9). Each time a user logs on, there will be an H drive shown in My Computer and in the Explorer, with a path to the user's home directory on LAWYER. After Sara enters the information, she clicks OK.

Figure 7-9

User
Environment
Profile screen
in the New
User section

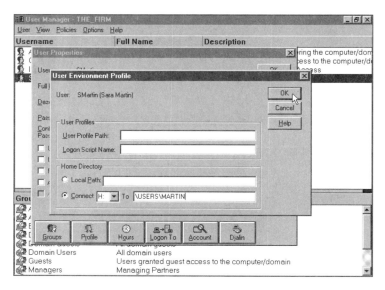

User **profiles** are needed in situations where users have early versions of Windows or where there are very inexperienced users. Profiles can be set up for each user to create a consistent desktop environment each time he or she logs on. The environment may be specific program groupings, a set of drive mappings for users on large networks with many servers, or a particular program that runs each time the user logs on. In working with the office members, Sara knows they prefer to set desktop options independently from their workstations, rather than to have the desktop controlled from the server. She does not plan to have user profiles on the firm's network.

A default user profile, USERDEF, is provided by NT Server as an example and is located in the server directory, \WINNT\SYSTEM32\CONFIG.

A **logon script** is a set of commands that automatically run each time the user logs on to the domain. A summary of the commands is provided in Table 7-4.

Table 7-4

Example script
commands

Script Command	Function
Homepath	Establishes the path to the user's home directory
Homedrive	Sets a drive letter for the home directory
Username	Specifies the user's logon name
Userdomain	Specifies the domain to which the user belongs
OS	Specifies the workstation's operating system
Processor level	Specifies the type of processor in the workstation
Homeshare	Used for home directories on a shared drive

If a logon script exists for a user, it is downloaded from the server at each logon. Scripts are kept in the server directory \WINNT\SYSTEM32\REPL\IMPORT\SCRIPTS. The following script commands would set Sara's home directory to drive H, specify the home directory path, and specify her logon name so she would not have to type it:

```
USERNAME=SMARTIN

HOMEDRIVE=H:

HOMEPATH=\USERS\MARTIN
```

Sara does not plan to create logon scripts for users, because the network environment at the firm is simple. If she were managing a larger network with multiple servers and a large number of users, logon scripts might be of use. Further, Sara can set the home drive and path using the bottom parameter on the screen in Figure 7-9.

THE HOURS BUTTON

Sara can set up the user accounts so they cannot access the server during system time on Thursday evenings from 8:00 to 10:00 P.M. She does this by clicking the Hours button on the screen shown in Figure 7-7. A screen with dates and times appears, where she can block out the system time. Figure 7-10 shows this screen, where Sara is practicing blocking out system time on her account. First she clicks the area box for 8PM and drags the cursor through the 10PM box. With 8PM-10PM blocked on the screen, Sara clicks the Disallow button to prevent logon during this time range. Because she does not really want to disable her own account, she clicks Cancel. If this were another user's account, she would click OK.

 As system administrator, you should enable access during all hours to the domain from your personal account as well as from the Administrator account. This gives you alternate access in case there is a problem with the Administrator account.

Figure 7-10

Logon Hours screen with 8PM–10PM disallowed for system time

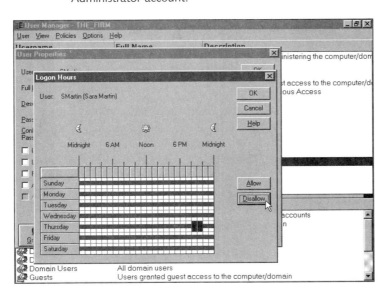

THE LOGON TO BUTTON

Back on the New User screen, Sara clicks the button labeled Logon To. This shows the Logon Workstations screen, where Sara can limit where a user can log on to the domain. For example, Sara could set her own account so it can only be accessed from her computer. She would do this by defining her workstation name as different from her login name and entering her workstation name in one of the text boxes on the screen in Figure 7-11 (see Chapter 4 for information about setting up a workstation name).

Figure 7-11

Logon
Workstations
screen in the
New User
section

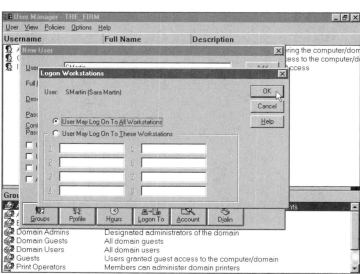

Sara may want to restrict account access to specific workstations in the future, but for now this will be limiting as she is setting up the network. She wants to be able to log on to any account from any workstation to keep flexibility for troubleshooting problems. For now, she clicks the radio button labeled User May Log On To All Workstations, as shown in Figure 7-11, and saves the change by clicking OK.

THE ACCOUNT BUTTON

The Account button on the New User screen (shown previously in Figure 7-7) is used to expire an account. This is a useful option when temporary employees, business auditors, or visitors need an account created for a specific period of time. The account can be set to expire on a given date by clicking the radio button labeled End of and entering the expiration date. The account is expired at the end of the specified working day. Sara clicks the Never radio button because she does not want to expire her account (see Figure 7-12).

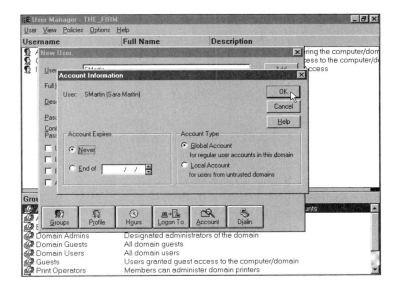

Figure 7-12

Account
Information
screen

An account also can be designated as global or local. A **global account** is one that has normal domain membership and is recognized by other domains when it is in a trusted domain. All the accounts Sara is creating are of this type. When the branch offices are added, she wants accounts to be recognized by other domains. A **local account** is one that is defined only to the home domain and is not recognized by other domains. The local account option is used for situations where the user would never access another domain, such as when creating student accounts in an academic lab domain where access to administrative domains must be restricted. Sara clicks the Global Account radio button and then clicks OK.

THE DIALIN BUTTON

The Dialin button on the New User screen is for controlling remote access to the domain, such as from dial-in modems. Remote access can be granted or disallowed, as shown in Figure 7-13. The firm will have dial-in access in the future, when modems are purchased to attach to LAWYER. Sara clicks Grant Dialin Permission to User, which causes the bottom portion of the screen to activate. These are "call-back" security options for dial-in access so LAWYER's modems can call back the accessing workstation after the initial request to log on is received. This enables LAWYER to verify the call is from a known location. The call-back can be set from the workstation's modem or from a prearranged number used by LAWYER. For the present, Sara does not want to enable call-back until there is time to test remote access when this is set up. She clicks No Call Back and then clicks OK.

Figure 7-13

Dialin
Information
screen

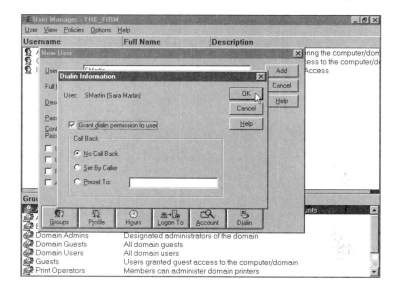

SAVING CHANGES

Sara is back on the New User screen, only now she is finished setting up her user account. She glances over the information on the screen to be certain it is accurate and then clicks OK to save it. She can verify her work by checking for the account on the User Manager screen. As Figure 7-14 shows, Sara's account is created and ready to use.

Figure 7-14

Verifying that
the SMartin
account is
created in User
Manager

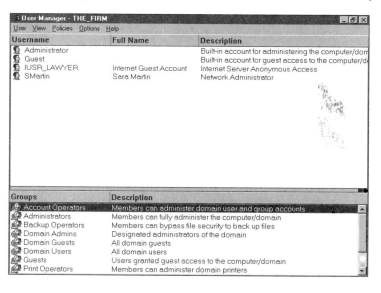

THE NEW ACCOUNT SETUP WIZARD

To compare the Setup Wizard to User Manager, Sara uses the former to create Anne Nishida's account. The information Sara uses to create the account is similar to that for creating her own account, except that the Setup Wizard obtains the information in a series of continuous steps. These are described by the following presentation of steps and screens.

1. On the Administrative Tools menu, Sara clicks the Administrative Wizards option and then clicks Add User Accounts (see Figure 7-15).

Figure 7-15

Administrative Wizards menu

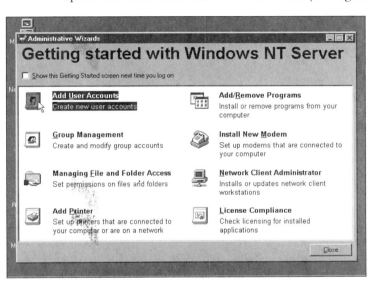

2. On the following screen, Sara checks to be certain the domain name is THE_FIRM and clicks Next (see Figure 7-16).

Figure 7-16

Domain name entry screen

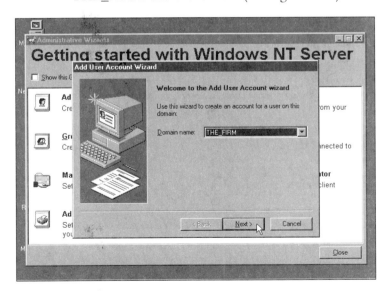

3. Sara enters Anne Nishida's full name, user account name, and position and then clicks Next (see Figure 7-17).

Figure 7-17

User account name information

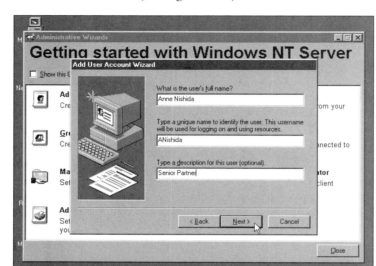

4. The next screen calls for the account password information, which Sara enters. Then she clicks Next (see Figure 7-18).

Figure 7-18

Password entry screen

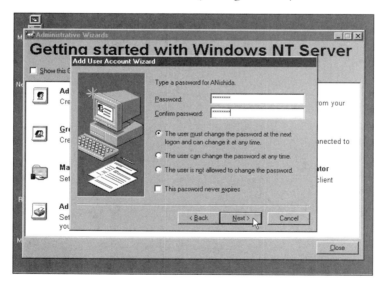

5. Sara does not yet have the managers group created, so she clicks Next on the screen to add Anne to a group (see Figure 7-19).

Figure 7-19

Adding a new user to groups

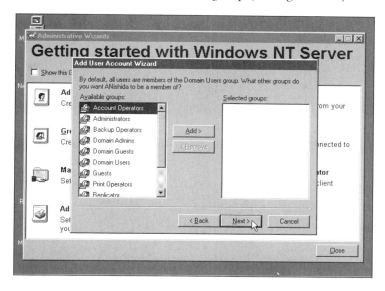

6. Sara puts a check in the box to create a home directory and clicks Next (see Figure 7-20).

Figure 7-20

Setup options

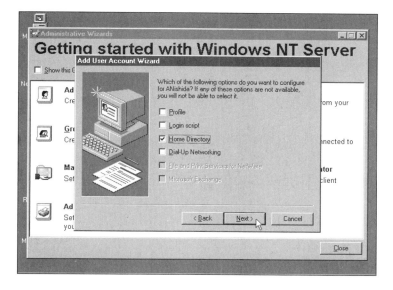

7. Because Anne's home drive is on LAWYER, Sara clicks On Another
   Computer and enters the drive letter H plus the path \USERS\NISHIDA.
   Sara clicks Next to continue (see Figure 7-21).

Figure 7-21

Designating a
home directory

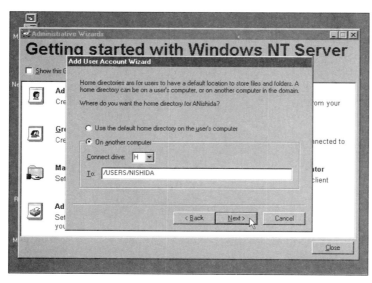

8. Sara clicks the radio button for restrictions and checks time restrictions (see
   Figure 7-22). Then she clicks Next.

Figure 7-22

User
restrictions

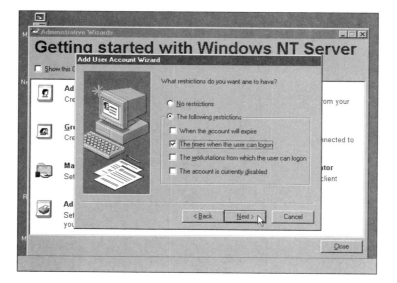

9. Sara sets the system time restrictions for Thursdays between 8:00 and 10:00 P.M. and clicks Next (see Figure 7-23).

Figure 7-23

Setting time restrictions

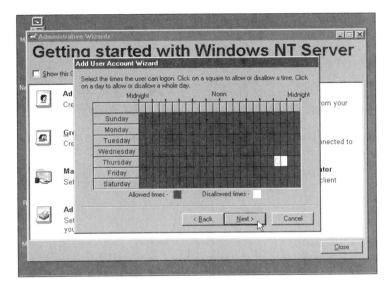

10. Sara clicks Finish to add Anne's account (see Figure 7-24).

Figure 7-24

User account information is entered and the wizard is ready to add it

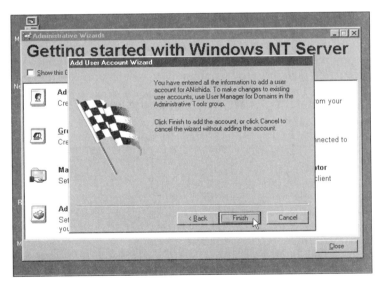

CREATING GROUPS

Sara is ready to set up the Managers and Business groups. The Managers group will be global so it can span domains in the future and so it can be a member of the Business group. Sara starts with the Managers group. First she clicks the New Global Group option on the User menu on the User Manager screen (see Figure 7-25).

Figure 7-25

The menu selection to create a new global group

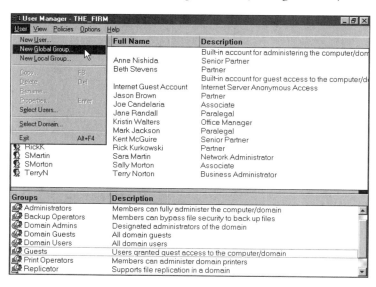

Next, Sara enters the group name and a description of the group in the text boxes at the top of the screen. She highlights the five members, one at a time, in the Not Members box and clicks Add to move each into the Members box on the left of the screen (see Figure 7-26). All the members she adds appear in the Members box when she is finished, and she clicks OK to save the group.

Figure 7-26

Creating a new global group

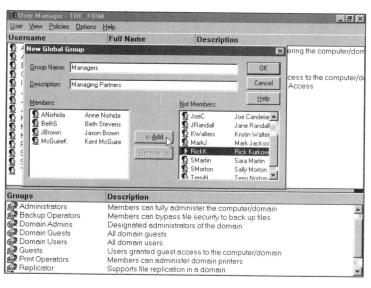

THE GROUP MANAGEMENT SETUP WIZARD

Another way to create new groups is to use the Group Management Setup Wizard shown on the screen in Figure 7-15. Sara tries this wizard to set up the Business group, as illustrated in the following steps.

1. Sara clicks the Group Management Setup Wizard and clicks the radio button labeled Create a New Group and Add Members. Then she clicks Next (see Figure 7-27).

Figure 7-27

Creating a new group using the Group Management Wizard

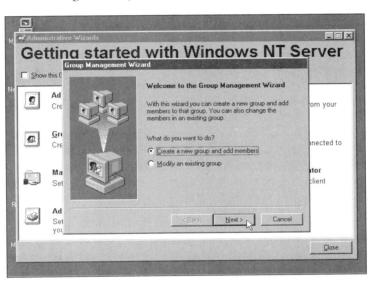

2. Sara enters Business as the new group name and types a description. She clicks Next to continue (see Figure 7-28).

Figure 7-28

Entering the group name and description

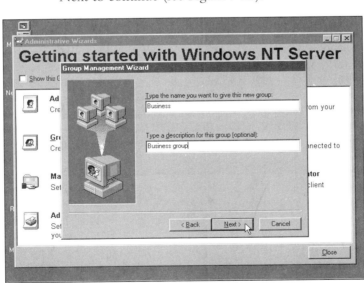

3. She clicks the radio button for Local Group and then clicks Next (see Figure 7-29).

Figure 7-29

Specifying the type of group

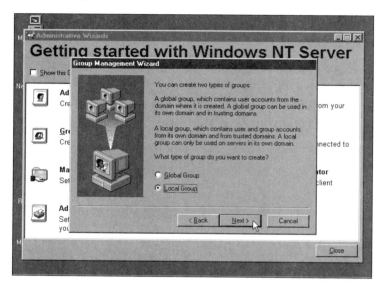

4. Sara highlights Managers and clicks Add. She repeats these steps to add Kristin Walters and Terry Norton, and then she clicks Next to continue (see Figure 7-30).

Figure 7-30

Adding group members

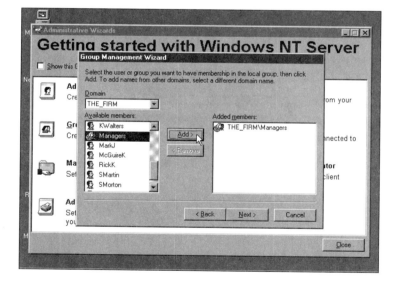

5. She clicks Finish to add the group to the domain (see Figure 7-31).

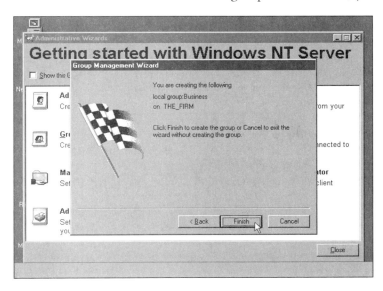

RIGHTS

With the new groups created, Sara wishes to assign rights to each group. Rights are assigned by using the Policies menu on the User Manager screen (see Figure 7-4). Sara clicks Policies and then clicks User Rights. NT Server has a wide range of rights that can be assigned. Sara clicks the Down Arrow to view the rights selections in the drop-down box, as shown in Figure 7-32.

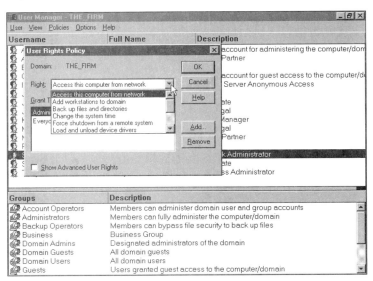

Rights grant privileges to perform functions such as accessing the server, adding workstations to the domain, changing the system time, and backing up files. Only members of the Administrators group have authority to grant rights. The rights can be granted to users, groups, or a combination of both, but the easiest way to administer rights is through groups.

Two levels of rights can be granted. The regularly used rights are described in Table 7-5. These rights apply to everyday users and groups and appear in the drop-down box shown in Figure 7-32. More complex rights can be assigned by clicking the box labeled Show Advanced User Rights. The advanced rights are for programmers and system developers who have technical access needs, such as debugging programs, gaining access to operating system internals, and controlling memory swapping. Sara is not planning to use the advanced rights, as she is not writing programs at this expert skill level.

Table 7-5

User rights

Right	Typically Granted To	Description
Access this computer from network	Users of workstations and servers	Privilege to connect to a computer, such as LAWYER, from a connection on the network
Add workstations to domain	Administrators	Ability to add a server or NT workstation to an existing domain with capability to interact with domain users, resources, and global groups
Back up files and directories	Administrators, backup operators, server operators	Includes permission to read all files and directories to be able to back them up
Change the system time	Administrators, server operators	Privilege to reset the server's time clock
Force shutdown from a remote system	Administrators, server operators	Reserved but not yet available on NT Server
Load and unload device drivers	Administrators	Privilege to copy in or remove device drivers for the server
Log on locally	Administrators, backup operators, server operators	Ability to log on to the server from the server console
Manage auditing and security log	Administrators	Privilege to specify what to audit and to maintain the audit logs kept on system and user activities
Restore files and directories	Administrators, server operators	Permission to write to any file or directory on the server
Shut down the system	Administrators, server operators	Privilege to shut down the server
Take ownership of files or other objects	Administrators	Ability to take ownership of files and directories created by another user

GRANTING RIGHTS TO A GROUP

The Business and Managers groups, by default, have rights to access LAWYER from the network, but Sara wants to practice assigning this right using these groups as test subjects. The other rights in Table 7-5 are used for administrator or operator groups. Sara highlights the right labeled Access This Computer From Network and clicks the Add button to show a list of groups in the domain, as shown in Figure 7-33. Sara scrolls down the list of groups to Business, which she highlights. Next, she clicks the Add button. The Business group appears in the bottom box, Add Names, to verify it has been selected. Sara repeats the process for the Managers group and clicks OK. She clicks OK again on the User Rights Policy screen to save the changes.

Figure 7-33

Granting rights to the Managers group

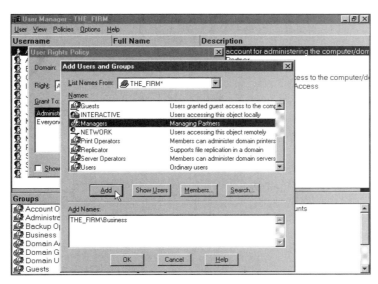

SARA'S NEXT ASSIGNMENT

Applications and services are the lifeblood of a network, and Sara starts work setting these up in the next chapter. Before she installs the applications, she needs to plan their location on the file server. Each application should have a distinct location for easy management, such as when performing upgrades and isolating problems. Also, applications and other files need security to help the firm honor licensing and confidentiality requirements.

Sara begins Chapter 8 by creating a directory design for applications and shared files. She places security on the directories, making them available to her newly created network accounts. Also, she secures the network system files so they cannot be altered or damaged by accident. With security in place, Sara loads the software applications. All these tasks bring the server closer to release for prime time.

KEY CONCEPTS SUMMARY

Much of this chapter focuses on account and group creation. The following concepts are important to these processes.

account lockout This security measure prohibits logging on to an NT server account after a specified number of unsuccessful attempts.

global account This account type has regular domain membership and can be recognized by other domains.

home directory This directory is located on a file server as a default location to store a designated user's files.

local account This account type is recognized and used only in the home domain.

login script This file contains a command set that runs each time a user logs on to a server.

permissions Access capabilities for reading, viewing, and changing files or directories.

profile This setup file creates a specified desktop environment on a workstation at the time a user at that station logs on to a server.

rights Access privileges to perform different levels of activities, such as log on to a server, shut down a server, create user accounts, and load server drivers.

SUMMARY OF WINDOWS FUNCTIONS

Accounts and groups are created and managed from two places on Windows NT servers: the User Manager and Setup Wizards. The capabilities of these tools to manage accounts and groups are summarized in the following paragraphs.

Setup Wizards The Setup Wizards unite setup steps into one program function, guiding you in a logical sequence from step to step. In this chapter, Setup Wizards are used to create an account and a group.

User Manager for Domains You can employ the User Manager to create accounts, set account parameters and restrictions, create user account policies, create groups, and establish rights.

REVIEW QUESTIONS

1. Account lockout is which of the following?
    a. When an account cannot be accessed because a user has not paid his or her bills
    b. When a given number of bad logon attempts have been made
    c. When a user cannot remember his or her account name
    d. When the server is protected from remote access

2. Account policies are set from
    a. The User Manager Policies menu.
    b. The User Manager Accounts menu.
    c. The Server Manager Group menu.
    d. The Server Manager Policies menu.

3. Local groups can be members of global groups.
    a. True
    b. False

4. The ability to shut down a server is a/an
   a. Right.
   b. Permission.
   c. User Manager function.
   d. Administrative wizard.

5. Which group typically has the privilege to take ownership of a file?
   a. Domain users
   b. Administrators
   c. Server operators
   d. Global operators

6. The replicator is a
   a. Predefined local group.
   b. Predefined global group.
   c. Predefined account.
   d. None of the above.

7. The privilege to read a file is a
   a. Right.
   b. Permission.
   c. Default function.
   d. Global privilege.

8. A local account can be used in more than one domain.
   a. True
   b. False

9. From where is a new account set up?
   a. User Manager
   b. New Account Wizard
   c. Server Manager
   d. All of the above
   e. Both a and b

10. "Log on Locally" is the right to
    a. Log on to the server from the network.
    b. Log on to the server from its console.
    c. Log on to a remote print server.
    d. Access a local modem.

11. Call-back is used by which of the following?
    a. Remote access services
    b. The audit log to make a security check
    c. NetBEUI to test a workstation on the network
    d. All of the above
    e. Both a and c

12. NT Server account restrictions can be set up to allow logons from only designated workstations.

   a. True

   b. False

13. A requirement to have passwords of seven characters or more is

   a. A group policy.

   b. An account policy.

   c. A user policy.

   d. A group right.

14. Which of the following can be used in a logon script?

   a. Homepath

   b. Username

   c. Temppath

   d. All of the above

   e. Both a and b

15. The logon script is loaded from the workstation.

   a. True

   b. False

16. USERDEF is a/an

   a. Default profile.

   b. Default logon script.

   c. Account ID in NT Server.

   d. Account lock key.

17. Domain Guests is a/an

   a. Local group.

   b. Global group.

   c. Account group.

   d. Account type.

18. Restrictions on the hours when an account can access the server are set from

   a. The User Manager screen.

   b. The New Account Wizard.

   c. The Group Management Wizard.

   d. All of the above.

   e. Both a and b.

19. Domain resources should be assigned to which of the following?

   a. Local groups

   b. Global groups

   c. Domain users

   d. All of the above

   e. Both a and b.

20. Advanced user rights are needed for
   a. Client/server users.
   b. Backup operators.
   c. Expert programmers.
   d. Server operators.
21. Which of the following groups have authority to grant rights?
   a. Administrators
   b. Server operators
   c. Backup operators
   d. Managers
   e. All of the above
   f. Both a and b.

THE HOLLAND COLLEGE PROJECT: PHASE 7

Bob Watson is very pleased with your work and requests that President Jackson promote you to network administrator. Your promotion will become official as soon as the paperwork is completed, within two days. Congratulations on your fine progress!

The next test is to set up user accounts and groups on the administrative and English and writing lab servers.

ASSIGNMENT 7-1

What account policy recommendations would you make to Bob Watson for the administrative and lab servers? Record your policy recommendations in the following tables.

Administrative Server Policies	
Policy	**Your Recommendation**

Lab Server Policies	
Policy	**Your Recommendation**

 ASSIGNMENT 7-2

Set up accounts for the business branch including Reuben Asimow, Angela Miles, Jackie Herrera, Sherry Parks, Dave Whitefeather, Janice McKinney, Randy Thomas, and Ryan McKim. Set up half of the accounts using the User Manager and half using the New Account Setup Wizard. Answer the following questions about how you set up the accounts.

- Would you restrict any of these accounts to particular workstations? Why or why not?
- Would it be useful to have logon scripts for any of these users? Why or why not?
- Would it be useful to create profiles for any of these users? Why or why not?
- Do you plan to establish home directories? If so, explain your plan.
- Which tool is easier, User Manager or the Setup Wizard?

 ASSIGNMENT 7-3

Explain the difference between global and local groups. What is the difference between global and local accounts? In Assignment 7-2, did you create global or local accounts? Why?

ASSIGNMENT 7-4

Write a plan for creating lab accounts so any student on campus can have access. Answer the following questions:

- How would you set up user names?
- How would you set up passwords?
- What account restrictions would you use?
- What hours would the server be available?
- Would the accounts be global or local?

 ## ASSIGNMENT 7-5

Create a group through the User Manager with the following characteristics:

- Group name = Operators
- Type of group = global
- Members = Backup operators and server operators

Create a group using the Administrative Wizards with the following characteristics:

- Group name = Auditors
- Type of group = global
- Members = guests

Which tool is easier for you to use? Why?

 ## ASSIGNMENT 7-6

Create a group called Overseers. Add the following rights to the group and describe how you added them:

- Change the system time
- Restore files and directories
- Shut down the system
- Add workstations to the domain

ASSIGNMENT 7-7

Bob Watson has asked you to set up a group consisting of the president, vice-presidents, and Steve Gaudio, the executive assistant to the president. They will be working on confidential information about the college's five-year plan, the budget, and personnel matters. Describe how you would set security restrictions on these accounts to help protect access. Also, describe how you would set up their group.

 ASSIGNMENT 7-8

In a lab, practice the following and record where you completed the task:

Task	Where Completed
Expire an account	
Disable an account	
Set up account lockout for seven bad logons	
Add an account to the Backup Operators group	
Grant the account rights to log on locally	
Restrict the account from remote access	
Change the account's password	

SERVER MANAGEMENT: DIRECTORIES, PERMISSIONS, AND SOFTWARE APPLICATIONS

Sara is working on the server when Joe Candelaria stops in to visit and ask how the work is going. She enthusiastically tells him the user accounts are set up and it won't be long until he can work from the server. Joe is pleased and wishes her well. Before continuing with new work, Sara decides to glance over the accounts and groups in User Manager for one more check. From the User Manager, she reviews the 12 user accounts and 2 groups. She randomly examines two accounts, JBrown and BethS, to be sure the home directory and time restriction information are entered. She checks the members of the Business and Managers groups and verifies the assigned rights.

After reviewing her work, Sara turns to planning for the server directories and permissions. In this chapter, she completes the design for all directories, including the application software directories. She assigns directory properties and security so information can be shared on the network. Toward the end of the day, Sara reviews issues that affect loading software onto a server. She finishes by loading Microsoft Office and, with Kristin's help, testing her software installation.

AFTER READING THIS CHAPTER AND COMPLETING THE EXERCISES YOU WILL BE ABLE TO:

- DESIGN A DIRECTORY STRUCTURE FOR A SERVER.
- SET DIRECTORY ATTRIBUTES.
- SET DIRECTORY PERMISSIONS.
- TAKE OWNERSHIP OF A DIRECTORY.
- CREATE A SHARE.
- SET SHARE PERMISSIONS.
- INSTALL APPLICATION SOFTWARE ON A SERVER.

DIRECTORY STRUCTURE

Sara realizes it is easy for a hard drive to become cluttered and disorganized with different versions of files and software. Many PC users keep all their files in the computer's root directory, or they load all application software into the same directory. Many application software programs use an automated setup that suggests a directory for new programs, but some users still have difficulty organizing files. A chaotic file structure makes it difficult to run or remove programs, as well as to determine the most current versions.

Sara is well aware of the necessity to have a carefully designed file structure from the start, especially on the server because it impacts the entire office. Already she has created the home directories for the account setup. Beyond these directories, she needs a place for the following:

- Software applications
- Confidential files shared by the management group
- The firm's accounting software
- The legal time accounting software
- Files to be shared by the entire office

In deciding how to allocate disk directories for these files, Sara has a mental list of criteria to follow. For instance, the **root directory** should not be cluttered with files or too many directories. Each software application should have its own directory or subdirectory, so updates and software removal are easy to administer. For easy access control, similar information should be grouped, such as the accounting systems. Windows NT Server system files should be kept separate and protected so important files are not accidentally deleted by a user. Directories should have names that clearly reflect their purpose. Considering these criteria, Sara plans to have six primary directories besides those already created by the NT Server setup program. The six directories are:

- *Users* for home directories
- *App* for software applications such as Lotus 1-2-3, WordPerfect, and legal time accounting
- *Msoffice* for Microsoft Office applications
- *Manage* for the managers' group
- *Public* for openly shared files such as research, office correspondence, court dates, and schedules
- *Ntserver* for server utilities

 The **root directory** is the highest-level directory, with no directories above it in the tree structure. On DOS and Windows systems, the root directory of the hard drive often is represented by C:\ and the first network drive as F:\.

Each major directory has subdirectories to keep grouped files or application software separate. For example, the App directory has subdirectories for Lotus 1-2-3, WordPerfect, the wills and bankruptcy forms software, and all other applications other than Microsoft Office. Msoffice has subdirectories for Word, Excel, Access, and other Microsoft applications.

Figure 8-1 is a diagram of the directory structure Sara is implementing from the root, with an example of the subdirectories under the App main directory.

Figure 8-1

THE_FIRM
directory
structure

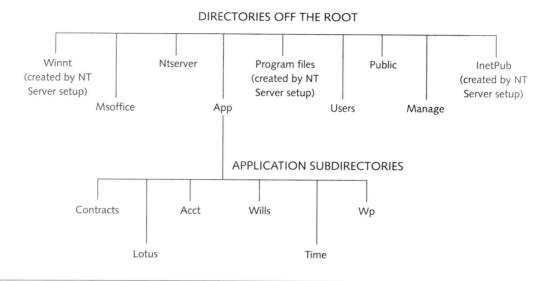

DIRECTORIES OFF THE ROOT

Winnt (created by NT Server setup) | Ntserver | Program files (created by NT Server setup) | Public | InetPub (created by NT Server setup)

Msoffice — App — Users — Manage

APPLICATION SUBDIRECTORIES

Contracts — Acct — Wills — Wp

Lotus — Time

VIEWING DIRECTORIES

Sara has already created three of the new directories, Users, App, and Ntserver, from the administrators account. She created App and Ntserver earlier in the day while experimenting with directory setup and decided to keep both after composing the directory design. She used My Computer on the desktop to create the new directories. Continuing to work, Sara logs on to the Administrator account and clicks My Computer to view the server directories, as shown in Figure 8-2. The directories created by NT Server are InetPub, Program Files, and Winnt. InetPub is for Internet Web pages, graphics, and other files for Web publishing. The Program Files directory has three subdirectories with applications that come with NT Server. The Accessories subdirectory has third-party applications, such as ImageVue, which is used for computer graphics. The Plus! subdirectory has the Internet Explorer, which is a browser for accessing files on the Internet. And the Windows NT subdirectory has Microsoft applications, including WordPad for small word processing tasks, a calculator, an automatic dialer for modem connections, and MS Exchange for e-mail.

Figure 8-2

Server
directories in
My Computer

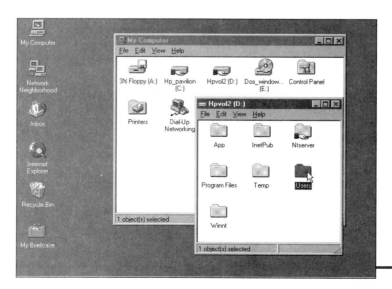

Sara double-clicks the Users folder to view the home directories, as shown in Figure 8-3. The directories are arranged alphabetically across the screen, ready to store the users' files. Later, Sara places security on each folder so it can be accessed only by the user.

Figure 8-3

User home directories

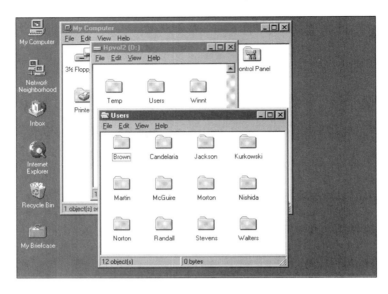

CREATING A FOLDER

Sara exits the Users subdirectory display and returns to the screen shown previously in Figure 8-2. She clicks the File menu, New, and then Folder to create the Public directory. Figure 8-4 shows the menu options to create a folder.

Figure 8-4

Creating a folder

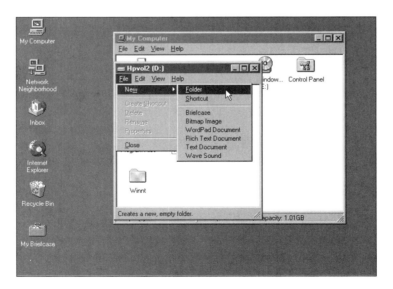

A new file folder appears on the screen with a box underneath in which to enter the new title. Sara types "Public" and presses [Enter], as shown in Figure 8-5.

Figure 8-5

Entering a new folder name

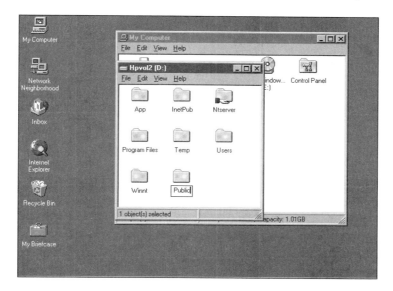

If a directory name is entered incorrectly, Sara can reenter it by clicking the directory folder with the right mouse button and, from the Options menu, selecting Rename. The directory name is highlighted so you can enter a new name or correct the existing one. You save changes by pressing [Enter].

When creating directories, be certain the structure is well-designed and the names are correctly entered from the start. It's confusing and time-consuming to change directory names after users have built paths to the original ones.

DIRECTORY PROPERTIES

With the Public directory created, Sara sets the directory properties. She highlights Public and clicks File on the menu bar at the top of the screen. From the File menu, she selects Properties. There are three properties tabs for any directory: General, Sharing, and Security. The General tab contains descriptive information about the directory and directory attributes, the Sharing tab enables the directory to be shared with network users, and the Security tab is for setting directory permissions. Sara uses each tab in the following sections.

GENERAL PROPERTIES

The General tab shows descriptive information about the directory, such as type of **object**, location, size, and number of files or folders contained within the directory (see Figure 8-6). The folder name and creation date also appear on the screen. The bottom of the screen has directory **attributes** that can be assigned. Attributes are directory and file characteristics and should not be confused with NT File System permissions.

Use of attributes is retained in NTFS as a carryover from earlier DOS-based systems and to provide a partial migration path to convert files and directories from a Novell NetWare file server. DOS and NetWare systems use file attributes as a form of security and file management. The attributes, except for backup purposes, are largely ignored by NT administrators in favor of rights and permissions. Attributes are stored as header information with each directory and file, along with other characteristics including volume label, designation as a subdirectory, date of creation, and time of creation. Table 8-1 provides a comparison of attributes for DOS, NetWare, and NT.

Objects are NT Server entities that have properties and exist as a single unit. Files, directories, subdirectories, printers, user accounts, and groups are objects.

Figure 8-6

General directory properties

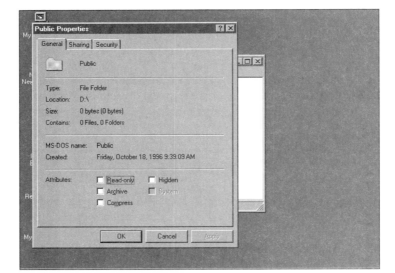

As Table 8-1 shows, directory and file attributes available in NTFS are Read-only, Archive, Compress, Hidden, and System. If Sara checks Read-only, the directory is read-only, but not the files in the directory. This means the directory cannot be deleted or renamed from the MS-DOS command line. Also, it cannot be deleted or renamed by a user other than one belonging to the Administrators group. If an administrator, such as Sara or Kristin, attempts to delete or rename the directory, a warning message states the directory is read-only and asks whether to proceed. Most NT network administrators leave the read-only box blank and set the equivalent protection in permissions instead, because the read-only permissions apply to the directory and its files.

Table 8-1

MS-DOS,
Novell NetWare,
and Windows NT
attributes
comparison

MS-DOS Attribute	Netware Attribute	Windows NT Equivalent Attribute	Purpose of Attribute
Read only (R)	Read only (RO)	Read only (R)	Prevents directory or file from being changed or deleted
Archive (A)	Archive (A)	Archive (A)	Directory or file is new or changed and needs to be backed up
No equivalent	No equivalent	Compress (C)	Compresses files to save disk space
System (S)	System (SY)	System (S)	File is used by the operating system and should not be viewed with ordinary list commands—used by NetWare directories but not NT directories
Hidden (H)	Hidden (H)	Hidden (H)	Directory or file cannot be viewed with ordinary list commands
No equivalent—file is not flagged with an R	Read-write (RW)	No equivalent—file is not flagged with an R	Directory or file can be viewed, changed, or deleted
No equivalent	Copy inhibit (C)	Handled through NTFS permissions	Cannot copy a file
No equivalent	Delete inhibit (D)	Handled through NTFS permissions	Cannot delete a directory or file
No equivalent	Execute only (X)	Handled through NTFS permissions	Can only execute a file (run the program)
No equivalent	Indexed (I)	Handled by the NT operating system	Flags large files for fast access
No equivalent	Purge (P)	Handled by the Recycle Bin	Purges deleted directories and files so they cannot be salvaged
No equivalent	Rename inhibit (RI)	Handled through NTFS permissions	Cannot rename a directory or file
No equivalent	Read audit (RA)	No equivalent	Can be assigned but has no function in NetWare 3.1 and later systems
No equivalent	Shareable (SH)	Handled by creating a network share	Files can be accessed by more than one user at a time
No equivalent	Transactional (T)	Handled by NTFS through directory and file recovery options	For recovery of data files after a system interruption, such as a power failure
No equivalent	Write audit (WA)	No equivalent	Can be assigned but has no function in NetWare 3.1 and later systems

Archive is checked to indicate the directory or file needs to be backed up, because the directory or file is new or changed. Most network administrators ignore the directory Archive attribute, but instead rely on it for files. Files, but not directories, are automatically flagged to archive when they are changed. File server backup systems can be set to detect files with the Archive attribute to ensure these files are backed up. The backup system ensures each file is saved following the same directory or subdirectory scheme as on the file server. Sara does not need to check the Archive attribute for the directory, as all new and changed files will automatically have it. Sara works on backup procedures in Chapter 11.

A directory and its contents can be stored on the disk in compressed format, which is a property of the NT File System, as Sara found in Chapter 5. This attribute is used when disk space is limited or for directories that are accessed infrequently, such as those used to store old fiscal year accounting data. Compression saves space, but it takes longer to access information because each file must be decompressed before it is read. The Public directory will be used frequently and Sara does not want to compress these files, so she leaves the box unchecked. If Sara had chosen the attribute, all files in Public would be compressed.

Sara also would have the option to compress files in subdirectories. Subdirectories are not automatically compressed along with the directory's files, unless this option is checked. If she wanted to compress the directory files and the files in its subdirectories, Sara would check Compress and click the Apply button. A message would appear warning that all files in the main directory will be compressed, accompanied by a box to check for compressing files in subdirectories (see Figure 8-7).

Figure 8-7

Compressing files and subdirectories

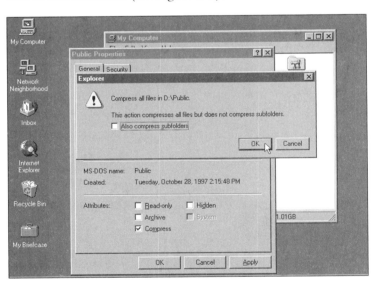

Directories can be marked as Hidden to prevent users from viewing their contents. For example, one college network administrator placed zip code verification software on a network, but kept the directory hidden while several users tested it. After testing was completed, the Hidden attribute was removed. Sara wants all to be able to view the Public directory, so she leaves this attribute unchecked.

The Hidden attribute can be defeated by any Windows 95 or Windows NT Workstation user by selecting to view hidden files from the View menu in Explorer or My Computer.

The System attribute is deactivated for directories and cannot be set. This attribute is used on system files to make them hidden and read-only for protection against accidental deletion.

DIRECTORY AND PERMISSION SECURITY

Like many network administrators, Sara prefers to set directory security before sharing a directory so files are not accessed before the administrator is ready. Sara clicks the Security tab on the Public Properties screen in Figure 8-6. There are three security options: Permissions, Auditing, and Ownership (see Figure 8-8). Permissions control access to the directory and its contents. Auditing enables the administrator to audit activities on a file, such as the number of times the file has been read or changed. Sara investigates auditing later, in Chapter 10. Ownership designates the directory owner who has full control of that directory.

Figure 8-8

Security tab

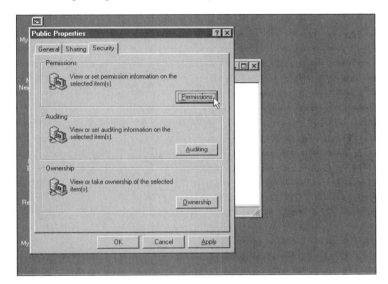

Permissions are set on objects such as directories, subdirectories, files, and shares. Shares are a resource object, such as a directory or a printer, that can be made available to network users. Because permissions can be set at several levels, there needs to be a way to determine what permission applies. For example, permissions on a directory may be different from permissions set on the network share of that directory. Or permissions on a file may be different from those of its parent directory. When there are multiple permissions, a principle of least allowed access applies as a way to err in favor of greatest security. For example, Sara might set up a directory share for Public allowing full permissions. At the same time, she might set the actual directory permissions to allow no access. It's unlikely she would make this mistake, but if she did, users would have no access to the directory.

Permissions can be set on individual files within a directory. However, managing these exceptions can become time-consuming and confusing. Instead, create a subdirectory for exceptions for easier management.

Ownership of a directory or subdirectory gives the owner entire control, including the ability to set permissions. Many network administrators limit ownership to the Administrators group, except for a few situations. The directories typically owned by users include subdirectories within their home directories and subdirectories within publicly shared directories. Users can create and own subdirectories within a directory where they have appropriate permissions. When there are user areas on a server, it's wise to monitor available disk space so the disk does not fill up too quickly.

PERMISSIONS

Sara clicks the Permissions button first. The Directory Permissions screen in Figure 8-9 has two check boxes at the top.

Figure 8-9

Setting directory permissions

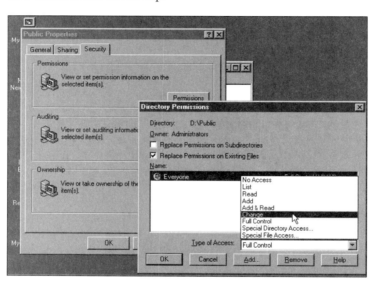

The first check box sets permissions on all subdirectories, and the second sets permissions on all files. Sara has the option to check one or both boxes. Because there are no subdirectories in Public, she checks only Replace Permissions on Existing Files. From this point on, the permissions she sets apply to the directory and its files. The wide range of permissions that can be set on a directory are defined in Table 8-2.

Table 8-2

Directory and
file permissions

Permission	Access and Abbreviation	Description	Applies To
No access	None	There is no access to the directory for any users other than the owner	Directories and files
List	Read and execute files (RX)	Can list files in the directory or switch to a subdirectory, but cannot access new files added to the directory	Directories only
Read	Read and execute files (RX)	For existing and new files; can read their contents and can execute program files	Directories and files
Add	Write and execute files (WX)	Can write new files in the directory and execute program files, but cannot view the directory files	Directories only
Add and read	Read, write, and execute files (RWX)	Ability to read files, add files, and execute program files, but cannot modify the file contents	Directories only
Change	Read, write, execute, and delete files (RWXD)	Ability to read, add, delete, execute, and modify files	Directories and files
Full control	All directory and file permissions	Can read, add, delete, execute, and modify files plus change permissions and take ownership of directories	Directories and files

The permission with the broadest range of capabilities is full control. This permission is the default assigned to a directory at the time it is created. Most network administrators change full control to another permission, so the ability to take ownership and assign permissions is kept with the Administrators group. Sara clicks the Down Arrow to display the permission options and highlights Change, permitting users to read, add, delete, execute, and modify files, as shown in Figure 8-9. She clicks OK to accept the changes.

From the same screen Sara has the option to specify which groups can access the directory with these permissions. She could add a group by clicking Add and select a group from the list of groups. She also can remove a group by highlighting the group and clicking Remove. The group Everyone, which includes all domain users, is set as the default. Sara wants all users to be able to access the Public directory, so she leaves Everyone. When she creates the Manage directory, she plans to remove Everyone and add Managers to restrict access to the Managers group only. In setting permissions, Ryan suggests the following guidelines to Sara based on Microsoft's recommendations:

- Protect the Winnt directory and subdirectories from users by specifying no access.
- Protect server utility directories, such as for backup software, with access permissions only for administrators and operators.
- Protect applications directories by specifying Add and Read permissions so users can run applications and write temporary files but not alter files.

- Create publicly used directories using Change, so users have broad access except to take ownership and set permissions.

- Provide users full control of their own home directories.

- Remove the group Everyone from access to confidential management-level directories, including payroll and accounting directories.

Always err on the side of too much security. It is easier, in terms of human relations, to give users more permissions later than it is to take away permissions.

The Special Directory Access and Special File Access options enable Sara to customize directory or file access beyond the standard permissions. For example, by clicking Special File Access, she could click Read and Write access only or Delete and Execute only. Sara calls Ryan to discuss these possibilities, and Ryan recommends staying with the standard permissions (see Figure 8-10) unless a unique situation arises, such as for special software installation requirements. For example, there might be a situation where a program only stores setup parameters in the program files directory and the network administrator wants to remove users' ability to change the setup file or to create their own customized setup. This may be necessary to ensure that everyone uses the program identically. In this case, the administrator could make the directory execute only through Special Directory Access. While they are on the telephone, Sara also questions Ryan about Access Not Specified and Ryan tells her this means files cannot be accessed.

Figure 8-10

Special file access

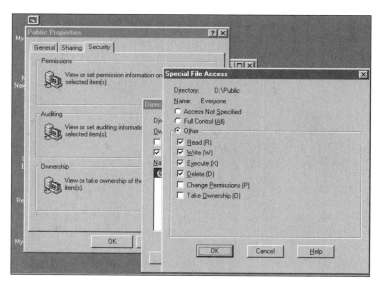

Sara notices the screen shows the permission levels associated with the Change permission, because this is how she has the directory set up. She does not want to alter any checks, so she clicks Cancel and then clicks OK to exit the Directory Permissions screen.

To help keep track of the assigned directory permissions, Sara is creating a spreadsheet, as shown in Table 8-3. The table also shows examples for the App subdirectories.

Table 8-3

Sara's spreadsheet showing assigned permissions for directories

Directory/ Subdirectory	Permissions	Reason for Permissions
APP	Add & Read for Everyone	Users need to read and execute files and add setup or temporary files, but should not change files
APP/ACCT (for the accounting software)	Change for the Business group only	Business group only has the full range of permissions to access, modify, read, and delete files
APP/CONTRACTS (for contracts and tax forms software)	Add & Read for Everyone	Users need to read and execute files and add setup or temporary files, but should not change files
APP/LOTUS (for Lotus 1-2-3)	Add & Read for Everyone	Users need to read and execute files and add setup or temporary files, but should not change files
APP/TIME (for the legal time accounting software)	Change for the Business group only	Offers the full range of permissions to access, modify, read, and delete files exclusively for the Business group
APP/WILLS (for the wills and bankruptcy forms software)	Add & Read for Everyone	Users need to read and execute files and add setup or temporary files, but should not change files
APP/WP (for WordPerfect)	Add & Read for Everyone	Users need to read and execute files and add setup or temporary files, but should not change files
INETPUB	Full control for Administrators group only	Access restricted to Administrators group until there is an Internet connection and Internet applications are developed
MANAGE	Change for Management group only	Broad ability to control and change information protected for the Management group
MSOFFICE	Add & Read for Everyone	Users need to read and execute files and add setup or temporary files, but should not change files
NTSERVER	Full control for Administrators group only	Protected for use by the Administrators group because it contains server utilities
PROGRAM FILES	Full control for Administrators group only	Access restricted for use by the Administrators group until program options are explored
PUBLIC	Change for Everyone	Broad sharing of files in a public area
USERS	Change for Everyone	Open access to all users at the directory level with access restricted per each subdirectory
USERS/all subdirectories	Full control set on each sub-directory for the designated user	Each user has full control over his sub directories directory for the designated user or her home directory
WINNT	Full control for Administrators group only and no access to others	System files are protected for access by the Administrators group

OWNERSHIP

With permissions set for the Public directory, Sara moves on to check the ownership. Directories are first owned by the account that creates them. In this case, the Public directory is owned by Administrators, because this is the account Sara is using for all setup work on the server. Directory owners have full control over the directories they create. Ownership can be transferred by having Full Control Permission. This permission enables a user to take control of a directory and become its owner. Taking ownership is the only way to shift control from one account to another. The Administrators group always has the ability to take control of any directory, regardless of the permissions.

On the Securities tab (Figure 8-8), Sara clicks the Ownership button to check the Public directory. The next screen shows the directory name and Administrators as the owner (see Figure 8-11). If Sara needed to take ownership, she could do so by clicking Take Ownership. Instead, she clicks Close to exit the screen. There may be instances when Sara needs to take ownership of a user's home directory or subdirectories within the home directory, if a user leaves the firm.

Figure 8-11

The Owner
dialog box

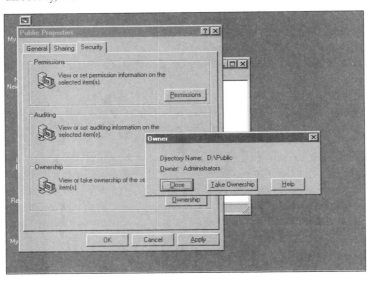

SETTING UP A DIRECTORY SHARE

With the Public directory permissions and ownership set up, the final step is to share the directory on the network so users can map a drive to it. Sara does this by clicking the Sharing tab on the Public Properties screen in Figure 8-8. As Figure 8-12 shows, the Sharing tab has two main options: to share or to not share the directory. Sara clicks the radio button Shared As and enters "Public" as the name of the share. In the Comment box, she types a note saying that this directory is for general sharing. She clicks the radio button Maximum Allowed, which enables as many accesses as there are client access licenses. The other option, Allow _____ Users, would enable her to specify a limit to the number of simultaneous users. This is one way to ensure the licensing restrictions for software are followed. For example, the firm has only two licenses for the legal time software. When Sara creates the App/Time directory for this software, she sets the Allow _____ Users parameter to 2 so the license requirement is honored.

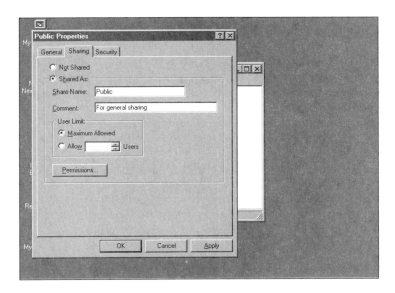

Figure 8-12

Creating
a share

Sara clicks the Permissions button to set the share permissions. There are four share permissions:

- No Access prevents access to the shared drive for the specified group.

- Read permits groups or users to read and execute files.

- Change enables users to read, add, modify, execute, and delete files.

- Full Control provides full access to the directory including the ability to take control or change permissions.

Before setting the share permissions, Sara first checks that the specified group is Everyone. She can add a group by clicking the Add button and selecting a group from the list of groups. Or she can remove a group by highlighting it in the list box and clicking Remove. She leaves the group as Everyone and clicks the Down Arrow for Type of Access, as shown in Figure 8–13. She selects the permission, Change, to replace the default, which is Full Control. She clicks OK to save the changes and clicks OK again from the Sharing tab.

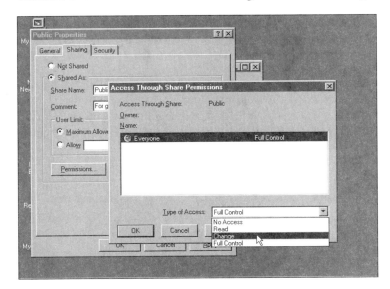

Figure 8-13

Share
permissions

SETUP WIZARD

An alternative to using My Computer for setting directory properties is to set them through the Administrative Wizards option in Administrative Tools. The Setup Wizard called Managing File and Folder Access uses the same process Sara has just covered, but the user is taken through it step by step.

INSTALLING APPLICATION SOFTWARE

Sara closely reads her forum group and newsgroup messages about software installation. Reading the experiences of others has taught her several lessons about installing software on a network. There are several important issues to consider before installing the software. These include the following:

- Software licensing
- Network compatibility
- Network performance
- Location of temporary files
- Software testing
- Loading software from the network
- MS-DOS based software

Application software is licensed to the user as explained in the software licensing agreement. The network administrator should carefully read and follow the licensing agreement before loading software. Some companies offer site licensing for unlimited access to the software through the network. Others restrict software licensing to groupings, such as "5-packs" or "10-packs." Some come with **license monitoring** built into the software, whereas others rely on the network administrator to monitor use, as Sara is doing through share restrictions on the legal time accounting software.

 License monitoring involves creating a mechanism to ensure network users do not access software in numbers larger than the software license allows.

Besides monitoring license use, the network administrator also is responsible for copy protecting the software as much as possible. This is accomplished in two ways. One is to set permissions on software directories so it is difficult to copy the software from the network, such as protecting program files with a special permission of execute-only. Many software applications cannot be fully protected due to their run-time requirements, such as creating individual setup files. Therefore, the second way to protect software is often the best. This is to fully educate network users on their responsibility to honor software licensing, an activity that will be easier for Sara because she's working at a law firm.

Some applications, such as desktop publishing programs, are not designed to run from a network. In these cases, the best solution is to consult with the vendor about how to adapt the software for a network, if possible. These systems are few in number, but they do exist. Sara's news group advisors suggested she check all applications to be certain they are **network compatible**.

Network-compatible programs are designed for multi-user access, often with network capabilities such as options to send files through e-mail.

The network load generated by an application is another issue. Some database applications create high levels of traffic, particularly if the entire database is sent each time a user wishes only to examine a small amount of information. Database reporting tools also may generate high traffic. Graphics and computer-aided design programs are other examples. Traffic is not likely to be a problem on a network as small as the firm's, but it is important to closely monitor network activity associated with applications.

Some applications create temporary or backup files while the application is running. For example, Microsoft Word creates backup files so work can be restored after a power failure or computer problem. It is important to determine what extra files are needed to run an application and where to store them. For example, Word backup files can be directed to the user's home directory through Word setup. Sara plans to teach each user in the firm how to create automatic Word backups and to write the backup files to his or her home directory. As she teaches, she plans to show how to delete old temporary and backup files no longer needed.

Sara is planning to test each software installation before releasing it to the users. She will test it from her own account and from two test accounts she is creating with the same permissions as any user in the office. She also plans to ask Kristin to help test in order to be sure the software works well with several accounts actively using the software. She regards the tests as important to determine that the software is working and that the permissions are correctly set.

Some applications, such as Microsoft Office, provide the option to install software application files from the network onto each client workstation. Another way is to install client software so application files are loaded from the server each time the application is run. The second way might take a few seconds longer to run the application, because the files are shipped over the network instead of loaded from the user's hard drive. The advantage is a significant savings in disk space on the workstation. Sara is opting to teach users to select network installations to leave workstation disk space open for other uses.

Some organizations have MS–DOS software applications to load onto the network. Difficulties that may arise from this software include memory management problems, **swap space** requirements, lock files that lock the application to one user at a time, and drivers that are not compatible with Windows 95 or Windows NT. Often the best solution is to avoid networking these applications, instead running them independently on individual workstations. If it is necessary to run the application from the network, it is wise to fully test to be sure the application does not interfere with other NT Server operations.

Some applications use "**swap space**" on a hard disk to store data for manipulation or because the data won't fit in memory. Check to be sure you know where the application writes the swap space and that it deletes old swap space.

Sara has read about instances where software does not work properly in Windows 95 or Windows NT due to updates in **application program interfaces (APIs)** from Microsoft. APIs are portions of the operating system that perform specific functions or provide links to the operating system, such as for mail services or network communication services. Microsoft is standardizing the APIs for both Windows 95 and Windows NT through a common set of programming interfaces called WIN32, to address this issue. However, some applications might still introduce problems. Most vendors develop "fixes" for these problems, which are available through the Internet. Sara's news group sources emphasized calling the software vendor about problems with an installation, to find out whether the vendor has a quick solution.

 More and more software companies offer software through the Internet. Eventually most software will be purchased and loaded directly through the Internet instead of from disks or CD-ROMs.

THE REGISTRY

NT Server keeps information about software, drivers, users, multi-user information, and other parameters in a database called the **Registry**. For example, many software applications use an initialization, or ".ini," file to obtain configuration information each time the application starts. The initialization file holds customized information about parameters used, such as where temporary files are written, which toolbars or buttons should appear, and what type of printer is used.

Modern applications that use a setup.exe file to install programs are designed to interface with the NT Server Registry to store configuration information automatically. Making use of the Registry for software applications offers several advantages such as the following:

- Configuration information is available for a multi-user environment.

- Configuration information is kept stable through a managed database.

- Software licensing can be managed through the Registry.

- Software pieces are tracked for easier removal or upgrades.

- Important software information can be backed up and restored in one place.

- The Registry can be a single repository for configuration information that formerly was kept in the config.sys, win.ini, and system.ini files on each workstation.

Sara's forum and newsgroup advisors recommended taking advantage of the Registry each time software is loaded on the server. Sara follows the advice and loads the software from the Control Panel using the Add/Remove Programs icon. Another way to load programs via the Registry is to use the Add/Remove Programs Wizard from the Administrative Wizards menu. Both ways take the installer through the same setup screens. Earlier, Sara practiced adding a program by installing the Internet Information Server from the Windows NT Server CD-ROM. Now she is ready to install Microsoft Office.

INFORMATION CONTAINED IN THE REGISTRY

The Registry database stores information about the server in a hierarchical fashion, similar to a directory, subdirectory, and file structure. The top of the hierarchy is composed of five root keys: HKEY_LOCAL_MACHINE, HKEY_CURRENT_USER, HKEY_USERS, HKEY_CLASSES_ROOT, and HKEY_CURRENT_CONFIG. The root key

HKEY_LOCAL_MACHINE contains information about the server hardware, operating system information, SAM information, and information about the software installed on the server. HKEY_CURRENT_USER has information about the user logged on to the Registry from the console, such as Control Panel settings, screen settings, folders, and preference settings. HKEY_USERS contains user profile information about user accounts that can log on to the server console, such as the account currently logged on. HKEY_CLASSES_ROOT stores information about which application to open when a given file is opened from the NT Explorer, such as opening Word for files with the extension .doc. HKEY_CURRENT_CONFIG contains information about the server hardware configuration, which is used each time NT Server boots.

Within each root key lies a subkey, similar to a subdirectory within a directory. Subkeys may contain additional subkeys. For example, the root key HKEY_CURRENT_USER contains the five subkeys HARDWARE, SAM, SECURITY, SOFTWARE, and SYSTEM. Further, the subkey HARDWARE has subkeys consisting of DESCRIPTION, DEVICEMAP, OWNERMAP, and RESOURCEMAP, as shown in Figure 8-14 (from the Registry Editor, which Sara uses later in this chapter). Some keys are stored as a set within the Registry, because they contain related or dependent functions. When this is the case, these sets are called hives. For example, all information within the root key HKEY_LOCAL_MACHINE and the subkey SOFTWARE is a hive stored as an NT Server system file called SOFTWARE. This Registry hive contains information about software such as shared configurations, utility file locations, toolbar setup, and a large range of other parameters.

Figure 8-14

Subkeys within a root key

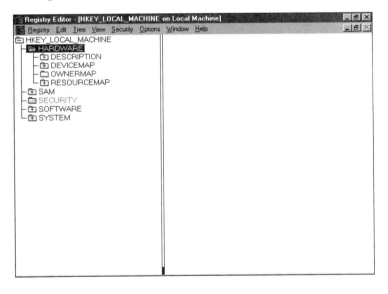

Value entries are stored within a subkey and define a particular characteristic to the Registry. There are values stored for hardware and software parameters. For example, after Sara installs Microsoft Office, there will be a Registry value for the default dictionary used, as shown in Figure 8-15 on the following page (also an example from the Registry Editor). In Figure 8-15 the subkeys are shown on the left side of the screen and the value for the default dictionary is on the right side of the screen. There are three components for each value. The first is the value name, which is 1 in Figure 8-15. Next is the value data type, which specifies the format of the value such as binary, two-byte word, text, data, or multi-valued. The data type REG_SZ in Figure 8-15 is in text format. Last is the actual data value, such as CUSTOM.DIC as in Figure 8-15. In the sections that follow, Sara installs Microsoft Office. Later, she uses the Registry to change a shared configuration parameter.

Figure 8-15

An example
Registry value

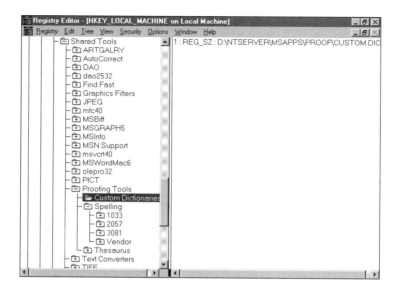

INSTALLING MICROSOFT OFFICE

To install Office, Sara places the Microsoft Office CD-ROM in the server's CD-ROM drive. She accesses the Control Panel from the Start menu and clicks Add/Remove Programs. She sees a screen with two tabs, one labeled Install/Uninstall and the other labeled Windows NT Setup (see Figure 8-16). She uses the Install/Uninstall tab to load Office. The other tab enables her to add or remove a system software component, such as the NT Accessories mentioned earlier.

Figure 8-16

Installing
software

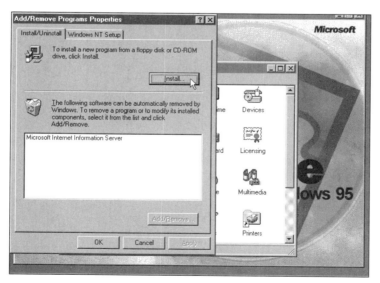

Sara clicks the Install button to begin the installation. She is asked to insert the installation disks or CD-ROM, which is already done. She clicks Next, as shown in Figure 8-17, and the Microsoft Office Setup program then guides her through each step, such as where to write the files on the server, which program pieces to install, and whether to install the practice files. Sara instructs the Office Setup to write to the Msoffice directory and to use the full setup for Word, Excel, Access, PowerPoint, and other Microsoft software. She also spec-ifies the number of licenses purchased for the network installation. Sara completes the installation and calls Kristin to ask her to arrange a time to help test the Office software.

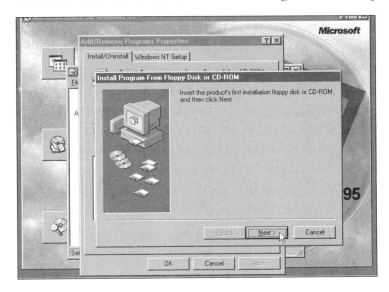

Figure 8-17

Inserting a new software disk or CD-ROM

MANAGING AN APPLICATION FROM THE REGISTRY

Because the firm has many WordPerfect 5.1 for DOS documents with the file extension .WP5, Sara wants to set Word so it automatically recognizes these as WordPerfect documents. Thus, when one is opened, Word will automatically identify the format, convert the file, and import it into Word. Sara can set this as a default shared parameter within the Registry, by using the Registry Editor. The Registry Editor is an executable file, REGEDT32, located in the Winnt\System32 directory on NT Server. Sara starts the program by clicking it from the NT Explorer. To start, Sara sees five cascaded windows, each representing a root key, as shown in Figure 8-18.

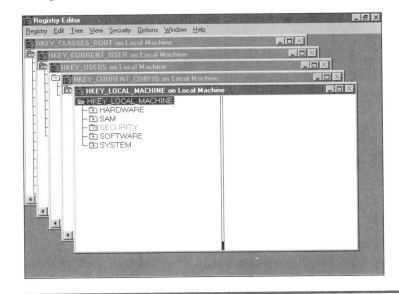

Figure 8-18

Registry Editor root key windows

From this point, Sara uses the following steps:

1. Sara clicks on the screen for the root key HKEY_LOCAL_MACHINE and clicks the SOFTWARE subkey.

2. Under SOFTWARE, she double-clicks MICROSOFT, which contains a large range of subkeys for the Microsoft Windows and Office applications.

3. The Microsoft Office 95 parameters shared by users are contained in the subkey SHARED TOOLS, which Sara double-clicks.

4. Sara double-clicks the subkey TEXT CONVERTERS, which is listed under SHARED TOOLS.

5. Next, she double-clicks the subkey IMPORT, which is under TEXT CONVERTERS.

6. She double-clicks the subkey WRDPRFCTDOS under the IMPORT key (see Figure 8-19).

Figure 8-19

Selecting a subkey

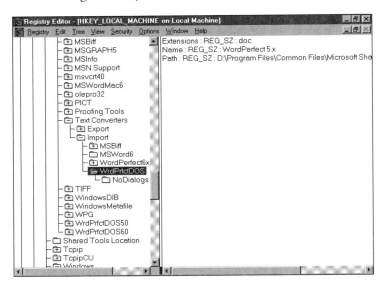

7. On the right side of the screen, Sara finds the value that controls the file Word uses to convert WordPerfect for DOS files. The name, data type, and value components are EXTENSIONS, REG_SZ, and DOC.

8. Sara double-clicks the value and a box appears where she can change DOC to WP5.

9. She enters the new value in the box and clicks OK (see Figure 8-20).

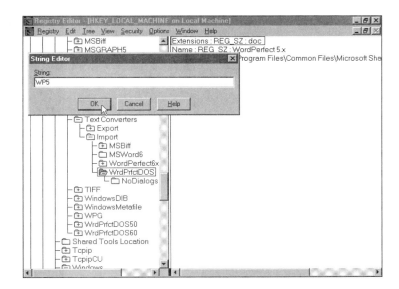

Figure 8-20

Changing a
Registry value

10. Sara clicks the Registry menu in the top left corner of the screen and clicks Exit to leave the editor.

When first trying the Registry Editor, click the Options menu and click Read Only Mode, to eliminate the risk of making a change you don't intend.

Only use the Registry Editor to modify a parameter when you are certain about the changes you intend to make, such as from a Microsoft technical note. An entry mistake in the Registry can cause a program to no longer run or result in a problem booting the server.

REMOVING AN APPLICATION

Removing a software application is a straightforward process with the help of the Registry and the Add/Remove Programs utility. For example, to remove a program Sara would access the screen in Figure 8-16 and highlight the application to remove, such as Microsoft Internet Information Server, and click Add/Remove.

SARA'S NEXT ASSIGNMENT

Sara spends several days loading software and testing it with Kristin's help. As they test the software, they also test the network cable installation. Sara and Kristin test from their offices and from different offices throughout the firm while attorneys are in court or out of town. With each software installation, they test with one user connected to detect any obvious problems such as the wrong permissions. Next, they test with two or more connections, depending on how many additional workstations are available in the office for testing.

When Sara finishes the installations, she is ready to work on setting up print services for the office. In the next chapter Sara has three printers to set up as network resources. Each printer becomes a share requiring Administrator management through permissions. Further, she allocates permissions to the print operators group, so there are several people designated to manage the printers. Also, she learns about print servers and printing options for the future.

KEY CONCEPTS SUMMARY

The terms reviewed in the following paragraphs relate to issues for directory setup and software installation.

application program interface (API) Functions or programming features within a system that programmers can use for network links, links to messaging services, or interfaces to other systems.

attribute A characteristic associated with a directory or a file used to help manage access and backups.

license monitoring A process used on network servers to be certain the number of software licenses in use does not exceed the number for which the network is authorized.

network compatible Software that can operate in a multi-user environment using network or mail communication APIs.

object Single entities, such as files, directories, and printers, within NT Server with property information stored in the SAM or Registry on each entity.

Registry A database used to store information about program setup, configurations, devices, drivers, and information used by NT Server.

root directory The highest level directory on a disk volume and is home to files or lower level directories and subdirectories.

swap space Temporary disk storage used by an application to supplement memory requirements and manipulate data.

SUMMARY OF WINDOWS FUNCTIONS

Windows NT Server has several utilities to help in setting up directories, managing security, and installing application programs. These utilities are available through wizards, the Control Panel, and My Computer.

Add/Remove Programs The add/remove programs capability is accessed from two places, the Control Panel or the Administrative Setup Wizards. This utility enables the network administrator to install programs while utilizing the Registry functions. It also makes program removal easy, because the Registry tracks the program pieces.

Managing File and Folder Access Setup Wizard This wizard is used to set directory and file attributes, permissions, ownership, and create a share.

My Computer The File menu for a folder in My Computer provides the ability to set directory properties which include attributes, creating a share, share permissions, directory permissions, and ownership.

Registry Editor This utility enables the network administrator to change or delete values contained within the Registry.

REVIEW QUESTIONS

1. What is the typical directory name for the NT Server system files?

    a.   SERVER

    b.. SYSTEM

    c.   WINNT

    d.   LOGON

2. Setting limits on access to a share is one way to help honor software licensing.

    a.   True

    b.   False

3. The X in a directory permission means:

    a.   Execute.

    b.   Example.

    c.   Read and run.

    d.   Write.

4. Which of the following permissions includes the ability to change permissions?

    a.   Full control

    b.   Read

    c.   List

    d.   Add

5. Which of the following is a tool to change permissions?

    a.   My Computer

    b.   Managing File and Folder Access Wizard

    c.   The audit log

    d.   All of the above

    e.   Both a and b.

6. Ownership of a directory can be assigned by the present owner to the new owner.

    a.   True

    b.   False

7. Which of the following permissions provide the ability to execute a program file?

    a.   Read

    b.   Add

    c.   Add & Change

    d.   All of the above

    e.   Both a and b.

8. Which of the following permissions includes the ability to modify a file in a directory?

    a.   Read

    b.   Change

    c.   Add

    d.   All of the above

    e.   Both a and b.

9. The Ownership Wizard is used to manage file and directory ownership.

    a.   True
    b.   False

10. Where is application software configuration information kept?

    a.   The Registry
    b.   The SAM
    c.   In an API
    d.   In the APP directory

11. What is the default permission assigned to a directory when it is created?

    a.   No access
    b.   List
    c.   Read
    d.   Change
    e.   Full control

12. When a directory attribute is set to read-only this means:

    a.   All files in the directory are read-only
    b.   New files added to the directory are read-only
    c.   The directory cannot be deleted
    d.   All of the above
    e.   None of the above

13. When the compress attribute is checked on a directory it compresses:

    a.   Existing files in the directory
    b.   New files added to the directory
    c.   Subdirectories as requested
    d.   All of the above
    e.   Both a and c.

14. What account group can always take ownership of a directory?

    a.   Managers
    b.   Administrators
    c.   Global Users
    d.   Guests

15. Which of the following is not a directory share permission?

    a.   No access
    b.   List
    c.   Change
    d.   Full control

16. Permissions can be customized by using which of the following?

    a.   The Registry editor
    b.   Special directory access

    c.   Ownership manager

    d.   None of the above

17. The system attribute can be assigned to a directory.

    a.   True

    b.   False

18. Which of the following is not a property for a directory?

    a.   Ownership

    b.   Attribute

    c.   Permission

    d.   Audit parameters

    e.   Expire

19. The Registry can take the place of:

    a.   Parameters in Config.sys.

    b.   Initialization files.

    c.   Device drivers.

    d.   All of the above.

    e.   Both a and b.

20. Which of the following are examples of NT Server objects?

    a.   Printer

    b.   File

    c.   Directory

    d.   All of the above

    e.   Both a and b.

21. From where is a directory share set up?

    a.   Server manager

    b.   User manager

    c.   My computer

    d.   All of the above

    e.   Both a. and c.

THE HOLLAND COLLEGE PROJECT: PHASE 8

With the user accounts and groups set up, your next task is to create a directory structure for the Administrative server and one for the English and writing lab server. For the administrative server, Bob Watson is asking you to create server areas for the following types of people:

- The executive group consisting of the President, Vice Presidents, and Steve Gaudio

- The business branch under Reuben Asimow, Vice President of Administration

- The instructional branch under Howard Victor, Vice President of Instruction
- The college auditors

Also Bob has purchased software for you to install on both servers, which he asks you to do in the assignments that follow.

ASSIGNMENT 8-1

Design a directory structure for the administrative server. Assume that you have decided to give each user a home directory on the server and include the server areas already requested by Bob Watson. As you design the directory structure include a design for application software including Microsoft Office and the VT emulator for accessing the DEC VAX administrative computer.

Also note that Howard Victor has asked Alice Yasui to contact you about placing the financial aid packages on the server. And the President's executive assistant, Steve Gaudio, wants to put his FoxPro database on the server. It will be used by the president and vice presidents as well as by Steve.

Finally, include in your design a place for server utilities you will likely obtain in the future and for the C++ compiler you now have on your PC.

ASSIGNMENT 8-2

Design a directory structure for the English and writing lab server. As you design the directory structure take into account that you will be installing the following software on the server:

- WordPerfect
- Microsoft Office
- Lotus 1-2-3
- SAS

Note that Bob is asking you to install SAS on this server because the faculty along with Howard Victor have decided to hold a statistics class in the lab each semester. After you complete the directory design, answer the following questions:

- Did you decide to include an area for server utilities? Why or Why not?
- Assume that the English faculty, the writing composition faculty, and the statistics faculty would like to put assignments on the server and have students turn in assignments via the server. How would you add to the directory design to accommodate their requests? What recommendations would you make to the faculty to help them implement this service?
- Assume that Bob Watson has purchased Encarta to make accessible from the server's CD-ROM drive. How would you set up the directory structure to enable access for Encarta? What licensing considerations should you discuss with Bob?

- How would you add an area for Howard Victor who would like to place on the server the student handbook, the college catalog, and the list of courses offered for the academic year.

 ASSIGNMENT 8-3

In a lab, practice creating a directory from the root directory. Explain what tool you used to create the directory. Next, complete the following tasks on the directory and briefly explain the steps you took to complete each task.

Task	Explanation of How the Task was Completed
Hide the directory and then un-hide it	
Check the default permissions already assigned to the directory and report what they are	
Remove access to the directory for the group Everyone	
Assign a permission level of add & read to a group other than Everyone	
Change the add & read permission level and assign the permission of execute only	
Share the directory on the network, but limit it to two users at a time	
Assign the read permission to the share	
View the directory on the network to be sure it is available as a share	
Practice taking ownership of the directory, even though you already own it	
Make the directory read-only and then try to delete it	

ASSIGNMENT 8-4

In a lab, practice creating a directory for the financial aid software used by Alice Yasui. Note that the college owns two licenses for this software, one for Alice and one for Dimitri Kasakav. Address the following questions about how you would set up the directory:

- What permissions would you place on the directory?
- Would you recommend changing ownership from Administrators? If so, how would you do it?
- How would you share the directory on the network?
- Since the software does not have built-in license monitoring, how would you have the server monitor access?
- How would you prevent students from viewing the contents of the directory on the network?

 ASSIGNMENT 8-5

Also in the lab, practice creating a directory to accomplish Howard Victor's request to make the student handbook, college catalog, and list of courses available to any users of the English and writing lab. Answer the following questions about how you would set up the directory:

- What permissions would you put on the directory?
- How would you share the directory?
- Would you restrict access or permissions in any way?
- What procedures would you recommend to Howard for moving new information to the directory and for updating the existing files?

 ASSIGNMENT 8-6

Assume that a user has created a subdirectory in his or her home directory that occupies 40 MB of disk space. The user has given permissions for that directory to no one else, including the administrators group. He or she has now left the organization and you are responsible for checking the directory in case it has valuable data, and then deleting it. Describe the steps you would take to accomplish this task.

ASSIGNMENT 8-7

Bob Watson has asked you to put an accounting package on the server in the English and writing lab for use by an evening accounting class. In the table below, describe the steps you would take to install the software.

STEP 1:
STEP 2:
STEP 3:
STEP 4:
STEP 5:
STEP 6:
STEP 7:
STEP 8:
Additional Steps or Comments about the Installation:

ASSIGNMENT 8-8

In a lab, practice installing two software packages that your instructor has made available. Use the Control Panel to install one of the packages. Use an Administrative Wizard to install the other. Describe, in general, the steps you took to install each package.

 ASSIGNMENT 8-9

Assume you have just installed a report generator package to use on the network. Windows 95 users can run the package flawlessly, but Windows NT Workstation users experience problems with some function keys and hot keys. Explain the steps you would take to resolve this problem.

 ASSIGNMENT 8-10

Assume you are reading messages from an NT Server newsgroup and you notice one from a new network administrator. This administrator has installed a software package intended for organization-wide use, but only the Administrators group can access it. Also note that the administrator already advised users they could access the software, and several users are upset that they cannot. What advice would you give this administrator to fix the problem? What advice would you give in terms of following a different approach next time?

CHAPTER NINE

SERVER MANAGEMENT: PRINTERS

So far, the directory structure Sara created is accommodating all the software she is installing. Lotus 1-2-3, WordPerfect, the accounting packages, and the legal forms software are housed in their own subdirectories under the App directory. The Microsoft Office products each have a subdirectory under Msoffice. Sara is setting permissions on the directories and is creating directory shares for the office users. Kristin is proving to be a reliable testing associate, helping to test each software package from several workstations throughout the office.

An important strength of their testing approach is that the network connections are now tested from every workstation location. Sara has encountered only one workstation, in Rick Kurkowski's office, with intermittent connection problems. This was due to a faulty RJ-45 connection on the cable attached to the NIC. Sara called the cable contractor, who found the problem by using test equipment and replaced the connector.

Print services are next on Sara's agenda. This morning, Anne Nishida surprised Kristin and Sara by delivering a laser printer to Sara's office. Anne purchased the printer at a discount from the city's largest law firm, which ordered an extra by mistake. Kristin and Sara briefly discuss where to put the printer, deciding to attach it to the file server. Confidential information such as paychecks can be sent to the printer, which will be in the same unoccupied room as the server. The room will be locked when checks are printing.

AFTER READING THIS CHAPTER AND COMPLETING THE EXERCISES YOU WILL BE ABLE TO:

- EXPLAIN PRINT SPOOLING.
- INSTALL A PRINTER AND PRINTER DRIVERS.
- SHARE A PRINTER ON A NETWORK.
- MANAGE PRINTER PROPERTIES.
- SET PRINTER SHARE SECURITY.
- VIEW, PAUSE, CANCEL, AND RESUME PRINT JOBS.

NETWORK PRINTING

Network printing is often viewed with apprehension by network administrators. Multi-user computer systems are known for having a maze of printing utilities to install printer drivers, set up print services, and accommodate special forms. On these systems, maintaining printers is tedious, problem-ridden work, and this work sometimes is ignored by administrators in favor of easier and more interesting tasks. But to network users, printing is one of the most critical network services.

Sara is cheered by reading newsgroup and forum comments about how much network printing has evolved as operating systems have improved, especially with NT Server. For instance, Microsoft has made printer setup intuitive by sharing printers as objects, in the same way directories are shared. Printer shares are created, named, and made available to the network with the same permissions as are used by directories. Second, printer setup is performed in one place within the operating system. And last, all new printers are installed step by step through the Printer Setup Wizard, making it difficult for the network administrator to make an error.

AN OVERVIEW OF PRINTING

The network printing process on NT Server LANs begins when a user decides to print a file. For example, in the firm, a Word user prints a file, which goes to the printer designated in the user's Printer Setup configuration within Word. The Printer Setup may direct the printout to the user's printer or to any network printer available through a **printer share** for which the user has permission. A printer share can be a workstation sharing a printer, a printer attached to the file server, or a printer attached to a print server device.

A **printer share** is an object, like a directory, made available to network users for print services. The printer is offered from a server, workstation, or print server device.

Several manufacturers offer print server devices that connect directly to the network without the need of an attached PC. These devices eliminate dependence on a PC, which may be shut off or inconveniently located. Some print servers are small boxes that connect to the network at one end of the box and to one or more printers at the other. Another kind of print server is a card that is mounted inside the printer, with a network port similar to an NIC on the card. Figure 9-1 shows examples of printer server devices.

Some print server devices generate a large amount of network traffic because they frequently poll to determine whether print jobs are waiting. These devices may contribute to bottlenecks on busy networks.

Figure 9-1

Print servers

When the printout goes to a printer share, it is temporarily **spooled** in specially reserved RAM or disk storage and held until it is sent to be printed. Spooling frees the server CPU to handle other processing requests in addition to print requests. NT networks spool on the computer providing the print services. For example, when Mark's workstation is sharing its laser printer, spool space is made available on his workstation for other office users' print jobs. Print jobs are usually printed in the same order as received, unless an administrator or print operator changes the order due to a high-priority situation. The network administrator can disable spooling, but this is rare because it defeats the value of background print services, which free server resources for other tasks.

 Spooling is a process working in the background to enable several print files to go to a single printer. Each file is placed in temporary storage until its turn comes to be printed.

When its turn comes, the print file is sent to the printer along with formatting instructions. The formatting instructions are provided by a **printer driver** that holds configuration information for the given printer. The formatting and configuration information includes instructions to reset the printer before starting, information about printing fonts, and special printer control codes. The printer driver resides on the computer offering the printer services. For example, if Mark's printer is shared, those who use the shared printer will print via the driver set up in Mark's printer share settings.

 A **printer driver** is a file containing information needed to control a specific printer for best results. It is either provided through the computer operating system or obtained from the manufacturer.

When the user selects to use a printer share, his or her document is formatted for the driver on that share. The printer can start printing the file as soon as the first page is received, or it can be instructed to print the file only when all pages have been received. The advantage of printing immediately is that printing starts sooner than waiting for the entire print file to be spooled. The disadvantage is in offices where there are constant print requests. In this case, a pause at a workstation sending a print job may result in another job printing pages in the middle of the first job. If this is a problem, it is better to have the printer share wait until the entire file is spooled. This instruction is set by the owner of the network printer, such as the network administrator.

Figure 9-2 shows a summary of printing stages.

Figure 9-2

Printing stages

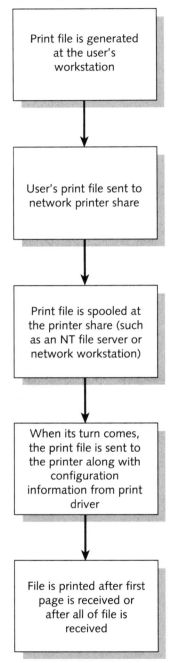

Print file is generated at the user's workstation

User's print file sent to network printer share

Print file is spooled at the printer share (such as an NT file server or network workstation)

When its turn comes, the print file is sent to the printer along with configuration information from print driver

File is printed after first page is received or after all of file is received

SETTING UP AND SHARING A NETWORK PRINTER

Sara has three network printers to set up: one connected to the server, one to Mark Jackson's workstation, and one to Jane Randall's workstation. The printers are located to enable convenient access by all members of the office, giving Mark and Jane particularly close access because they do the most printing. Sara is considering print servers for the future, as the budget allows. Until then, connecting the printers to the three computers is an inexpensive solution she can implement immediately.

Sara starts with the server printer. First, she locates an extra printer cable in her office and shuts down the server. She connects one end of the cable to the parallel port on the server and the other end to the printer. She checks the printer documentation to determine how to print a test page by pressing a given sequence of buttons on the printer.

Sara starts the printer and prints the test page, to verify that the printer works. The test page looks good, so she turns on the server. Sara logs on as Administrator, so the new printer share is owned by this account. Once on, she clicks Start and then Settings. The Settings menu has three selections: the Control Panel, Printers, and Taskbar. Sara could click the Control Panel and then the Printers icon. It's faster, however, to click Printers directly from the Settings menu, as shown in Figure 9-3.

Figure 9-3

The Printers folder

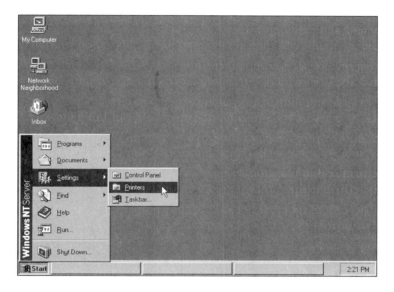

STEP 1: STARTING THE PRINTER SETUP WIZARD

Sara double-clicks Add Printer to start the Printer Setup Wizard (see Figure 9-4).

Figure 9-4

Adding a printer

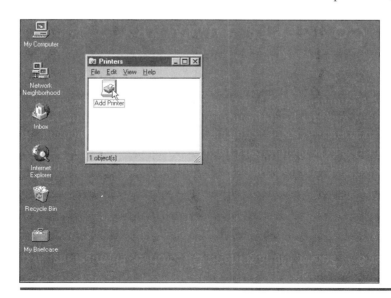

The beginning setup screen is where you specify whether the printer to be set up and administered is on the server or on another computer on the network, as shown in Figure 9-5. Because the printer is connected to the server, Sara clicks My Computer and then Next.

Figure 9-5

Designating
the printer
location

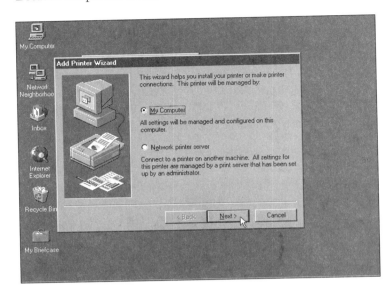

STEP 2: PRINTER PORT SETUP

The next screen is where Sara specifies the computer port used by the printer. Port selections include parallel port options LPT1, LPT2, or LPT3. Serial port options are COM1 through COM4. The printer already is connected to LPT1, and Sara clicks this option, as shown in Figure 9-6. There are two buttons near the bottom of the screen, Add Port and Configure Port. The Add Port option is used for specialized ports on some large servers, such as DEC computers. Most installations, such as Sara's, do not need this option.

Figure 9-6

Specifying the
printer port

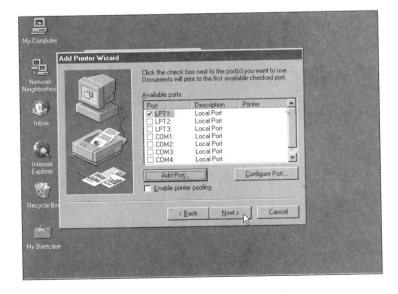

The other button on the screen, Configure Port, is to set the time-out parameter, as shown in Figure 9-7. The time-out is the amount of time the server will attempt to send a file to the printer when the printer is not responding. If the printer does not accept the file within the specified time, the server sends a message to the user that the printer is not responding and provides options to retry or cancel the request. The default time-out is 90 seconds, which is sufficient for the firm's setup. Sara clicks the Configure Port button to view this option and clicks Cancel to return to the port selection screen in Figure 9-6. She clicks Next for the next screen.

In an office where there are large print files, such as for desktop publishing, it may be necessary to increase the time-out to 120 seconds or more. This is especially true where the workstations take longer to process a print file because they have too little memory.

Figure 9-7

Printer
time-out

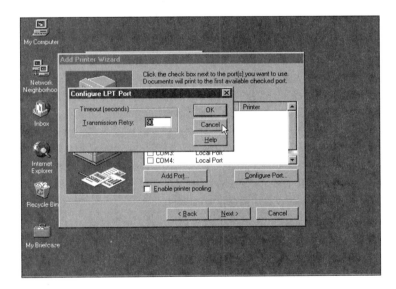

STEP 3: PROVIDING PRINTER DRIVER INFORMATION

On the next screen, Sara specifies the brand and type of printer (see Figure 9-8 on the next page). This enables the wizard to implement the appropriate printer driver. The NT Server Setup CD-ROM contains a large number of drivers for nearly all printers made by brand-name manufacturers. If she had a newly released printer, Sara would need a printer driver disk from the vendor and would click the Have Disk button.

The printer purchased by Anne is made by Hewlett-Packard. Sara clicks the Down Arrow on the left side of the Manufacturers list box until she sees HP, which she highlights. She clicks the Down Arrow in the Printers list box until she reaches HP LaserJet 5Si, and then she highlights this choice. Sara ignores the Have Disk button, because the wizard will find the driver in the Winnt directory or will request the Setup CD-ROM, if the driver is not already available from Winnt. She clicks Next to move to the next screen.

Figure 9-8

Specifying
printer
manufacturer
and model

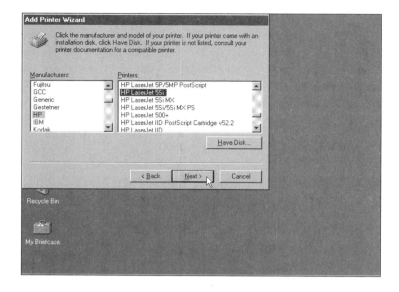

STEP 4: ENTERING THE PRINTER NAME

The next step with the wizard is a screen where Sara enters the name of the printer. Sara is giving careful attention to the selection of the name, because it is used to identify the printer to others as a network resource. The name should include characteristics that clearly identify the printer to anyone who has access to use it. Through her newsgroup, Sara has learned some common guidelines for naming a network printer, such as the following:

- Use a name that is understood by users.

- Identify the location or owner of the printer in the name, such as the room number or an abbreviation for the owner.

- Identify the brand or type of printer.

Sara is using the name Law_5Si for the server printer. This name combines an abbreviation for the server name LAWYER (indicating the printer is located near LAWYER) with the type of printer. She enters the name and clicks Next, as shown in Figure 9-9.

Figure 9-9

Entering the
printer name

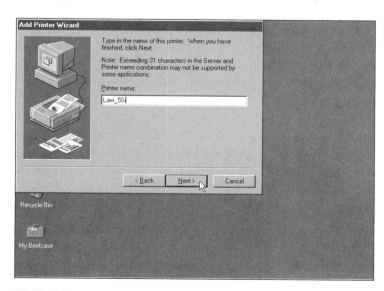

STEP 5: CREATING A PRINTER SHARE

On the next screen, Sara has the option to designate the printer as shared. She clicks the Shared button, which activates other parameters on the screen. Law_5Si is entered by default as the printer share name. Sara could name the share differently, but it's less confusing if the share name is the same as the printer name. She also highlights Windows 95 as the operating system to be used to access the printer share, because Windows 95 is on all the user workstations (see Figure 9-10). Windows NT also is set automatically, because it is the operating system on the server. Sara clicks Next to continue with the installation.

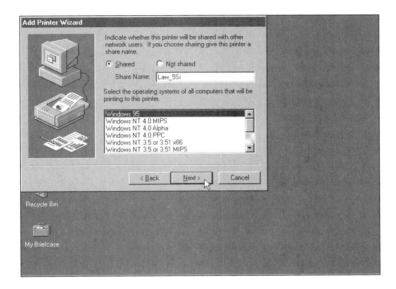

Figure 9-10

Creating a printer share

STEP 6: PRINTING A TEST PAGE

The last option in the Setup Wizard is to print a test page to be certain the printer is communicating with the server. Sara clicks Yes and then Finish to print the test page, as shown in Figure 9-11.

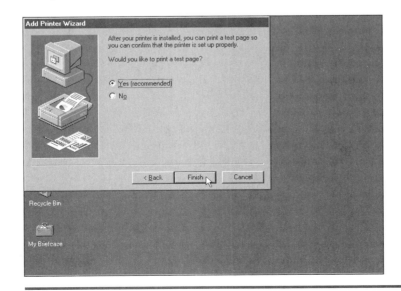

Figure 9-11

Requesting a test page

The test print completes successfully, and Sara clicks Yes on the next screen to finish (see Figure 9-12).

Figure 9-12

Test page
completed

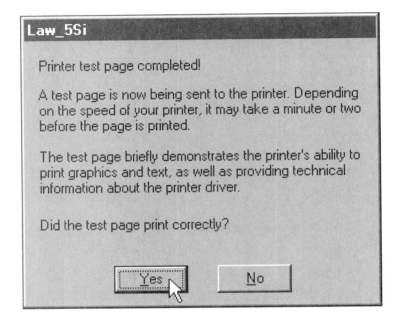

Sara's successful installation is verified by the appearance of an icon for the new printer, called Law_5Si. This icon appears alongside Add Printer in the Printers folder, as shown in Figure 9-13.

Figure 9-13

The new icon
for Law_5Si

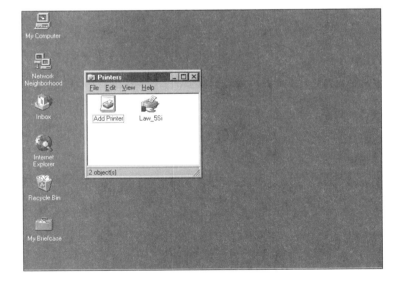

ADDING A WORKSTATION PRINTER TO SHARE

Sara ran the Printer Setup Wizard at Mark Jackson's and Jane Randall's computers quite some time ago so they could use their laser printers. She used the wizard that comes with Windows 95. When she set up the workstations for networking (see Chapter 4), she flagged the printers to be shared on the network. Now, Sara can complete their installation as network printers by using the Printer Setup Wizard from LAWYER.

From the Administrator account, Sara starts the wizard and goes to the screen in Figure 9-5. On this screen she clicks the radio button labeled "Network printer server". The next screen is where she designates the printer as a shared domain resource (see Figure 9-14).

Figure 9-14

Installing a printer share on a workstation

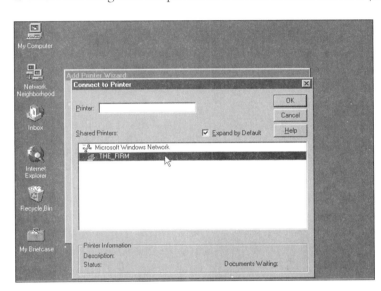

Sara double-clicks THE_FIRM to display the printers. Then she enters Mark Jackson's printer name in the text box entitled "Printer" and clicks OK. On the next screen Sara specifies whether this printer will be the default for the programs run from the server. Sara clicks No, because the server uses its printer as the default, and then clicks Next (see Figure 9-15).

Figure 9-15

Specifying a share is not the default for the server

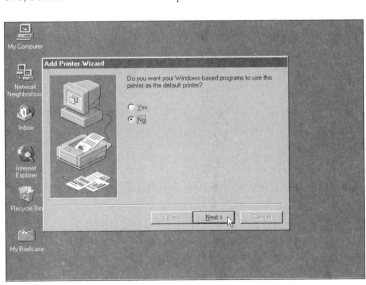

The last screen is where Sara decides whether to print a test page, which she chooses to do. Sara repeats the same process for Jane Randall's printer. Note that the port and printer driver information are already installed on Mark's and Jane's workstations.

MANAGING PRINTER SERVICES

Sara manages the printer services through the Printer folder (shown in Figure 9–13). For example, to manage the shared printer Law_5Si, the server printer she just installed, Sara double-clicks the Law_5Si icon. The next screen, entitled Law_5Si (see Figure 9–16), is where she manages the following functions:

- Sharing information
- General printer information
- Printer port setup
- Printer scheduling
- Security
- Device settings
- Pausing print jobs
- Deleting print jobs

To start, Sara chooses to view the sharing information for the printer, by selecting the Printer menu. Next, she clicks Sharing, as shown in Figure 9–16.

Figure 9-16

Selecting to view printer sharing information

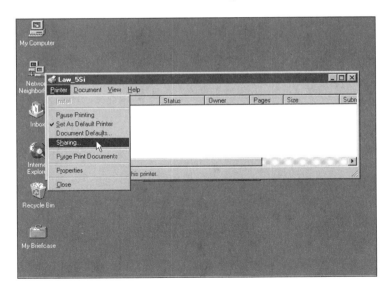

SHARING

Sara views the printer properties screen with the Sharing tab in the front, as shown in Figure 9-17. The other printer properties tabs are General, Ports, Scheduling, Security, and Device Settings. The sharing information is the same as what Sara viewed in Figure 9-10. From the sharing tab, Sara can remove the printer share or rename it. Also, she can install drivers for additional operating systems, such as a DEC Alpha workstation running Windows NT or earlier versions of the NT Server operating system. Sara has nothing to change, so she clicks the General tab.

Figure 9-17

The printer
Sharing tab

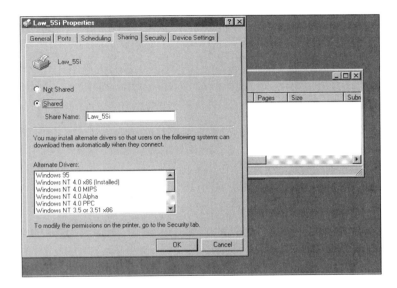

GENERAL PRINTER SPECIFICATIONS

The top portion of the General tab holds reference information about the printer (see Figure 9-18).

Figure 9-18

The printer
General tab

The Comment box is used to store special notes about the printer that might describe a particular feature, a common operational problem, or information about special use. Below the Comment box is a place to specify the location of the printer. This is convenient information for a large organization where there may be several dozen network printers. Where there are many printers, comments in these boxes help current or new network administrators to have ready documentation about printers. The Driver list box and New Driver button are used to install a new driver, in the event the printer is upgraded or replaced with a different model.

The Separator Page button is what Sara would use to place a blank page at the beginning of each printed document. This helps designate the end of one printout and the beginning of another, so printouts do not get mixed together. The Print Processor button is used to specify print formats for different environments. The default format is "winprint" for documents printed within Windows 95 and NT. Other formats include "raw" or "text" with automatic form feed codes at the end of each document. This would be used for some documents printed from UNIX or DOS workstations. Also, there is a button to print another test page to help diagnose printing problems.

PORT SPECIFICATIONS

Next, Sara clicks the Ports tab. The printer port options are similar to those shown in Figure 9-6, with a few additional features: Enable bidirectional support and Enable printer pooling (see Figure 9-19). Bidirectional support is checked as a default, because many printers, such as Sara's HP, now have **bidirectional** capability. This means there is a two-way flow of data on the cable between the printer and the computer. Data are sent to the printer from the computer, and the printer is able to communicate back with the computer for flow control, data buffering, and coordinating communications. **Pooling** printers is the ability to link two or more printers to one printer share object, used in high-volume printing. Sara leaves this option disabled. After viewing the port options, Sara clicks the Scheduling tab.

Figure 9-19

The printer Ports tab

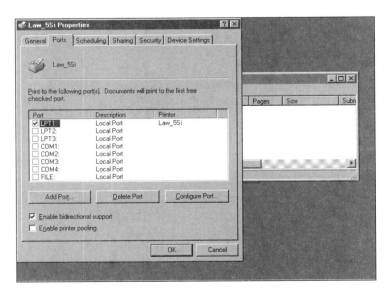

Before you connect a printer, consult the manual to determine whether the printer is bidirectional. If so, the printer requires a special bidirectional cable, and the printer port may need to be designated as bidirectional in the computer's BIOS setup program.

PRINTER SCHEDULING

The Scheduling tab allows Sara to have the printer available at all times or to limit the time to a range of hours, as shown in Figure 9-20. Sara leaves the default, which is to make the printer available at all times. She can set the priority higher to speed print turnaround for a particular printer. For example, if the server is managing several printer shares, one may be set for higher priority because it prints payroll checks or is used by the company president.

Figure 9-20

The printer Scheduling tab

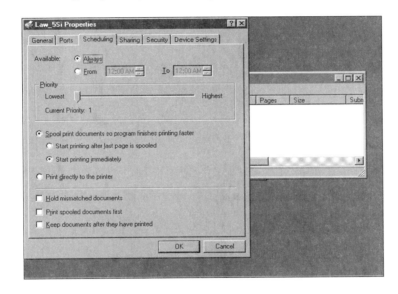

The screen provides the option to use spooled printing or to bypass the spooler and send print files directly to the printer. It works best to spool print jobs so they are printed on a first-come, first-served basis and to enable background printing so the CPU can work on other tasks. Printing directly to the printer is not recommended, unless there is an emergency need to focus all resources on a specific printout. Print spooling also helps ensure that jobs are printed together, so a long Word document is not interrupted by a one-page print job. Without spooling, such an interruption can happen if the one-page job is ready to print at the time the Word job is pausing to read the disk. The spool option is selected by default, with the instruction to start printing before all the pages are spooled. This is an appropriate option for Nishida and McGuire, where most print files are not resource-intensive and there is infrequent contention for printers, reducing the odds of intermixing printouts. If there is a problem with pages intermixing from printouts, Sara can reset this option later.

The "Hold mismatched documents" option causes the system to compare the setup of the printer to the setup in the document. For example, if the printer is set in the share as a Hewlett-Packard 5Si and the document is formatted for a plotter, the print job is placed on hold. The job doesn't print until the document is released by the user, a member of the Print Operators group, or an administrator.

The "Hold mismatched documents" option is a good way to save paper in a heterogeneous situation, such as a student lab, where users have very differently formatted print jobs. One mismatch situation can use hundreds of pages printing one character per page.

The option labeled "Print spooled documents first" enables jobs that have completed spooling to be printed no matter their priority. Where there is high volume printing, this speeds the process by reducing the wait for long print jobs to spool. This also is a good option for the firm, to reduce the wait whenever there is high demand on printers.

The "Keep documents after they have printed" option enables the network administrator to re-create a printout damaged by a printer jam or other problem. For example, if a large number of paychecks are printing and a printer problem strikes in the middle of the printout, this critical option makes it possible to reprint the damaged checks. However, this option should be accompanied by a maintenance schedule to delete documents no longer needed. Sara checks "Hold mismatched documents" to save paper, and she checks "Print spooled documents first" to reduce the chances of printing bottlenecks. After making these selections, she clicks the Security tab.

SHARE PERMISSIONS

The Security tab is identical to the tab in Figure 8-8 for Directory permissions. This is because a printer share is treated as an object similar to a directory. As Figure 9-21 shows, there are three security buttons: Permissions, Auditing, and Ownership.

Figure 9-21

The printer Security tab

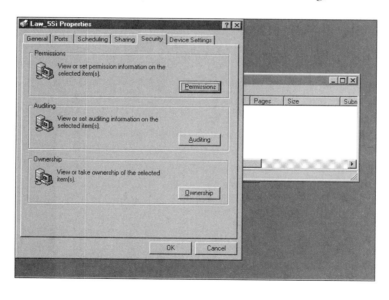

Sara clicks the Permissions button to view the default settings. Four security permissions can be assigned as follows:

- No Access, which prevents using the printer share

- Print, which enables users to print and manage their own print requests

- Manage Documents, for pausing, deleting, or restarting any document submitted to the printer share

- Full Control, for changing sharing properties or deleting the printer share

Sara wants the Everyone group to have permission to print, which is already set by default. This gives each office member the ability to print on the server's printer. Also, a user can pause or end his or her own printout, but not someone else's. Full control of printers is normally reserved for those trained in managing printer setups, such as the network administrators. This permission includes the ability to set up, modify, and delete printer shares. Print Operators and Server Operators also have this permission through the default settings. Mark and Jane are members of the Print Operators group, but Sara wants them to have Manage Documents authority instead of Full Control. This centralizes share management with Sara and Kristin, consistent with their defined duties to administer the network. With Manage Documents permission, Mark and Jane can stop or delete documents but not modify the printer shares. Sara clicks Print Operators and changes their authority, as shown in Figure 9-22. Sara repeats the process for Server Operators, even though this group has no members at present. After changing the printer permissions for Server Operators, she clicks OK to save the changes.

Figure 9-22

Changing printer permissions

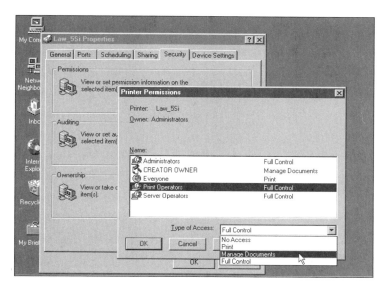

Back on the Security tab, Sara plans to wait to use printer auditing until she can focus on managing server logs in Chapter 10. The Auditing button enables Sara to have a log of all print jobs, for the purpose of locating a print problem or a security problem. For example, if Kristin believes she is experiencing problems sending printouts, Sara can use auditing to determine when and how frequently the problem occurs. The Ownership button is identical to the one used for directories. The Administrators group already owns the printer share by default. Finished with the security settings, Sara clicks the Device Settings tab.

DEVICE SETTINGS

This tab enables Sara to specify printer settings such as printer trays, memory, and paper size (see Figure 9-23). She leaves the defaults for the printer, with the first one, Auto Select, set to automatically choose the paper tray per the instructions in each user's document setup. Memory is 4 MB, which is standard for this printer. The automatic setting for paper size is Letter, which can be overridden through the setup in the document sent to the printer. Finished setting the properties of the Law_5Si printer, Sara clicks OK.

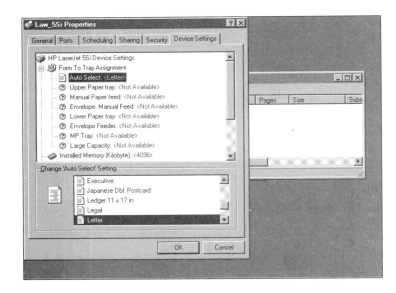

Figure 9-23

The printer Device Settings tab

PRINTER MANAGEMENT SCREEN

Back on the printer management screen for Law_5Si, Sara is interested in viewing it with an active print job. She creates a test print job in the WordPad utility and sends it to Law_5Si. Figure 9-24 shows the printer management screen with the active print job. The screen shows the name of the job, its current status, the owner, the number of pages, the size of the print file, and the time of submission.

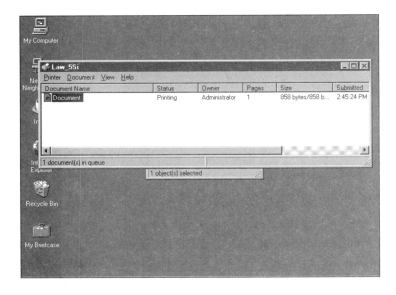

Figure 9-24

The printer management screen

To provide time to view the document management options, Sara turns off the printer before the job arrives so the job does not print immediately. She highlights the document and then selects the Document menu, as shown in Figure 9–25.

The following options from the Document menu are available:

- Pause, to hold the document so it will not print until the Resume instruction is clicked

- Resume, to continue printing a paused document

- Restart, to send a Restart command to the printer, which attempts to restart printing after the printer has been taken off line and subsequently put back on line

- Cancel, to remove a print job so it does not print

- Properties, to view properties of the print document, such as size and owner

Figure 9-25

Pausing a print job

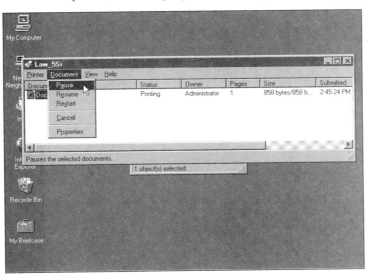

Sara experiments by pausing the document and resuming it after turning the printer back on. These are the same print management options that will be used by Mark and Jane when they exercise their Print Operators group permissions.

Canceling a printout only works if all or part of the job is still in the spooler. Once the job is sent to the printer, it is necessary to shut off the printer to stop the job.

SARA'S NEXT ASSIGNMENT

After testing the Law_5Si printer setup, Sara tests the setup for the printers connected to Mark's and Jane's computers. While she is testing, Ryan stops by and tells Sara about the print server card he purchased for a laser printer at his firm. Sara can purchase the same card, one for each of the three Hewlett-Packard printers used by the the firm. The card installs inside the printer and directly attaches to the network. The advantage of the card is that the printer can be located anywhere, without attaching it to a workstation or server. Each card comes with print server software that interfaces with NT Server, enabling shared printers exactly as Sara has just created. Sara feels she already has an economical solution but will consider using one or more print server cards as funds become available.

Sara and Ryan agree she is very near the point of releasing the server to the users. Before she does, Sara wants to complete the list of tasks she outlined at the start. The next task on the list is to set up monitoring for system events, activity audit logs, and other monitoring information. She wants to have information available to help manage and tune the server, plus to catch problems as they occur or to eliminate problems before they occur.

KEY CONCEPTS SUMMARY

The key concepts discussed in this chapter are presented in the following paragraphs.

bidirectional port This type of printer port enables two-way data communications between a printer and the computer to which the printer is attached.

pooled printers Two or more printers associated with one printer share.

printer driver A file with configuration and control code information for a printer.

printer share This shared object is available to the network from a workstation, server, or print server device to enable specified users the option to print on an attached printer.

spool A background process of storing a print file until the printer is free to print the file, making it possible to route several print files to one printer at the same time.

SUMMARY OF WINDOWS FUNCTIONS

Printer management in NT Server is primarily controlled through the Printer folder and the Printer Setup Wizard, as described below.

Printers Folder This folder has an icon to add printers to set up printer configuration and driver information, as well as to create shared network printers. Once a printer is added, a new icon is created with properties for managing the print services for that printer.

Printer Setup Wizard Printers are added by using this wizard either from the Administrative Wizards menu or from the Add Printer icon in the Printers folder.

REVIEW QUESTIONS

1. Configuration information about a printer is contained in which of the following?
   a. Printer profile
   b. Printer driver
   c. Printer manager
   d. All of the above
   e. None of the above
2. Temporarily saving print files on disk until they can be printed is part of
   a. Printer swapping.
   b. File negotiation.
   c. Print spooling.
   d. Print spawning.

3. Bidirectional printing requires a specialized printer cable.

    a. True

    b. False

4. A shared printer on a server can be set from which port?

    a. LPT1

    b. LPT2

    c. COM1

    d. COM2

    e. All of the above

    f. Only a and c

5. Which of the following is not a printer share permission setting?

    a. No Access

    b. Full Control

    c. Change

    d. Manage Documents

6. Printer drivers are loaded from which of the following?

    a. A server directory

    b. A disk provided by the printer manufacturer

    c. The NT Server CD-ROM

    d. All of the above

    e. Both b and c

7. All printers connected to the server must be shared.

    a. True

    b. False

8. The separator page is enabled from which of the following printer properties tabs?

    a. Security

    b. Sharing

    c. General

    d. Scheduling

9. All shared printer setups require spooling a document completely before starting to print.

    a. True

    b. False

10. When setting up an NT Server printer share for UNIX-based clients, which format would you most likely use?

    a. Raw

    b. Wintext

    c. Uuencoded

    d. FTP

11. Canceling a print job is one way to stop printing after the job has been sent to the printer.

   a. True

   b. False

12. Which of the following can be set from the printer properties Device Settings tab?

   a. Paper size

   b. Print port

   c. Print auditing

   d. All of the above

   e. Both a and b

13. The default permission for the Print Operators group when a printer share is created is

   a. Change.

   b. Print.

   c. Full Control.

   d. No Access.

14. NT Server views a printer share as

   a. Private.

   b. An object.

   c. A user account.

   d. A domain account.

15. Assume you have just upgraded the memory in a network printer. Where would you tell NT Server about the amount of memory now in the printer?

   a. The Device Settings tab

   b. The General tab

   c. The Scheduling tab

   d. NT Server will automatically detect the memory upgrade

16. What happens when a mismatched document is detected by a printer share set up to look for mismatches?

   a. The document is automatically deleted.

   b. The document is automatically held.

   c. The document is immediately sent to the printer.

   d. The document is automatically reformatted.

17. Where would you look to find out the size of a document waiting to be printed?

   a. In the Server Manager

   b. From the Printers folder

   c. In the Printer Wizard

   d. Print document size information is not available

18.   What command is used to print a document after the job has been paused?

   a.   Resume

   b.   Reset

   c.   Retry

   d.   Reprocess

19.   A printer share can be set to keep documents after they have been printed.

   a.   True

   b.   False

20.   A printer share always must be named for the type of printer.

   a.   True

   b.   False

21.   Who owns a printer share?

   a.   All shares are owned by the Administrators group.

   b.   All shares are owned by the Print Operators group.

   c.   The printer share is originally owned by the account that sets up the printer.

   d.   The domain owns the printer share.

THE HOLLAND COLLEGE PROJECT: PHASE 9

Bob Watson is purchasing four new laser printers for the administrative users in the Hoyt Administrative Building. He wants to make one printer available for the president, giving Steve Gaudio capability to use the printer as well. Another printer will be shared by the vice-presidents. The third is to be shared by the business units under Reuben Asimow, and the fourth will be shared by the Student Services staff and the registrar, who work for Howard Victor.

Also, Bob would like you to turn the two laser printers in the English and writing lab into network printers. The specifics of your assignments unfold in the sections that follow.

ASSIGNMENT 9-1

Study your network design scheme for Hoyt as developed in Assignment 2-2. Describe where you would put the four new laser printers. Answer the following general questions about how you would set up the printers.

   ■   Would you create any new groups for the printers, or would you try to use groups already created in Chapter 7? What groups would you use? What printer share permissions would each group have?

   ■   Would you designate users as Print Operators?

   ■   Would you attach any of the printers to the server?

■ Would you recommend that Bob purchase print server cards for any of the printers?

■ Would you recommend sharing any existing printers?

ASSIGNMENT 9-2

You want to develop a naming scheme for the shared printers. Explain the general guidelines for the naming scheme you will use. In the following table, enter names for the four new administrative printer shares and for the two you will create in the lab. Provide a brief description of why you have selected each particular name.

Printer Share Name	Reason for Name

ASSIGNMENT 9-3

In a lab, create a printer share using one of the names from Assignment 9-2. Set up the printer share using each of the requirements listed in the following table and explain where you found the print management option to complete the requirement.

Requirement	How Accomplished
Add the printer to the server	
Designate the printer to be used from LPT2	
Designate the name of the printer share	
Print a test page	
Set the time-out for 60 seconds	
Print separator pages with each printout	
Give Manage Documents permission to the Server Operators and Print Operators groups	
Hold documents that mismatch	
Make documents wait until fully spooled before printing	
Set default printing to legal-size paper	

ASSIGNMENT 9-4

Use the Internet to research print server devices available on the market. Approximately what are the costs of print servers? Would one or more print servers be of value in the English and writing lab? Would they be of value for the Hoyt Administrative Building?

 ## ASSIGNMENT 9-5

Assume that Bob Watson is receiving reports of printer problems in the student lab. One problem is that paper is being wasted because printouts often have only one or two characters per page. Also, the server seems to periodically slow down or stop when jobs print. Explain the steps you would take to solve these problems.

 ## ASSIGNMENT 9-6

Assume you have set up the lab printers and students are complaining that some pages of one printout are mixing in with pages of another printout. Describe the steps you would take to resolve this problem.

ASSIGNMENT 9-7

In a lab, go through the steps you would follow to connect a bidirectional printer to a server or workstation for use on the network. Record the steps in the table provided here.

Steps Needed to Connect a Bidirectional Printer

ASSIGNMENT 9-8

Send one or more print jobs to a shared printer and practice the following tasks, recording how you accomplished each in the table provided.

Task	How Completed
Pause a document	
Resume a document	
Cancel a document	
View the size of a document	
Determine the document owner	
Check to determine whether a document is held	

CHAPTER TEN

SYSTEM MONITORING

Sara arrives in the office early to check on the attorneys who are preparing for court appearances. No one is reporting a computer problem, so Sara turns to work on the server, printing a memo using her Law_5Si printer share. As the print job finishes, Sara checks the Network Neighborhood icon to confirm that all three printer shares are available. Next, she views the Law_5Si printer icon in the Printers folder, checking the sharing properties one more time. Then she reviews the permissions to ensure the Everyone group has print capabilities.

Satisfied, Sara spends the morning getting acquainted with the tools for monitoring the server. She learns about services that manage functions on the server, including how to stop and start them. She uses the Task Manager to view software applications and the server resources they require. Also, she adjusts the virtual memory allocation and learns where to view users of the server. Later, she tries the Performance Monitor to view the CPU and disk load on the server and checks the server event logs. These are just the first steps in learning to monitor a server. Performance monitoring is an ongoing process as the network administrator grows in knowledge of the system. In this chapter, Sara gets a taste of the monitoring tools. When she releases the server to the users in Chapter 12, she uses these tools for more complex troubleshooting and tuning.

AFTER READING THIS CHAPTER AND COMPLETING THE EXERCISES YOU WILL BE ABLE TO:

- EXPLAIN THE FUNCTION OF THE DEFAULT SERVER SERVICES.
- VIEW, START, AND STOP SERVICES.
- DETERMINE THE SIZE AND NUMBER OF PAGING FILES.
- SET UP PAGING ON A SERVER.
- VIEW AND STOP SERVER PROGRAM TASKS.
- USE THE PERFORMANCE MONITOR TO GATHER SERVER PERFORMANCE INFORMATION.
- ACCESS AND USE THE SERVER EVENT LOGS.
- AUDIT LOGON AND ACCESS EVENTS ON THE SERVER.

MONITORING ISSUES

Monitoring the performance of multi-user systems is a complex process. Many factors interact to affect the overall performance of a server. These range from the speed of the CPU to the efficiency of applications. Problems in one area can disguise problems in another. For example, a poorly written software application may require extensive CPU time. The first symptom of the problem may be high CPU utilization, causing the network administrator to initially believe the CPU needs to be upgraded. Sara is researching these types of performance issues with Ryan, with her newsgroup and forum members.

As a starting point, she learns there are several areas to monitor on an NT server. Each area plays a significant role in a server's response and is monitored through the tools included with NT Server. These basic areas are the following:

- Server services that are started or stopped
- Number of users on the server
- Software applications in use
- Virtual memory settings
- RAM management
- CPU load
- Disk response

ESTABLISHING PERFORMANCE BENCHMARKS

Sara's advisors say the most important place to start is to get to know the normal performance of a server by establishing **benchmarks**. Benchmarks provide a basis for comparing data collected during problem situations with data showing normal performance conditions. This creates a basis upon which to diagnose problems and identify changes. Benchmarks are acquired in several stages:

1. Generate statistics on CPU, disk, memory, and I/O with no users on the system, to establish a baseline for comparison to more active periods. Keep a spreadsheet and performance charts of this information.

2. Use performance monitoring to establish slow, average, and peak periods. Keep records on these periods.

3. Each time a new software application is installed, gather performance statistics on slow, average, and peak periods during its use.

4. Establish benchmarks to track growth in use of the server, such as increases in number of users, increases in software applications, and increases in the average amount of time users are on the system.

Sara feels some of the best advice is to frequently review the performance information. Performance indicators can be confusing at first, so the more you spend time observing them, the better you'll understand them. For example, viewing the CPU utilization the first few times does not tell you much, but viewing it over a longer period, noting slow and peak periods, helps develop knowledge about how CPU demand varies for that server.

A **benchmark** is a measurement standard for hardware or software used to establish performance tolerances under varying loads or circumstances.

NT SERVER SERVICES

NT Server automatically starts a range of system services that run in the background as the server is operating. Many of these are default services provided with NT. Other services can be installed or added by the network administrator from the NT Server Setup CD-ROM or from independent software sources. Many services are automatically started when the server boots, and others are started manually as needed. There are several default services that provide for messaging, logging, scheduling, server, and printer activities. If the server is having performance problems, Sara has the option to stop an unneeded service to ease the load. For example, the ClipBook Server or the Directory Replicator might be disabled because they're not currently used by Nishida and McGuire. The default services are described in the following paragraphs.

The Alerter service is used to send a notification when a problem is detected at the server, such as a failed NIC, a disk problem, or a hung service. Notification is sent to anyone designated by the network administrator, but typically would be sent to those who would fix the problem such as the Administrators and Server Operators groups. Establishing who will be notified is done through the Server icon (as discussed later in this chapter) or the Server Manager. The Alerter service requires that the Messenger and Workstation services also are started.

The ClipBook Server enables users to share graphics images, files, and other information. Each entity, such as a picture or text, is stored as a page. The images are viewed by means of the ClipBook Viewer on the server. The ClipBook Viewer can store up to 127 pages for users to share. Any page within the viewer can be designated as a shared object, with shared permissions. The ClipBook Server requires the Network DDE service to be running as well.

Computers on a network can be viewed within NT by means of the Computer Browser service. The service is used by tools such as the Network Neighborhood, the User Manager, and the Server Manager to view computers. Services upon which the Computer Browser depends are the Server and Workstation services.

Another service, the Directory Replicator, copies files and directories from one server to another server or workstation. For example, the Directory Replicator is used to copy the logon scripts from one domain controller to another. Or it is used to replicate database files from one server dedicated to updating information to another server dedicated to creating reports using the same information, such as on a client/server system. The Directory Replicator works from an account created by the network administrator that performs the specified copying. The data copied to a server is "exported" and data brought in from another server is "imported." The directories or scripts designated for copying are set from the Server icon, as shown later in this chapter. The Directory Replicator relies on the Server and Workstation services.

EventLog is a critical monitoring service for network administrators. Server events, such as logon activity and hardware problems, are tracked and recorded in logs, which run from the EventLog service. The network administrator uses these logs to trace and solve problems.

The Messenger service provides communications to deliver messages, such as those sent by the Alerter. Also, this service is linked to e-mail and other applications that use messaging, including print and fax service messages. The Messenger requires that the Workstation service is working as well. Another service, Net Logon, interacts with the SAM to verify each account and password when a user logs on. Net Logon is used by each domain controller and also has responsibility for synchronizing the domain SAM databases. Like many other services, Net Logon requires that the Server and Workstation services are started.

The Network DDE and DSDM services provide capabilities to handle data exchange over the network between two programs. For example, data used by one program in a spreadsheet format may be linked for use by another using Microsoft Access. Or a graphics object in the ClipBook Server can be brought into Microsoft Word on a client workstation. The Network DDE service does not work unless Network DDE DSDM is already started.

NT LM and the associated remote procedure call services enable an application on a remote computer to access functions on NT Server, such as file transfer or messaging capabilities. The Remote Procedure Call service makes this option possible. The Locator service enables client applications to find functions they can access. And the NT LM Security Support Provider enables access security to the functions.

The Schedule service enables the Administrators group to run jobs at specified times through the command, AT. For example, the service can be used to run a database update at a given time each day. Another use is to automatically reset the NT server's system time once each week from an Internet time server.

The Server service is critical to enabling shared services on NT Server such as shared printers, directories, and network services. Without the Server service, users cannot access and use the server as a server. Another critical service is the Spooler, which enables printer services at the server, as discussed in Chapter 9.

The UPS service is used when an uninterruptible power source (UPS) is connected to the server to protect it from power failures. Many UPS systems have the ability to communicate with the server, such as to warn it that a power failure has occurred. To make communications possible, the UPS service also requires the Messenger service to be active. Sara sets up a UPS system in Chapter 11.

Last, the Workstation service enables the network administrator to use the server as a workstation. For example, Sara uses this service each time she logs on to the server as the Administrator to access the NT Explorer or WordPad. Table 10-1 provides a summary of the default services.

Table 10-1

Default services

Service	Description
Alerter	Sends notification of alerts or problems on the server to users designated by the network administrator
ClipBook Server	Server for the remote ClipBook Viewer, enabling ClipBook pages to be shared
Computer Browser	Keeps a list of computers and domain resources to be accessed
Directory Replicator	Creates a duplicate of specified directories on different computers, such as designated databases
EventLog	Enables server events to be logged for later review or diagnosis should problems occur
Messenger	Handles messages sent for administrative purposes
Net Logon	Maintains logon services such as verifying users who are logging on to the server and synchronizing the server SAMs
Network DDE	Enables dynamic data exchange on the network for objects such as graphics
Network DDE DSDM	Enables conversion of object formats across the network
NT LM Security Support Provider	Used for security on remote procedure calls from UNIX and other systems
Remote Procedure Call Locator	Used in communications with clients using remote procedure calls to locate available programs to run
Remote Procedure Call	Provides remote procedure call services
Schedule	A scheduler for NT Server to run designated programs or commands at a specified time
Server	Critical to the server for support of shared objects and for remote procedure call support
Spooler	Enables print spooling
UPS	For use with an uninterruptible power source used to supply power to the server
Workstation	For workstation activities at the server

MONITORING SERVER SERVICES

Services are viewed and controlled from the Services icon in the Control Panel. Sara double-clicks the Services icon, which resembles two gears meshed together. The Services dialog box is shown in Figure 10-1. Services appear in a list box containing three columns. The left column shows services listed alphabetically. The Status column indicates the condition of the service as follows:

- *Started* means the service is running.

- *Paused* means the service is started but is on hold to the users.

- A blank means the service is halted or has not been started.

The Startup column shows how a service is started. Most services are started automatically when the server is started. Some services are started manually because they may not be needed until a given time.

In Figure 10-1, the Directory Replicator service is not currently running and is set to start manually when needed by the administrator. The DHCP Client service is disabled because Sara chose not to install it when she generated the server. It is not needed because the firm's network doesn't use IP addressing or the TCP/IP protocol.

Figure 10-1

The Services
dialog box

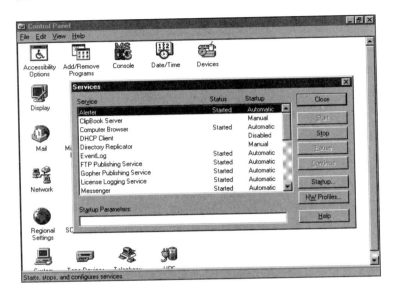

The buttons on the right of the screen are used to manage the services. For example, the Start button is used to manually start a service, such as the Directory Replicator. The button is not active in Figure 10-1 because the highlighted service, Alerter, is already started. The Stop button is used to stop a service. Ryan warned Sara to use Stop cautiously, because some services are linked to others. Stopping one service will stop the others that depend on it. For instance, stopping the Messenger service affects the Alerter. The system gives the administrator a warning when other services are affected by stopping a particular service.

 Many services are linked to the Server service, including logged on users. If it is necessary to stop the Server service, such as to diagnose a problem, give the users advance warning or stop the service after work hours.

The Pause button takes services off line to be used only by the Administrators or Server Operators groups. For example, if the ClipBook Server was sending error messages to users, Sara would pause the service so it would only be available to the administrator for testing until she resolved the problem. A paused service is restarted by highlighting the service and clicking Continue. The Startup button is used to change how a service is started. For instance, if Sara wants to make the Alerter a manually started process, she would click Startup, select Manual, and click OK. The last button, HW Profiles, is used to enable or disable a service for a given hardware unit. For example, the UPS service is disabled because there is no UPS hardware installed. The bottom of the screen has a box to enter special startup parameters. For example, if there is a service that only runs from a CD-ROM in drive E, then Sara would enter the drive letter and path in the box. She does not want to start or stop any processes at this time, so she clicks Close because she is finished viewing the screen.

Occasionally, a service does not start properly when the server is booted or hangs while the server is running. The Services icon provides a way to monitor this situation. For example, this morning Sara noticed a message at the server console that the Server service was suspended due to a problem. Sara was unable to log on to the server from her office. When she logged on to the console as Administrator, the logon process took four minutes. Also, when she checked the Printers folder for the printer share Law_5Si, the folder hung for a minute and aborted with a message that the Server service was suspended. Sara clicked the Services icon to view the currently started services. The screen showed the Server service as stopped. Sara started the service, which resolved the logon and print sharing problems.

MONITORING LOGGED ON USERS AND SERVER ACCESS INFORMATION

Network administrators frequently monitor the number of users logged on to the system for several reasons. One is to develop an indication of how many users are typically logged on at given times, which gives the administrator information about normal user load. Also, if a problem develops and the server needs to be shut down, the administrator can determine when the shutdown will have the least impact. Another reason is to be aware of security or misuse problems, such as an account in use when the owner is not at his or her workstation. On large networks, it's a good idea to frequently check the number of users on a server. An especially popular server may need to be expanded as more users log on for extended periods.

Sara is back on the Control Panel, where she clicks the Server icon to view information about connections to the server. On the next screen, shown in Figure 10-2, Sara sees there is one active session, which is hers. There are no open files, file locks, or named pipes because she is not using other programs. The Open Files information shows whether a file is in use. A **file lock** means no one else can access a specified file, and **named pipes** are open communication links.

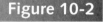

Figure 10-2

The Server dialog box

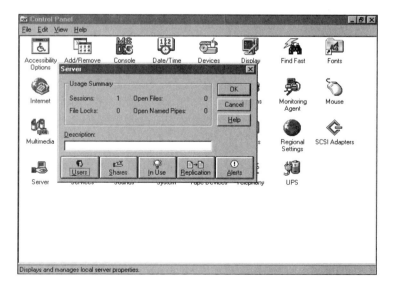

Locked files are those that are flagged as temporarily inaccessible because they are in use. Files in use are locked to prevent two users from updating information at the same time.

Named pipes are a communication link between two processes, which may be local to the server or remote, such as between the server and a workstation.

The Description text box allows for an optional description of the server computer, such as a name, brand, or location. Sara chooses to leave this blank, because there is only one server to remember on her network.

The buttons at the bottom of the screen are to view information about connections in use or to set service parameters. For example, when Sara clicks Users, a list appears of all users connected to the server along with a list of resources in use by each user, such as shared directories and printers. Sara is the only user and she is currently using Net Logon resources because she is logged on (see Figure 10-3). The Users button also enables Sara to disconnect one or more users. Sara might disconnect a user when his or her logon session is hung or to perform an emergency server shutdown.

Figure 10-3

The User Sessions dialog box

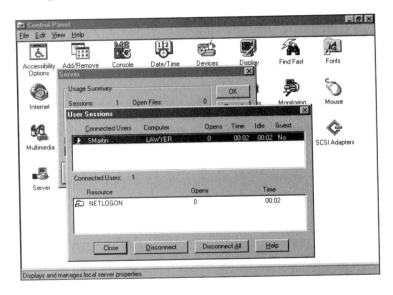

The Shares button enables her to view the same information, but by resource instead of by user. Again, Sara is the only one using NetLogon. When she opens the server to the office users, this screen will show those using resources such as Law_5Si and will provide the ability to disconnect a user (see Figure 10-4). Each resource is shown with an icon. The directory resource icon is a folder in a hand. The contents of drives C and D are shown as shared from the root by the dollar sign. The connector icon represents a named pipe, with IPC shown as a network communications pipe. A shared printer such as Law_5Si is shown with a printer icon.

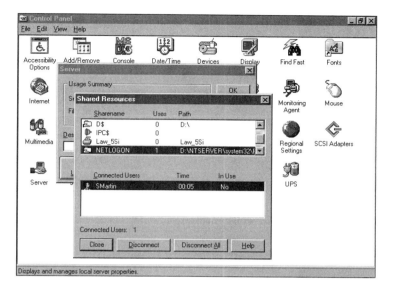

Figure 10-4

The Shared
Resources
dialog box

The In Use button in the Server dialog box (see Figure 10-2) provides information about all resources such as printers that are currently being used (Figure 10-5).

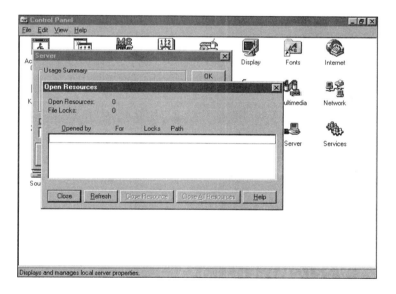

Figure 10-5

The Open
Resources
dialog box

The Replication button enables the network administrator to designate information about replication services, such as the path to logon scripts and the domain controller that will receive them (Figure 10-6).

Figure 10-6

Directory
Replication
dialog box

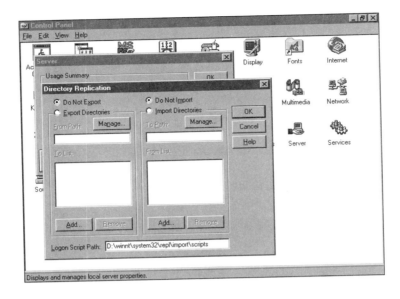

The Alerts button is used to specify which users should receive warning messages about problems at the server. On the screen shown in Figure 10-7, Sara enters her user name, clicks Add, and clicks OK. She clicks OK again to close the Server dialog box.

Figure 10-7

Adding users
for Alert
messages

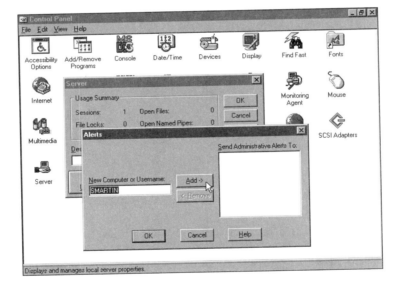

MONITORING APPLICATIONS WITH THE TASK MANAGER

Not all software applications are designed equally. Some have an extremely inefficient design that places unnecessary demands on the server. For example, an application may generate excessive network traffic by transporting more data than it needs between the server and the client. Another source of demand is reports that run against a database, requiring the system to read all the records in the database instead of the limited few needed for the report. An inefficient program is often signaled by high CPU, memory, or disk utilization each time the program runs.

Some applications advertised to be client/server-based are not truly designed according to these standards and can be inefficient when using server and network resources. For example, client/server design is intended to efficiently spread the workload between server and clients, but some applications place excessive work on the server or use poor database design at the server. Check on actual performance before you buy.

Sara uses the Task Manager to view applications running on the server. She accesses the Task Manager by pressing [Ctrl]+[Alt]+[Del] while logged on as Administrator. After pressing this key combination, she has the following options:

- Lock Workstation, to secure the file server console from access

- Change Password, to change the Administrator account password

- Logoff, to exit the Administrator account

- Task Manager, to view information about tasks and services currently running

- Shutdown, to shut down the server

- Cancel, to return to the NT Server desktop

Sara clicks the Task Manager button. A screen appears with tabs for Applications, Processes, and Performance. The Applications tab, shown in Figure 10-8, shows all the software applications running from the server console. Any application can be stopped by highlighting that application and clicking the End Task button. If an application were hung (no longer responding to user input), Sara could click End Task to release more resources for the server. The Switch To button switches to a different application than the one highlighted. The New Task button enables Sara to start another application at the console.

The bottom of the screen shows information about the highlighted task. For example, the applications running in Figure 10-8 are using 17 processes, 2% of the CPU resources, and almost 37 MB of memory. The processes relate to the number of threads or tasks a program is running that require CPU resources. In this instance, threads are in use, but they only require 2% of the CPU's time. The 37 MB of memory is a medium-level figure that is not taxing memory. If all applications were constantly using most of the CPU or memory resources, there would be reason for concern.

Figure 10-8

The Task Manager Applications tab

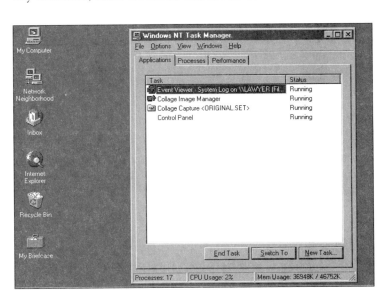

The Processes tab, shown in Figure 10-9, lists the processes in use by the system. The table shows the name of the process, the process ID (PID) used to identify the process to the operating system, the current percent of CPU use, the amount of CPU time the process has used, and the memory usage. In this example, the System Idle Process has 95% and taskmgr.exe (the Task Manager program) has 5%. This really means that only 5% of the CPU resources are in use. Sara could stop any process by highlighting it and clicking End Process.

Figure 10-9

The Task
Manager
Processes tab

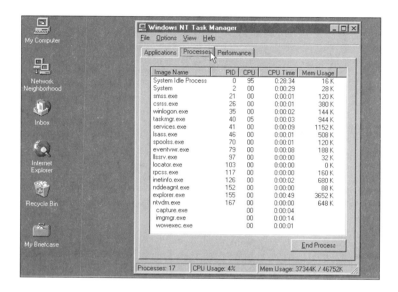

The Performance tab shows information about the server's performance, with the bar graph under CPU Usage showing 5% (see Figure 10-10).

Figure 10-10

The Task
Manager
Performance
tab

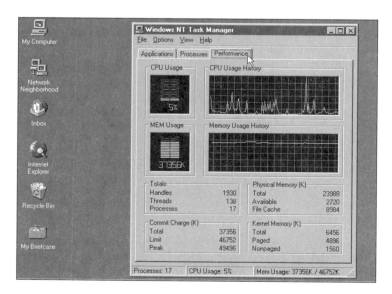

The CPU Usage History section represents the percent of CPU resources used over the past several seconds. Current and historical memory usage are displayed in the same way. The bottom four boxes show general information about the amount of server memory and memory in use. For example, handles are the number of objects in use, such as open files.

The threads are the number of code blocks executing, and one program may be designed to execute several threads at a time. The kernel memory is the amount of memory currently in use by the server operating system. Physical memory is the amount of RAM in the server, and commit memory is the amount of memory in use. For example, if the commit memory peak value is always at the limit, this means one or more applications are intensively using memory. It is a sign that memory needs to be increased or that parameters need to be adjusted in the programs. Sara particularly notes the box in the bottom-right corner, which has information about paging, a topic she looks at next. RAM has 1560 KB, and 4896 KB are paged onto disk, supplying information about paging performance. If there is constant use of paged memory, it may need to be expanded. Sara finishes viewing the Task Manager and closes it.

MONITORING RAM AND VIRTUAL MEMORY

The Task Manager is one tool that provides monitoring information about memory use on the sever. The memory has two components: RAM and virtual memory. The amount of RAM is important to server performance. Sara has 64 MB of RAM, which is likely sufficient for a small network like the firm's. Still, it is important to watch the server's use of RAM to be sure performance is acceptable. If the server frequently has all the RAM in service, it is time to consider upgrading to more. Or, if the Task Manager shows that a particular application dominates all memory, it may be necessary to consult the documentation for the application or the vendor.

Virtual memory is disk space used by NT Server to extend RAM when there is not enough for present tasks. Virtual memory acts like reserve memory to temporarily store program code or data not immediately in use by the processor. If NT Server needs more memory for current work, it **pages** data blocks from memory to previously reserved space on the disk. For example, on a Pentium processor such as LAWYER, data are paged in blocks of 4 KB. The reserved disk space is called the **page file**. For instance, the Event Viewer, which is used to access server log data, may require 75 MB of memory, but there are only 64 MB of RAM on Lawyer. The Event Viewer is still able to work by temporarily storing part of the information, which it is not currently using, in the page file. As soon as the information is needed for processing, it is read back into RAM. The amount of virtual memory allocated for a server should be at least as much as the amount of memory plus 12 MB. For example, LAWYER has 64 MB of memory and, therefore, should have 76 MB of disk space allocated for virtual memory.

The **page file** is disk space allocated for use as an extension of RAM, so the server continues to function when the requirement for RAM exceeds what is available. When information is moved to the page file, the process is called paging or swapping.

Increasing virtual memory is an economical way to extend resources, but is not as efficient as having additional RAM. If benchmarks show an ever growing amount of memory paging, it is time to consider purchasing a memory upgrade for the server.

CONFIGURING VIRTUAL MEMORY

Next, Sara checks the amount of virtual memory allocated to each drive on LAWYER. From the Control Panel, she double-clicks the System icon. Then she selects the Performance tab, as shown in Figure 10-11. The tab has two options, one to boost application performance and the other for allocating page file size for virtual memory. The first option is used to give the highest priority to the active application window on the server. For example, the active window now is System Properties. The sliding bar is used to increase or decrease the priority given to the active window. The default is to give maximum priority, which Sara leaves for now. Later, if she leaves an active monitor window open to diagnose a problem, she plans to reduce the priority to the middle, so the monitoring activities do not interfere with normal server functions provided to the users.

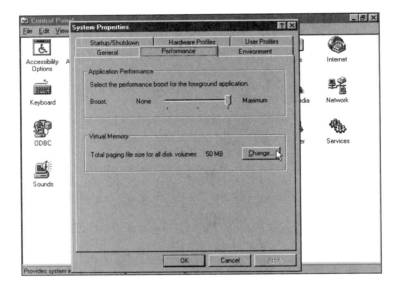

Figure 10-11

The System
Properties
Performance
tab

Sara clicks the Change button to view the size of each page file allocated for virtual memory. The page file on drive D is 50 MB by default, and there is no page file on drive C. Sara begins by modifying the page file on drive D by highlighting the drive. Next, she enters 76 MB in the Initial Size text box, which is the amount of RAM on LAWYER plus 12 MB, and she enters 95 MB in the Maximum Size text box (see Figure 10-12). The 95 MB for maximum page file size allows a 25% extra margin as needed for busy periods on the server. Sara plans to keep monitoring the server paging after users are on in full force, in case she needs to further expand the page file. She clicks the Set button to enter the change. She repeats the process to create a paging file for drive C. The new page file sizes will not take effect until Sara reboots the server.

Figure 10-12

The Virtual
Memory
dialog box

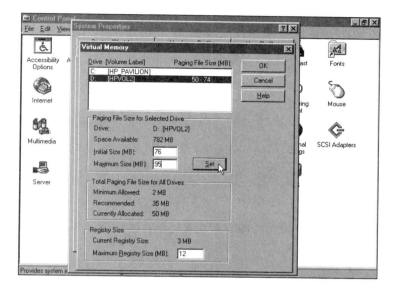

On multiple-volume servers, try increasing performance by creating a page file on each volume.

The paging blocks are stored in a file named pagefile.sys on the specified disk volumes.

The registry is entirely on disk as a database. Its size can be established at the same time as the page file. The maximum registry size typically is not sized larger than 25% of the page file size. Because the firm has a small network with relatively few applications to start, Sara is limiting the maximum registry size to 12 MB, which is about 20% of the size of a page file. Sara finishes setting the page files and registry size, checks her entries, and clicks OK.

MONITORING CPU AND DISK RESOURCES

Sara is especially concerned about monitoring the CPU response as a way to gauge the server load. The CPU response is often measured as a percent of utilization of the CPU. When the CPU is extremely busy, utilization may be over 90%, or it may be under 20% at relatively idle times. If the CPU utilization is frequently over 90%, this merits investigating to determine whether the problem is too little CPU or is related to something else. One source of excessive CPU utilization may be a program that is not working correctly.

Disk response reflects the demand on disk services. A critical step is to frequently monitor the amount of disk space available. No network administrator wants to be surprised by a full hard disk. A good rule to follow is to install more disk space before one or more volumes are 80% full. Volumes more than 80% full become less efficient in retrieving data and experience a high level of wear through constant data access. Also, volumes this full have a higher risk of disk failure than less full volumes. Extremely full volumes can seriously impair server performance if space is too limited for the allocated virtual memory.

Another factor in disk response on a multiple-volume system is excessive demand on one disk. Performance monitoring may indicate that the information on one disk is accessed with high frequency, whereas another disk is far less busy. This is a signal to move some of the files on the high-demand volume to another volume with low demand.

THE PERFORMANCE MONITOR

Sara monitors CPU, disk, and other resources by using the Performance Monitor. This utility can monitor many resources at the same time. Also, it runs several indicators about one resource simultaneously. There are literally hundreds of monitoring combinations within the Performance Monitor. Each monitored resource is an object. The tool monitors a wide range of objects such as cache, disk services, memory, protocols, paging, the processor, queues for objects, and hardware interrupts. The measures of performance are matched to the resource, such as percent of the object that is busy or number of requests made to the object. When first started, the Performance Monitor is a blank screen until an object is selected to monitor. The monitored data are displayed as a graph across the screen, and values continue to be plotted until the monitor session is stopped.

Sara starts the Performance Monitor from the Administrative Tools menu and clicks the Plus button on the button bar to access the Add to Chart dialog box as shown in Figure 10-13. The Computer text box lists LAWYER by default. The Object drop-down box contains processor by default, but any object can be selected by clicking the Down Arrow and highlighting the object. Sara is presently interested in monitoring the processor (CPU) load and so leaves Processor as the default.

Figure 10-13

Adding a
Performance
Monitor object

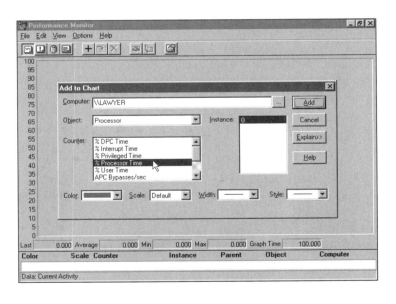

Each object has a list of **counters** to measure some quality of the object. Table 10-2 shows example counters used for monitoring the processor.

Table 10-2

Example processor counters in the Performance Monitor

Counter	Description
% DPC Time	Processor time used for deferred procedure calls, such as for hardware devices
% Interrupt Time	Time spent on hardware interrupts by the CPU
% Privileged Time	Time spent by the CPU for system activities in Privilege mode
% Processor Time	Time the CPU is busy on all non-idle activities
% User Time	Time spent by the CPU in User mode running software applications and system programs
Interrupts/sec	Number of device interrupts per second

Sara clicks the counter labeled "% Processor Time" to monitor the percentage of time the processor is busy. The Explain button provides a definition of each counter. Sara clicks the Add button to monitor statistics via the % Processor Time counter. Next, she clicks Done to view the Performance Monitor graph, as shown in Figure 10-14.

Figure 10-14

The Performance Monitor graphing screen

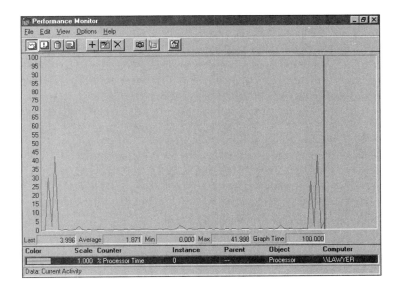

The vertical line extending from 0 to 100 indicates the current point and moves across the screen from left to right, drawing the graph behind. The 0 represents 0% busy. The statistics at the bottom of the screen show the following:

- Last is the current value of the monitored activity.
- Average is the average value of the monitored activity for the elapsed time.
- Min is the minimum value of the activity over the elapsed time.
- Max is the maximum value of the activity over the elapsed time.
- Graph Time is the amount of time to complete one full graph of the activity.

Counters are unique measurement options, such as percent busy or number of bytes per second, for a specific monitored object, such as the server memory or processor.

Sara clicks the Plus button on the button bar again to add more activities to the graph. From the Add to Chart dialog box shown in Figure 10-13, Sara highlights % Interrupt Time and clicks Add, and then she adds % User Time to the graph. Figure 10-15 shows the Performance Monitor with three activities graphed. Each one is graphed in a different color. Now the monitor is tracing the amount of processor time used for non-idle processes, the User mode activities, and the amount of processor time used for hardware interrupts. This gives Sara a picture of the load on the processor, including demand from hardware devices and users. For example, if there are high demands due to hardware interrupts, and all hardware is working properly, Sara would need to upgrade the CPU to handle the server hardware. This is not likely to happen now, but it might be a future problem if Sara adds more disks and a CD-ROM array.

Figure 10-15

Graphing multiple objects

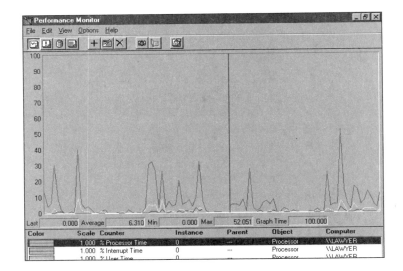

In studying the disk load, Sara would select the object Physical Disk and then choose a counter. To start, she collects information about the percent of time the disks are busy. She also gathers information about the disk requests waiting in queues until the disks are free. Sara uses this information in Chapter 12 to diagnose disk performance.

To establish benchmarks, Sara plans to track processor load, memory load, physical disk, and paging file information. She wants to gather data about how busy or full each object is and statistics about the maximum use for each. Information gathered by the Performance Monitor can be stored in a file to reference later. The data will give her information about whether the processor is fast enough, whether there is adequate memory and disk performance, and whether any paging adjustments are needed. Also, the monitoring will help her develop a knowledge of the normal server load and the load at peak times. With this knowledge, she will have an advantage in locating problems and in planning for growth as the server demand increases. In Chapter 12, Sara uses the Performance Monitor to troubleshoot problems by tuning the server.

Use the performance monitor to check specific areas of interest for a limited amount of time only. The Performance Monitor uses server resources and should not be left running continuously.

EVENT LOGS

Another way to track information about server activities is through the Event Logs option from the Administrative Tools menu. There are three event logs that continuously gather information: System, Security, and Applications. Each log shows individual events with the following information:

- An icon showing the severity of the event, such as error, warning, and information

- Date and time of the event

- Source of the event, which is the software application or hardware reporting it

- Category or type of event, if one applies, such as a system event or logon event

- Event number, so the event can be tracked if entered into a database

- User involved in the event, if applicable

- Name of the computer where the event took place

Sara accesses the system log first, as shown in Figure 10-16. The system log keeps information about components in the system, such as hard drives, drivers, NICs, CD-ROM drives, and other parts of the system. If a problem is detected, it is reported in the system log. Nonserious problems are reported as information, with a small "i" icon, such as when the system expects a CD-ROM to be loaded and it is not. More serious problems are reported with a stop-sign icon, such as when the Server service is unexpectedly not working or a disk drive has failed. To find out more about a particular event, Sara would click the event for a description. For example, if an NIC driver is loaded improperly, the description would say, "The following boot-start or system-start driver(s) failed to load:" followed by the name of the failed driver. Network administrators use the system log to quickly locate a problem, such as a driver failure, hardware failure, or service failure.

Figure 10-16

The system log

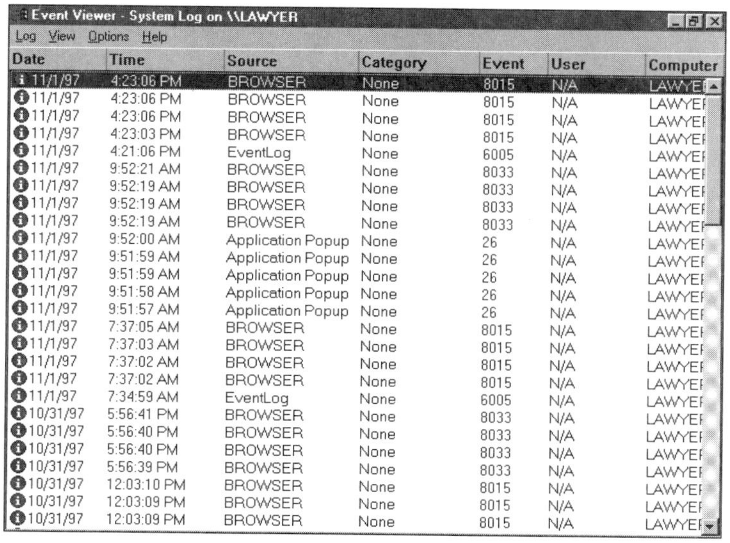

Next, Sara views the security log by clicking the Log menu in the upper-left corner of the screen and selecting Security. The security log contains information on successful and unsuccessful logon attempts, file and directory activity, shared object activity, and other information. For example, Sara can have the security log record all logon and logoff activity by selecting the Audit option under the Policies menu in the User Manager. Or she can record each time a directory or the files in a directory are accessed or changed by using the Auditing button on the Security tab for that directory and selecting to audit all read attempts. For example, if Sara wants to see how often the Public directory is accessed, she would follow these steps:

1. Display the Public folder in My Computer or the Explorer.
2. Click the **File menu** and click **Properties**.
3. Click the **Security tab**.
4. Click the **Auditing button**.
5. Check the boxes to audit subdirectories and files.
6. Add the Everyone group to audit.
7. Check the **Success** and **Failure boxes** for Read (successful or unsuccessful read).
8. Click **OK** to accept the changes and start auditing all read attempts of Public.

The security log is useful for tracing unauthorized logon attempts, checking for intruders, or determining who last accessed the payroll file. Figure 10-17 shows the security log.

Figure 10-17

The security log

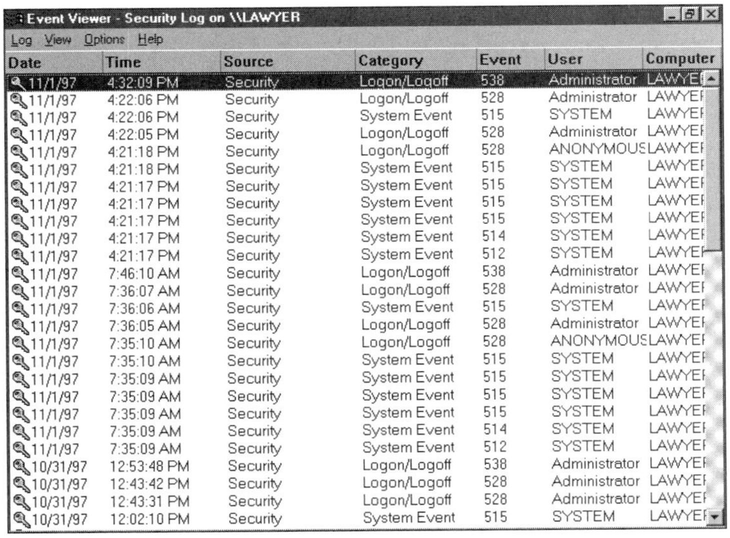

Date	Time	Source	Category	Event	User	Computer
11/1/97	4:32:09 PM	Security	Logon/Logoff	538	Administrator	LAWYE
11/1/97	4:22:06 PM	Security	Logon/Logoff	528	Administrator	LAWYE
11/1/97	4:22:06 PM	Security	System Event	515	SYSTEM	LAWYE
11/1/97	4:22:05 PM	Security	Logon/Logoff	528	Administrator	LAWYE
11/1/97	4:21:18 PM	Security	Logon/Logoff	528	ANONYMOUS	LAWYE
11/1/97	4:21:18 PM	Security	System Event	515	SYSTEM	LAWYE
11/1/97	4:21:17 PM	Security	System Event	515	SYSTEM	LAWYE
11/1/97	4:21:17 PM	Security	System Event	515	SYSTEM	LAWYE
11/1/97	4:21:17 PM	Security	System Event	515	SYSTEM	LAWYE
11/1/97	4:21:17 PM	Security	System Event	514	SYSTEM	LAWYE
11/1/97	4:21:17 PM	Security	System Event	512	SYSTEM	LAWYE
11/1/97	7:46:10 AM	Security	Logon/Logoff	538	Administrator	LAWYE
11/1/97	7:36:07 AM	Security	Logon/Logoff	528	Administrator	LAWYE
11/1/97	7:36:06 AM	Security	System Event	515	SYSTEM	LAWYE
11/1/97	7:36:05 AM	Security	Logon/Logoff	528	Administrator	LAWYE
11/1/97	7:35:10 AM	Security	Logon/Logoff	528	ANONYMOUS	LAWYE
11/1/97	7:35:10 AM	Security	System Event	515	SYSTEM	LAWYE
11/1/97	7:35:09 AM	Security	System Event	515	SYSTEM	LAWYE
11/1/97	7:35:09 AM	Security	System Event	515	SYSTEM	LAWYE
11/1/97	7:35:09 AM	Security	System Event	515	SYSTEM	LAWYE
11/1/97	7:35:09 AM	Security	System Event	514	SYSTEM	LAWYE
11/1/97	7:35:09 AM	Security	System Event	512	SYSTEM	LAWYE
10/31/97	12:53:48 PM	Security	Logon/Logoff	538	Administrator	LAWYE
10/31/97	12:43:42 PM	Security	Logon/Logoff	528	Administrator	LAWYE
10/31/97	12:43:31 PM	Security	Logon/Logoff	528	Administrator	LAWYE
10/31/97	12:02:10 PM	Security	System Event	515	SYSTEM	LAWYE

The application log shows information on software applications. Information is written to this log for an application, if the developer has designed the application to do so. For example, if the NT Explorer experiences a software error, this is reported in the application log. An error accessing a client/server database might be an error generating a report, reported in the log. Figure 10-18 shows the application log, which Sara selected it from the Log menu.

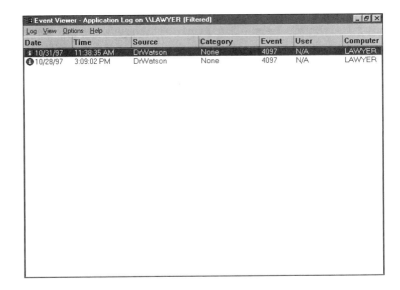

Figure 10-18

The
application log

TUNE BEFORE YOU UPGRADE

Most network servers experience dynamic variations in demand. For example, at one point, the demand may be to accommodate application requests for large numbers of users. At another time, the demand may shift to print services or Internet server services. Still later, the demand may be for frequent disk reads of large files for desktop publishing users. Modern network operating systems such as NT Server have several automatic tuning features to shift server resources to the current demand. No longer must you manually adjust the number of communication buffers, shift memory and disk resources for more users, or manually set a flag on large files for faster access. These and other tuning activities are automatically handled through the NT Server operating system.

In some areas the network administrator can intervene to troubleshoot performance problems, such as to expand virtual memory as demand grows. Applications that are demanding on the system can be scheduled to run at night, and inefficient applications can be replaced with better alternatives. Files on a busy disk can be moved to another disk. Unused server services can be stopped. Full system logs can be cleared and saved to disk. All these are options to try before purchasing more hardware, such as memory or disk drives. Sara examines these options in Chapter 12 after she has gathered benchmark data and opened the server to the users.

SARA'S NEXT ASSIGNMENT

Sara is not yet prepared to audit directory or shared object accesses, but she does want to monitor all logon and logoff attempts. She observes this option is already set by default in the security log. She also begins gathering CPU, memory, and disk information using the Performance Monitor. Sara collects this information at mid-morning and mid-afternoon each day while the server is still unavailable to the users. This provides her valuable information about the server when there is no load. When she releases the server to the users, she will continue to monitor, gathering information at peak and slow times.

In the next chapter, we follow along with Sara as she works on system maintenance. She is investigating backup procedures and wants to formalize them to ensure the firm's data are fully protected. Sara also wants to implement a UPS system for protection against power failures. Plus, Ryan warns Sara to develop procedures for regularly clearing system logs, a project she will tackle in the next chapter.

KEY CONCEPTS SUMMARY

Server performance monitoring is a complex process involving the development of measurement guidelines, monitoring techniques, and improving the use of memory resources. The following concepts relate to server performance and monitoring issues.

benchmark   A standard of measurement used to gauge the performance of a software or hardware system.

counter   A measurement option of a selected object, such as the processor or memory, within the Performance Monitor.

file lock   A way of protecting a file that is already in use from access by one or more additional users, guaranteeing only one data update can occur at a time.

named pipes   This communication link is a bridge between two processes, such as two programs on a server.

page file   Disk space reserved for use when memory requirements exceed the available RAM.

paging   This process takes place when the need for memory exceeds the amount of memory available and data blocks are temporarily written from memory to disk.

virtual memory   This is disk space allocated to link with memory to temporarily hold data.

SUMMARY OF WINDOWS FUNCTIONS

A wide range of NT Server tools are available to assist with performance monitoring. The following paragraphs summarize the NT Server tools described in this chapter.

Event Logs   These administrative tools give the network administrator historical information about server events such as hardware problems, unauthorized logon attempts, application program problems, number of successful logons, number of requests to access a specified directory, and other information about activities on the server.

Performance Monitor   This administrative tool is used to monitor server performance over a given period, tracking system, hardware, and software demands on the processor.

Server Icon   This icon is used to monitor connectivity and use information, such as the number of users connected, the resources used, open resources, controls on replication services, and users to receive alerts.

Services Icon   This icon shows services available to the server along with controls to start, pause, and stop selected services.

System Icon   Virtual memory and registry size are configured from the System icon.

Task Manager This tool is used to view information about programs and tasks started on the server. It shows what tasks are running, with performance statistics on the tasks, and enables the administrator to stop a task that is hung and that cannot be stopped in the normal manner.

REVIEW QUESTIONS

1. Which of the following is not a default service on an NT server?

    a. Messenger

    b. Net Logon

    c. Task Logon

    d. EventLog

2. Virtual memory on an NT server consists of:

    a. RAM

    b. Disk storage

    c. CD-ROM storage

    d. All of the above

    e. Both a and b

3. Server paging files should be how large?

    a. 100 MB or larger

    b. As large or larger than the amount of RAM plus 12 MB

    c. The same size as the registry

    d. The same size as the SAM

4. From where would you check to determine the number of users logged on to a server?

    a. The Server icon

    b. The Server User tool

    c. The System icon

    d. The Control icon

5. A hung program can be stopped from the Task Manager.

    a. True

    b. False

6. A named pipe is

    a. A communication link between two processes.

    b. An event log.

    c. A network protocol.

    d. An NIC driver.

7. From where would you be able to determine the percent of CPU utilization of a program running on the server?

   a. User Manager

   b. Task Manager

   c. Task log

   d. Program log

8. The paging file is called virtual.sys.

   a. True

   b. False

9. The Alerter service has the following purpose:

   a. To alert the CPU of a hardware interrupt request.

   b. To signal a program interrupt.

   c. To alert specified users about a detected server problem.

   d. To start the Task Manager.

10. File locking is used to

    a. Prevent security files from being accessed by anyone other than the Administrators group.

    b. Prevent two or more people from writing to a file at the same time.

    c. Lock out accounts after too many invalid logon attempts.

    d. Lock out nonessential hardware interrupts to the CPU.

11. As network administrator, you need to log off a user. What tool would you use?

    a. The Server icon

    b. The System icon

    c. The Event Viewer

    d. The Services icon

12. Information that an NIC on the server has failed would be reported in which of the following:

    a. Task Manager

    b. System log

    c. Application log

    d. User Manager

13. Only one paging file is allowed per NT server.

    a. True

    b. False

14. The server service can be stopped without much effect on users of an NT server.

    a. True

    b. False

15. To audit accesses of a particular folder on an NT server, the administrator would

    a. Use the Auditing button on the Security tab for that folder's properties.

    b. Use the Permissions button on the General tab for that folder's properties.

    c. Create a special event log for that folder.

    d. Set folder monitoring in the Performance Monitor.

16. A particular service on an NT server can be paused from

    a. The Services icon.

    b. The System icon.

    c. The Server icon.

    d. Services cannot be paused.

17. The Performance Monitor calculates average, minimum, and maximum data.

    a. True

    b. False

18. How many counters can be monitored at one time using the Performance Monitor?

    a. Only one

    b. Only two

    c. As many as are available to select from

    d. Monitoring counters are automatically determined by the operating system

19. You suspect that mail services running on the server are creating a heavy load at given periods of time. Where would you look to monitor these services?

    a. Task Manager

    b. Performance Monitor

    c. Application log

    d. All of the above

    e. Only a and b

20. Where would you look to find out whether someone is attempting to log on to the server with an invalid password?

    a. System log

    b. Security log

    c. Server log

    d. Application log

21. The Server icon provides information about the resources an account is using.

    a. True

    b. False

THE HOLLAND COLLEGE PROJECT: PHASE 10

You have just met with Bob Watson to discuss how to monitor the two servers at Holland College. Bob is asking you to investigate ways to monitor the servers as a means to anticipate and prevent problems. In the following assignments you experiment with monitoring and develop monitoring plans to use on both servers.

ASSIGNMENT 10-1

Develop plans to establish benchmarks for the Hoyt Administration Building and the English and writing lab servers. Outline your plans in the following tables in a step-by-step fashion.

Benchmark Steps for the Administrative Server
STEP 1:
STEP 2:
STEP 3:
STEP 4:
STEP 5:
STEP 6:
STEP 7:
Additional Steps or Comments:

Benchmark Steps for the Lab Server
STEP 1:
STEP 2:
STEP 3:
STEP 4:
STEP 5:
STEP 6:
STEP 7:
Additional Steps or Comments:

ASSIGNMENT 10-2

In a lab, work with virtual memory parameters in the following ways and record how you did the work.

Task	Explanation of How the Task was Completed
View the presently allocated virtual memory.	
Set the initial memory to 100 MB and the maximum to 120 MB for the existing page file.	
Create a page file on each server volume with the initial size of 100 MB and the maximum size of 120 MB.	
Set the registry maximum size at 25% of the page file size.	

ASSIGNMENT 10-3

Start four applications on the server, such as Event Viewer, WordPad, the Performance Monitor, and NT Explorer. Last, start the Task Manager and perform the following exercises.

Task	Explanation of How the Task was Completed (record any results)
Record the amount of CPU resources used for each task (current CPU and total CPU time).	
Record the status of each task.	
Determine how much memory is used via RAM and via disk storage.	
Stop a task, such as NT Explorer.	
Record how much of the CPU time is idle.	

ASSIGNMENT 10-4

Bob Watson calls and asks you to check on whether there were any failed attempts to access the server. Check for failed logon attempts and describe what you did.

Bob also wants to determine whether you can monitor the number of times the directory with payroll information is accessed. Set up a directory called Pay. In the process, set it up so information is generated each time Pay is accessed. Describe how you set the directory to report on the access attempts and where you would look to view the information.

 ASSIGNMENT 10-5

Set up the Performance Monitor to track % Processor Time and % Interrupt Time for the processor for 1 minute. Record in the following table the results of the monitoring.

Results for % Processor Time	Results for % Interrupt Time
Average utilization:	Average utilization:
Minimum utilization:	Minimum utilization:
Maximum utilization:	Maximum utilization:
Present utilization:	Present utilization:
Graph bar color:	Graph bar color:

 ASSIGNMENT 10-6

You suspect a hard disk is failing. Where would you look to gather evidence about the disk's condition? What would you look for?

 ASSIGNMENT 10-7

In a lab, after warning users, pause and then stop the Server service using the Task Manager. Describe what happens when you pause this service. What happens when you stop the service?

ASSIGNMENT 10-8

Practice the following tasks relating to monitoring users on a server.

Task	Explanation of How the Task was Completed (record any results)
Determine how many users are presently logged on.	
Determine the server resources used by each active user.	
Force log off a user.	
Set the Alerter to notify a particular user of each problem event detected on the server.	

CHAPTER ELEVEN

SYSTEM MAINTENANCE

Sara is monitoring the CPU with the Performance Monitor, gaining experience in viewing the charted statistics. She decides to test a space allocation utility she purchased. The new application unexpectedly hangs, causing Sara to check other windows for problems. Relieved, she determines the problem affects only the application she is testing, not the server. Sara starts the Task Manager, highlights the application, and ends it. She checks the application log and finds an entry reporting a run-time programming error for that application. She decides to call the application vendor later to find out about reported problems.

Sara returns to the Performance Monitor, printing the data collected over the past several minutes. She is rapidly developing a set of performance benchmarks on the server, taking advantage of the current low-usage period before the server is released to the users.

In this chapter, Sara completes several high-priority maintenance tasks in preparation for going live with the network. For example, she practices clearing and saving the event logs to save historical information about server problems. She works with disk maintenance procedures and fault-tolerance options. Also, she sets up the backup procedures using a tape rotation scheme. Sara has performed some backups already, but now she establishes procedures suitable for a production-ready server. Later, she connects an uninterruptible power supply (UPS) she purchased to protect the server.

AFTER READING THIS CHAPTER AND COMPLETING THE EXERCISES YOU WILL BE ABLE TO:

- MANAGE AND CLEAR EVENT LOGS.
- RESIZE EVENT LOGS.
- EXPLAIN DISK FAULT-TOLERANCE TECHNIQUES.
- VIEW STATUS INFORMATION ON SERVER DISKS.
- SET UP DISK MIRRORING AND DISK STRIPING.
- PERFORM DISK BACKUPS AND RESTORES.
- CREATE A TAPE ROTATION SCHEME.
- ATTACH A SERVER TO A UPS.

SERVER MAINTENANCE PROCEDURES

Unlike Sara, some network administrators pay little attention to maintenance procedures until a problem develops, at which point it takes much longer to fix the problem. Through the newsgroups and forums, Sara is reading about situations where servers are released too soon. Problems occur when a server is released before adequate time is spent on backup precautions, setting regular maintenance schedules, and ensuring reliable power. For example, one administrator experienced a disk failure and could not perform a restore due to a worn tape. The administrator had neglected to establish a **tape rotation** system, relying on the same tape set for all backups.

 Tape rotation is a system for performing backups using several tape sets at regular intervals.

Sara is composing the following list of essential maintenance items, profiting from the experiences of others:

- Maintaining event logs
- Disk maintenance and problem prevention
- Establishing production backup procedures
- Creating a tape rotation plan
- Installing a UPS
- Checking for viruses

MAINTAINING EVENT LOGS

Maintenance of the three event logs is a good starting point, because it is easy to implement. The event logs quickly fill with information about server and user activities, particularly logons. There are several ways to maintain the logs. One is to size each log to prevent it from filling too quickly. Another is to regularly clear each log before it is full. A third method is to have the logs automatically overwrite the oldest events when they are full. Sara receives conflicting advice on how long to keep log information. Several forum and newsgroup members recommend allowing the logs to overwrite the oldest events and not worrying about clearing or saving them.

Others, including Ryan, recommend saving the logs on a regular basis. Ryan clears and saves all three logs weekly, keeping the old log files on a log history tape. He keeps a file on tape for a year, deleting it after that time. Keeping the files has been useful in several instances when he has gone to an archived file to check security information for management. For instance, Ryan's firm audits the payroll file data to track the accesses. Two months ago, there was an error in the file due to the way the payroll was posted. At the request of management, Ryan was able to trace the date of the error in the security log so data could be corrected after that date. Another reason some network administrators keep old logs is to trace the occurrence of past hardware or software problems, such as problems with a tape or disk drive. This helps in diagnosing future problems and in taking preventive steps to replace a defective component.

Never underestimate the value of historical log information as an aid to tracing a problem, particularly a software data problem.

Sara adopts Ryan's approach, but she decides to keep the old event log data on disk so they are readily available, and until she feels sure the installation is working smoothly. All three event logs are sized at 512 KB by default. Sara has observed that the system and security logs are experiencing the most growth, with the system log already containing many entries. She increases the size of the system and security logs to 1 MB. She plans to watch all three logs to gain an idea of how much they grow due to server and user activities.

To increase the size of the logs, Sara starts the Event Viewer from the Administrative Tools menu. From the Event Viewer, she clicks the Log menu and selects Log Settings, as shown in Figure 11-1.

Figure 11-1

Log Settings option on the Log menu

The first drop-down box in the Event Log Settings dialog box enables Sara to select the system, security, or application log. Sara starts with the system log, which is the default. In the Maximum Log Size box she enters 1024 to indicate the number of kilobytes to allot (see Figure 11–2).

Figure 11-2

Entering event log settings

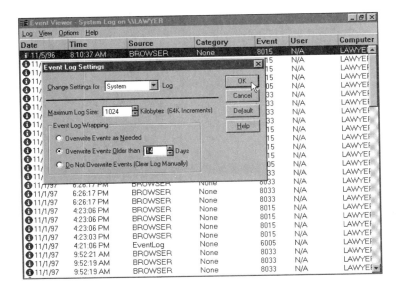

Next, Sara clicks the "Overwrite Events Older than" radio button and changes the value from 7 to 14 days. This option causes the log to save events for 14 days before overwriting them. Sara plans to clear and save each log every Thursday evening as part of her weekly maintenance routine. By setting the limit at 14, Sara allows herself a margin to miss clearing the logs for a week in case she is ill or on vacation. The alternative is to choose Overwrite Events as Needed, which overwrites the oldest events when the log is full. The Do Not Overwrite Events option keeps all event entries until the log is full or the administrator manually clears the log. Sara clicks OK to save her changes. She repeats the same steps for the security and application logs, but leaves the application log sized at 512 KB.

Next, Sara practices saving and clearing the event log. Each log is cleared individually by first displaying the log and then clicking Clear All Events on the Log menu (see Figure 11–1). Sara starts with the event log and sees a message box that reads, "Do you want to save this event log before clearing it?" She clicks Yes and enters the path and file-names, \Winnt\System32\Logfiles\evtnov1.evt, as shown in Figure 11–3. The LogFiles subdirectory already exists for this purpose. Sara names each file based on the file type, month, and week. The file types are .evt, .sec, and .app for event log, security log, and application log. EvtNov1 is the saved event log for the first week in November, and .evt is the default extension for a saved log. Sara clicks Save to save and clear the log.

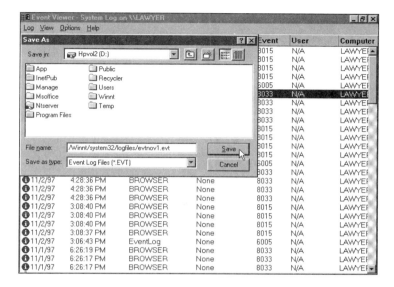

Figure 11-3

Saving an
event log

DISK MAINTENANCE

Server disk drives are the lifeblood of a system. It doesn't take long for the drives to be populated with vital information. Drives experience very high use and require planned maintenance. Designed to prevent problems or to enable recovery when a problem strikes, the maintenance activity falls into three categories: fault tolerance, disk management, and disk backups.

FAULT TOLERANCE

Fault tolerance is a hardware- or software-based system designed to provide redundancy in the event a failure occurs. To start, Sara has installed two SCSI pathways with two disks, to improve disk performance by spreading the load. As the load develops, she can use the Performance Monitor to determine the level of activity on each disk drive. If one drive has more activity than the other, she can equalize the load by reallocating the files between disks. Spreading the load helps to increase file access speed and to extend the life of the disks.

Fault tolerance has many faces, including disk redundancy, extra power supplies, uninterruptible power, data recovery methods, extra processors, extra data paths, and other methods to reduce the impact of a system failure.

Another fault tolerance option is to use **disk mirroring** to store redundant data. With disk mirroring, there are two separate drives for each volume of data. One is the main drive used to handle all of the user's requests to access or write data. The second drive contains a mirror image of the data on the first. Each time there is an update or deletion, it is made on the main drive and replicated on the second. If the main drive fails, the mirror drive takes over with no data loss. In disk mirroring, both drives are attached to the same disk controller or SCSI adapter. This is the technique's weak spot, because it leaves the data inaccessible if it is the controller or adapter that fails. Figure 11-4 shows an example of disk mirroring.

Figure 11-4

Disk mirroring

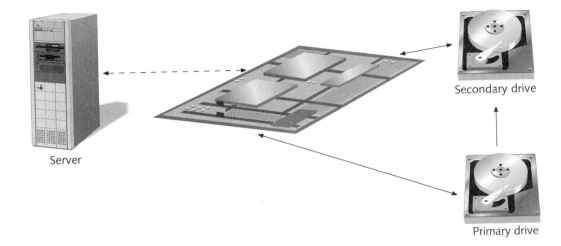

Disk duplexing is a way to combine disk mirroring with redundant adapters. Each disk is still mirrored by using a second backup disk, but the backup disk is placed on a controller or adapter that is separate from the one used by the main disk (see Figure 11–5). If the main disk, controller, or adapter fails, users may continue their work on the redundant one.

Figure 11-5

Duplexing with a redundant adapter

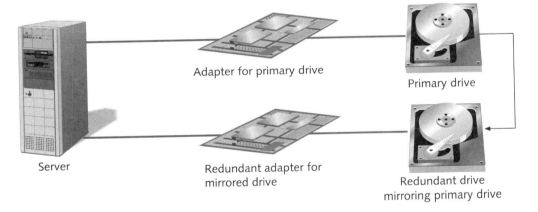

Another approach to disk redundancy is through the use of **redundant array of inexpensive disks (RAID)**. RAID is a set of standards for lengthening disk life and preventing data loss. There are six levels of RAID, beginning with the use of disk **striping**. Striping is the ability to spread data over multiple disk volumes. For example, part of a large file may be written to one volume and part to another. The goal is to spread disk activity equally across all volumes, preventing wear from being focused on a single volume in a set.

Striping with no other redundancy features is RAID level 0. NT Server supports level 0 as a means to extend disk life and to improve performance. Data access on striped volumes is fast on an NT server because of the way the data are divided into blocks which are quickly accessed through multiple disk reads and data paths. NT Server can stripe data across 3 to 32 disks.

A significant disadvantage to using level 0 stripping is that if one disk fails, you can expect a large data loss on all volumes.

RAID level 1 uses simple disk mirroring (sometimes called disk shadowing) and is commonly used on smaller networks. NT Server also supports level 1, but includes disk duplexing as well as mirroring. If there are three or more volumes to be mirrored or duplexed, this solution becomes more expensive than the other RAID levels. However, this option is sometimes preferred by network administrators because disk mirroring has better read and write performance than RAID methods other than level 0. Also, disk mirroring and disk duplexing offer the best guarantee of data recovery when there is a disk failure.

RAID level 2 employs an array of disks where the data are striped across all disks in the array. Also, in this method all disks store error correction information, which enables the array to reconstruct data from a failed disk. The advantages of level 2 are that disk wear is reduced and data are reconstructed if a disk fails. Like level 2, RAID level 3 uses disk striping and stores error correcting information, but the information is only written to one disk in the array. If that disk fails, the array cannot rebuild its contents.

RAID level 4 stripes data and stores error-correcting information on all drives, in a manner similar to level 2. An added feature is its ability to Perform checksum verification. The checksum is a sum of bits in a file. When a file is re-created after a disk failure, the checksum previously stored for that file is checked against the actual file after it is reconstructed. If the two don't match, the network administrator will know that the file may be corrupted. RAID levels 2 through 4 are not supported by NT Server because they do not offer the full protection found in level 5.

RAID level 5 combines the best features of RAID, including striping, error correction, and checksum verification. NT Server supports level 5, calling it "stripe sets with parity." Whereas level 4 stores checksum data on only one disk, level 5 spreads both error correction and checksum data over all of the disks, so there is no single point of failure. An added feature of level 5 is that a network administrator can replace a failed disk without shutting down the other drives. This level uses more memory than other RAID levels, with 16 MB recommended as additional memory for system functions. In addition, level 5 requires at least three disks in the RAID array. Recovery from a failed disk provides roughly the same guarantee as with disk mirroring, but takes longer with level 5.

 RAID arrays are offered as standard components on some hardware server systems. Due to market demand, watch for continuing advances in disk redundancy with newer levels of RAID.

Sara doesn't have a budget to purchase extra drives for mirroring or a full RAID drive unit. But she is researching the options. She wants to have time to follow the growth on LAWYER before making a proposal to Kristin and the management regarding their fault tolerance options. She and Kristin have already explained to management that a disk drive failure may involve some setup time when everyone is off the system as a replacement disk is installed and restored. Sara does have a disk drive as a spare in case there is a problem with the server or a workstation, and she would use the drive to replace one that has failed. She would reconstruct the lost files from backups. Sara considers proposing a RAID drive system as her first choice and disk mirroring as the alternate.

DISK MANAGEMENT

Setting up mirrored disks or RAID drives is performed from the Disk Administrator, a central tool for managing the server disk and CD-ROM drives. The Disk Administrator offers many powerful options in addition to fault tolerance. These include the following:

- Viewing status information about drives, including file system information
- Creating an NTFS partition on a new disk drive
- Combining two physical drives into one logical drive
- Changing drive letter assignments
- Formatting drives
- Extending a partitioned drive to include any free space not already partitioned

Sara starts the Disk Administrator from the Administrative tools menu. There are two views she can select from the View menu: Volumes or Disk Configuration. Figure 11-6 shows an example of the Volume information, with three different file systems detected by the Disk Administrator. It can detect volumes partitioned for FAT or NTFS. It detects CD-ROM drives and labels them as CD file systems (CDFS). The screen also provides information about the drive letter, the volume name, its capacity, the free space on the volume, the percent of space free, and whether it is set up for fault tolerance (mirroring or striping with parity). By providing all of this information in one place, the Disk Administrator is a good resource for monitoring the server drives. The network administrator can quickly see the remaining disk capacity, to keep abreast of the growth on a particular disk. In addition, this screen can help you verify that all drives are online and functioning, including CD-ROMs. If a drive is not available, the screen shows a message that the drive is offline.

Figure 11-6

Disk Administrator, Volume Information view

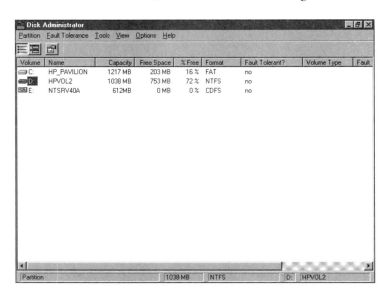

Each drive has a set of properties that can be viewed by highlighting the drive and clicking Properties from the Tools menu. The properties are similar to those for a directory, including general, tools, sharing, and security. The General tab shows information similar to the main view, but with a pie chart showing used space and unused space (see Figure 11-7). There is also a check box option to compress files on a volume, as long as it is NTFS-based. The same guidelines for compressing files apply here as for a directory, and Sara does not choose to compress files on any volumes. Compressed files take longer to access in a busy office such as the firm.

Figure 11-7

The volume properties General tab

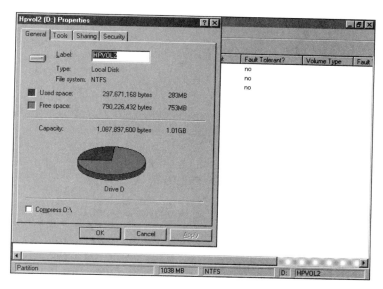

Sara clicks the Tools tab to view its options, as shown in Figure 11-8. She uses the Error-checking option to provide a check of the volume's integrity, in case a bad disk sector or track is suspected. This check can take several minutes on a large, full disk volume. The Backup Now button enables Sara to go into the administrative tools to back up the volume (see "Setting Up The Tape Backups" next). A disk **defragmenting** tool was not installed with NT Server, and so this button is deactivated. Sara plans to find a defragmenter shortly because it will help extend the life of the disks. Several vendors offer effective defragmenting software at a reasonable cost.

Defragmenting is a process of rearranging files on a disk to reduce pockets where there are no data. Disk wear is reduced by arranging files contiguously to reduce the work performed by disks to find data, and to improve disk response time.

Make system time available to periodically defragment disk drives. On a busy server, drives should be defragmented every week to two weeks. On less busy servers, defragment the drives at least once a month. Also, encourage users to defragment workstation drives once a month.

Figure 11-8

The volume
properties
Tools tab

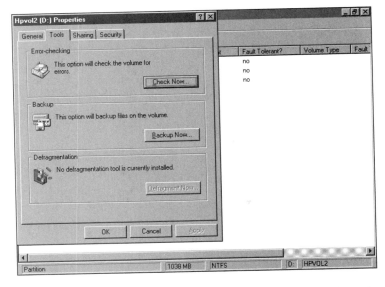

Next, Sara goes to the Sharing tab and verifies that the drive is available as a share to users on the network (see Figure 11-9). Share permissions for a hard drive cannot be set from the Permissions button, since the drive must be shared for administrative use. Sara discovers this when she clicks the Permissions button and receives a warning that the drive must be shared. If she wants to change the share to users, she could click the New Shares button, and enter a share name. She could also set permissions on the share for no access, read, change, or full control. The permissions enable her to control access to the entire disk from one place. Thus, if she wants to prevent access to a disk while she is setting it up for use, she would designate it as no access, so only the Administrators could use the disk and its files.

Figure 11-9

The volume
properties
Sharing tab

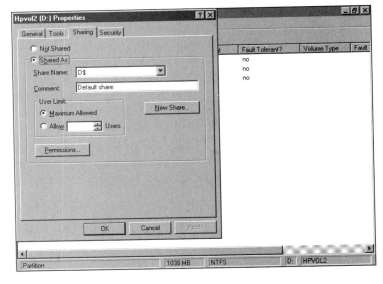

Sara moves on to the Security tab. Similar to a directory, she can set the complete range of permissions for groups and users to apply to the entire disk contents. The whole disk volume can be audited, although this would generate a large number of entries in the security log. The volume is already owned by the Administrator account. Should the Administrator need to take ownership of all files and directories at one time, he or she can do it from the Ownership button, as in Figure 11-10.

Figure 11-10

The volume properties Security tab

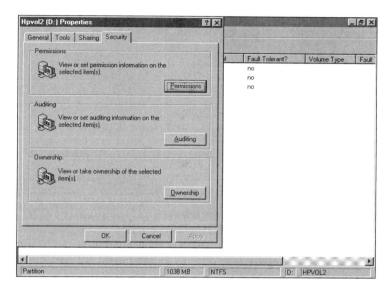

On the screen, as shown in Figure 11-6, Sara could partition a disk or delete a partition using selections from the Partition menu. As a precaution, NT Server will not let an administrator delete an active partition from which the server runs. Even so, it is wise to be careful on this menu so a data drive is not inadvertently partitioned. The Fault Tolerance menu option contains selections to create disk mirroring or to stripe drives in RAID arrays. For example, to create a mirrored set of drives, Sara would follow these steps:

1. Install the drive that will serve as the mirror.

2. Click **View** and select **Disk Configuration** to view the amount of free space on all drives (see Figure 11-11).

Figure 11-11

Creating mirrored drives

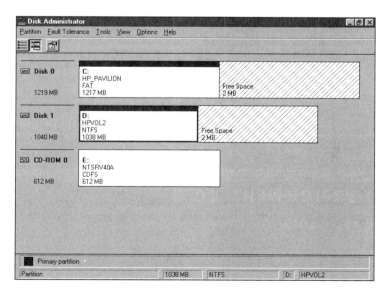

3. Designate the main drive partition.

4. Press **[Ctrl]** and simultaneously click a free area on another disk. The free area must be at least as large as the volume to be mirrored. This is disk space that currently is not partitioned, until it is designated as a mirror volume and partitioned for that purpose.

5. Click the **Fault Tolerance menu** and select **Establish Mirror**.

Creating a striped set of volumes with fault tolerance is just as easy, as outlined in the following steps:

1. Attach the RAID drive array to the server.

2. Display the Disk Configuration view.

3. Select the volumes to be striped by pressing **[Ctrl]** and clicking the free areas for striping. For example, if there are seven disks in a RAID array, Sara would click the free space (unpartitioned) available on each disk.

4. Click the **Fault Tolerance menu** and select **Create Stripe Set with Parity**.

DISK BACKUPS

Sara finishes with the Disk Administrator, but minimizes the window in case she wants to go back later. Her next interest is to develop a tape backup scheme. She has already installed the tape drive adapter in the server and attached the tape drive. Sara chose to put the tape system on the server instead of on her workstation because this allows her to back up the server's Registry, which is only permitted if the drive is attached to the server. Attaching the tape drive to the server also reduces network traffic because large files do not have to be sent over the network during backup sessions.

There are several types of backups to choose from. Most popular is a **full backup**, which backs up all volumes, directories, and files. One form of the full backup is to create an exact image of the disk files on tape. These backups, called image backups, are performed in binary format, storing the information bit by bit. Image backups are fast, but have the disadvantage that if only a few files on the hard disk were accidentally deleted or corrupted, all files must be restored from tape. Image Backups have no option to restore only selected files or selected directories.

A more widely used full backup procedure is file-by-file, which stores data as files on tape. In this format, the network administrator and backup operators can restore single files or selected directories as needed. The backup software that accompanies NT Server has file-by-file backup options, but no image backup capabilities. Backup software from tape subsystem vendors may come with image backup options. Sara has read that image backups are not recommended because they don't offer the flexibility of file-by-file backups.

The **incremental backup** is another backup method which backs up only those files that have changed since the previous backup, as indicated by the archive attribute on the file. Many organizations combine full and incremental backups because there is not enough time to back up all files after each workday. A popular method is to perform full file-by-file backups on a Friday night or a weekend day, when there is less activity on servers. During the week, incrementals are performed at the end of each workday. If a disk fails on Wednesday, the first restore step is to restore the volume from the weekend full backup, then to restore from Monday's incremental followed by Tuesday's incremental.

Backups are critical—never let a day pass without performing the regularly scheduled backups.

The NT Server backup software recognizes five backup options, which are variations of full or incremental backups. The first is called the normal backup, which is the same as a full file-by-file backup. The advantage of performing full backups each night is that all files are on one tape or tape set. Another NT option is the copy backup, which backs up only the files or directories selected. The archive attribute, only on new or updated files, is left unchanged. For example, if the archive attribute is present on a file, the copy backup does not remove it. Copy backups are used in exceptional cases where a backup is performed on certain files, but the regular backup routines are unaffected because the copy backup does not alter the archive bit.

NT has an incremental option that backs up only files that have the archive attribute. When it backs up a file, the incremental removes the attribute. A differential backup is the same as an incremental, but does not remove the archive attribute. Incremental or differential backups are often mixed with full backups. The advantage of the differential is that it restores only the most recent full backup and the most recent differential. This saves time over incremental restores, which require the full backup and all incrementals back to the last full backup.

The daily backup option backs up only files that have been changed or updated on the day the backup is taken. It leaves the archive attribute unchanged, so regular backups are not affected. A daily backup is valuable when there is a failing hard disk and little time to save the day's work to that point. It enables the administrator to save only that day's work instead of all changed files, which may span more than a day.

Sara decides to select normal backups for the close of each workday. Her backups take less than half an hour and fit on one tape. This is a good choice because she does not yet have fault tolerance disk protection. If a disk fails, the normal backup provides the fastest means to be back in action when a restore is needed.

Sara wants to establish a tape rotation method to ensure alternatives in case there is a bad or worn tape. One common tape rotation method is called the Tower of Hanoi procedure. This method rotates tapes so some are used more frequently than others. If one of the frequently used tapes is bad, a less frequently used tape is likely to be intact (although some recent data cannot be restored). Sara adopts the Tower of Hanoi method, using two sets of four tapes. In a given week the tapes are rotated Monday through Saturday, as shown in Figure 11-12.

Figure 11-12

Sara's tape rotation schedule

Sunday	Monday	Tuesday	Wednesday	Thursday	Friday	Saturday
1	2 Tape 1, Set 1 (Set 2 in Bank)	3 Tape 2, Set 1	4 Tape 1, Set 1	5 Tape 3, Set 1	6 Tape 2, Set 1	7 Tape 4, Set 1
8	9 Tape 1, Set 2 (Set 1 in Bank)	10 Tape 2, Set 2	11 Tape 1, Set 2	12 Tape 3, Set 2	13 Tape 2, Set 2	14 Tape 4, Set 2
15	16 Tape 1, Set 1 (Set 1 in Bank)	17 Tape 2, Set 1	18 Tape 1, Set 1	19 Tape 3, Set 1	20 Tape 2, Set 1	21 Tape 4, Set 1
22	23 Tape 1, Set 2 (Set 1 in Bank)	24 Tape 2, Set 2	25 Tape 1, Set 2	26 Tape 3, Set 2	27 Tape 2, Set 2	28 Tape 4, Set 2
29	30 Tape 1, Set 1 (Set 2 in Bank)					

Sara rotates the sets of four tapes every other week. The set not in use is carried to a bank safe-deposit box. This method has several advantages for Nishida and McGuire. First, tapes 3 and 4 in each set are used half as much as tapes 1 and 2. If there is a problem with tape 1 or 2, tapes 3 and 4 are likely to be useable. If any one tape in the set is bad, it is unlikely the firm will lose more than a single day of work. By having one complete set of tapes in a bank vault, the firm is protected if there is a fire, flood, or theft at the office. The most they would lose is a week of work.

Kristin asks Sara to present the tape rotation scheme to the managing attorneys for their approval. At the meeting, Anne is concerned about days when there is critical work that must be backed up at all costs. Sara recommends she be notified on these days so she can perform a differential backup to take to the vault for temporary safekeeping. Anne is satisfied with this answer and gives her approval along with the other managing partners.

SETTING UP THE TAPE BACKUPS

Earlier, Sara installed the tape subsystem through the Control Panel. She simply clicked the Tape Devices icon and then clicked Detect. She inserted the Windows NT Server CD-ROM, which the tape detect program used to load the tape driver. Now, when she starts the Backup option from the Administrative Tools menu, it automatically detects the tape drive each time the program starts.

Sara starts the Backup program and sees the Drives screen, as shown in Figure 11-13. She highlights drive C and clicks the Select option on the menu bar. Then she clicks Check to check the box in front of drive C. She repeats the process for drive D. Next, she clicks the Backup button under the menu bar. (The Backup option is also available from the Operations menu.) She opens the Backup Information dialog box and checks the box to backup the registry. Sara enters a description of the backup and enters Normal as the backup type. She clicks OK to start.

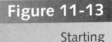

Figure 11-13

Starting backups

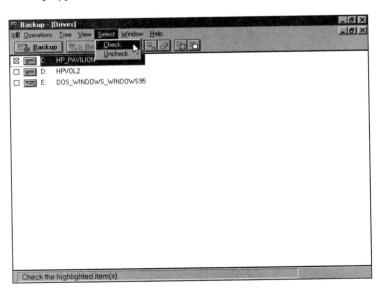

Sara's tape backup ends with a message that there is a problem with the tape. The tapes are already formatted, and Sara realizes the tape may need to be re-tensioned. She closes the error message and selects Retention Tape on the Operations menu. The tape is re-tensioned in under a minute, and Sara starts the backup again, which runs to a successful completion.

 Before starting a backup it may be necessary to format a new tape or re-tension new and used tapes. Both tasks are available on the Operations menu. Formatting deletes existing information and automatically re-tensions a tape. Tapes that have been used once should be re-tensioned before each backup to ensure the tape starts correctly.

Later, if Sara decides to install a new application, she may choose to back up the App directory first in case there is a problem with the install. To back up the directory Sara would remove the checks from the two drives on the screen shown in Figure 11-13 and double-click the drive containing the App directory. To back up the App directory, she would check its box and click the Backup button (see Figure 11-14).

Figure 11-14

Backing up the App directory

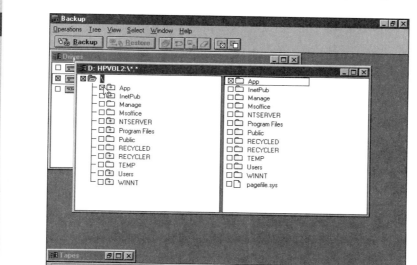

BACKING UP WORKSTATIONS

Sara intends to back up the users' workstations during her system time on Thursday nights. She plans to use the NT Backup utility for the workstations, performing a full backup on each station once a month. There will be a backup tape for every workstation, which Sara will replace once a year with a new tape. To back up a workstation, the workstation would need to be left powered on with the entire disk drive shared on the network for access by the Administrators and Backup Operators. Sara would temporarily map the drive to the server and perform a normal backup on that drive.

RESTORING A TAPE

If Sara needs to restore a tape, assistance is available using NT Server's catalog information. Each tape backup is cataloged to make it easy to refer back to a specific tape. The catalog contains information about the tape, including the tape label, the directories, and the files on the tape. To restore information, Sara would use the following steps:

1. Click **Catalog** on the Operations menu.

2. Select the tape or files to restore.

3. Click **Check** on the Select menu.

4. Check the backup sets to use.

5. Click **Restore** on the Operations menu.

UNINTERRUPTIBLE POWER SUPPLY

Sara was advised to purchase an uninterruptible power supply (UPS) for the server. A UPS is literally a box of rechargeable batteries that connects to a wall power outlet. Electrical devices are plugged into the UPS, so the devices continue to receive power when the main city power is out. A UPS is vital to protecting a server in several ways. First, it provides time to properly close files and shut down the server when city power fails. Without an orderly shutdown, server files or the operating system may be corrupted. Second, a UPS extends the life of the server and its components by shielding them from dramatic power changes. Disk drives are especially vulnerable to wear or damage during power failures. Third, many UPS systems have the ability to **condition power**, to protect the server from abnormal power conditions such as brownouts when power "sages" or "surges" but does not completely go out.

Power conditioning is provided by electrical circuits that take incoming power and regulate it to a consistent level regardless of fluctuations, thus protecting the devices attached to the conditioner.

There are two types of UPS systems: online and offline. An online UPS supplies power directly from its batteries. The batteries are continuously charging and supplying power. When city power goes out, there is no interruption to computers on the UPS because they continue to receive power from the UPS batteries, providing time to shut down systems. Most online UPSs also provide power conditioning.

The most damaging point of a power failure often is when power returns with an initial surge, stressing components within electrical devices.

Offline UPS systems, sometimes called stand-by systems, connect city power directly through to attached devices. They continuously monitor power for sages, or reductions in power levels. When a reduction is detected, the UPS switches to battery power, hopefully before the reduction becomes a power outage. Offline UPS systems are less expensive than online systems but do not offer the guaranteed protection needed for a file server.

Sara has an online UPS that is listed on Microsoft's hardware compatibility list. Her UPS has the ability to communicate information to the server, such as when it detects a power failure. Also, it can send a low-battery warning to the server. Sara powers down the server and attaches it to the UPS. The UPS has a serial communications cable that she attaches to the server's COM2 port. Sara also plugs the server monitor and tape drive into the UPS, because both provide critical server functions. She does not plug in the printer because it's a nonessential service that is easily resumed after a power failure.

Next, Sara provides information about the UPS to NT Server by selecting the UPS icon from the Control Panel. The dialog box shown in Figure 11-15 is used to establish communications with the UPS. Sara clicks the box labeled "Uninterruptible Power Supply is installed on" and then selects COM2. In the UPS Configuration section, she provides information about the UPS communications abilities. She clicks the boxes labeled "Power failure signal" and "Low battery signal at least 2 minutes before shutdown". These indicate that the UPS sends notification to NT Server when it detects a power failure and that the UPS sends a 2-minute warning before its batteries are too low to maintain the server. The lower-right boxes indicate that this UPS notifies the server within 5 seconds that a power failure has occurred and that users receive a message every 120 seconds warning of a shutdown.

Figure 11-15

Entering UPS parameters

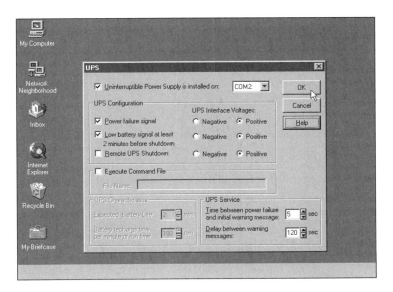

For the UPS interface voltages, Sara checks her UPS documentation to determine whether they are positive or negative. The voltages on her system are positive, so she clicks the Positive radio buttons. The Execute Command File option enables Sara to create a file of shutdown activities that runs automatically. She leaves this option blank for the present. Later she may want the file to automatically stop selected programs when a power failure occurs. Sara reviews the information on the screen and clicks OK to save it.

VIRUS PROTECTION

The term *computer virus* relates to three kinds of software programs that damage files on a server or workstation: viruses, Trojan horses, and worms. Sara is very concerned about protecting the server from invasion by any of these intruders. Viruses are program code that spreads into executable files, partition tables, system files, and other sensitive areas. As virus code spreads, it corrupts files, deletes data, and even prevents systems from booting.

A Trojan horse is program code hidden in software and set to strike on a given date or event, such as Halloween. It also damages files, data, and programs. The Trojan horse is usually packaged with a program that seems harmless, such as a computer utility or even a virus checker. Worms search for vulnerable entry points in a computer operating system, such as a Guest account that is not protected with a password. Once in, the worm grows within the operating system or duplicates files until the system fails.

The best precaution against these intruders is to purchase software from reliable vendors, avoiding free utilities or disks that have passed among several people. However, even software from a vendor may be infected, such as when disks are returned and reused. Careful network administrators run a virus scanner on all software before loading it on the server. But these efforts don't prevent a user from introducing a virus through his or her home directory. Two good methods for preventing viruses are to educate users to be careful about where they obtain software and to purchase a reliable virus scanning program.

Sara has purchased a virus scanning package for the server, with enough licenses to be used by everyone in the office. Before purchasing, she established the following criteria for the software:

- Easy to use
- Tests memory as well as disk drives for viruses
- Compatible with Windows NT and Windows 95
- Designed for network workstations and servers
- Has features to automatically schedule virus checking
- Updates are frequently sent, with scanning for new viruses
- Recommended by other network administrators

Part of the training for every user at Nishida and McGuire will be to run the virus scanner frequently, such as each morning, and to scan new files placed on a workstation or stored in a home directory. For example, a virus scanner can be started automatically from the Windows Startup folder to ensure the scanner runs each time a workstation is booted. Sara plans to encourage every user to scan computer memory as well as disk files, because a virus can be hidden to strike from a workstation's memory. Also, she plans to scan the server for viruses each day as part of her regular maintenance work.

SARA'S NEXT ASSIGNMENT

Sara sits in her office savoring the moment. She has reached the end of the preparations: The network is installed, the workstations are ready to connect, user accounts and groups are set up, directories and applications are in place, printers are working, backups are running, and the UPS is connected. In the morning, she and Kristin will begin training all the office users. Each will be trained in his or her office through several short sessions, allowing time to practice in between. Users will receive training on all of the following:

- Logging on
- Mapping drives
- Running software
- Using home directories
- Network printing

Sara's excitement leads her to call Kristin, who is equally pleased. Both know there will be many questions to answer and problems to address, but the new services make the work worthwhile. In the next chapter, Sara tackles server troubleshooting. She learns how to approach a range of server, printing, and network problems.

KEY CONCEPTS SUMMARY

Many of the key concepts in this chapter are related to disk management and disk backups. Other concepts relate to log maintenance and ensuring uninterrupted power. These concepts are presented in the paragraphs that follow.

conditioned power Power delivered from a conditioning device that takes city power and regulates it to a constant level for output to other electrical devices.

defragment A process that eliminates small pockets of empty space on a disk by arranging files contiguously.

disk duplexing This method for preventing lost data involves duplicating information from a main disk to a backup disk on a different controller or adapter.

disk mirroring A method that prevents data loss by duplicating data from a main disk to a backup disk.

fault tolerance The practice of creating redundant systems to have alternatives in the event of a hardware or software failure.

full backup A backup of an entire system including all system files, programs, and data files.

incremental backup A backup of new or changed files.

Redundant Array of Inexpensive Disks (RAID) Six levels of data protection that employ different combinations of striping, mirroring, storing correction data, and storing checksums.

striping This data storage method breaks up data files across all volumes of a disk set.

tape rotation This tape backup procedure uses multiple tape sets rotated for backups to reduce wear on tapes and to have restore alternatives, should there be a bad tape.

SUMMARY OF WINDOWS FUNCTIONS

In this chapter, Sara has learned to use several Windows utilities for system maintenance. These utilities, summarized in this section, are for maintaining event logs, establishing backups, managing disks, and creating fault tolerance.

Backup This tool is used to back up the contents of a server to tape. All information on the server disks can be backed up, or only selected directories and files can be backed up. The utility supports most standard backup methods including full, incremental, and impromptu backup needs. Restores also are performed from this utility.

Disk Administrator This administrative tool is used to manage disk activities such as fault tolerance, disk properties, partitioning, formatting, and assigning drive letters. Disk shares also are managed from this utility as well as permissions and auditing.

Event Viewer This utility enables the network administrator to view and manage the system, security, and application event logs. The logs can be resized, cleared, overwritten, and archived using the management options on the Event Viewer menu.

Tape Devices icon This Control Panel icon enables the network administrator to install drivers for tape drives that are attached to a server.

UPS icon This icon enables the server to recognize that a UPS is attached. It also is where the administrator defines communications abilities between the server and the UPS.

REVIEW QUESTIONS

1. Event logs have what default size?
    a.   100 KB
    b.   512 KB
    c.   1 MB
    d.   2 MB

2. From where are event logs maintained?
    a.   Event Viewer
    b.   User Manager
    c.   Backup log
    d.   Administrative Wizards

3. Fault tolerance is available only for disk drives on NT Server.
    a.   True
    b.   False

4. Which of the following NT backup techniques is used to save all files?

   a. Incremental

   b. Normal

   c. Copy

   d. Daily

5. Which backup techniques do not change the archive bit?

   a. Normal

   b. Daily

   c. Incremental

   d. All of the above

   e. Only a and b

6. Tape rotation is used to:

   a. Reduce tape wear.

   b. Provide an alternative for a bad backup tape.

   c. Enable off-site storage of backup tapes.

   d. All of the above

   e. Only a and c

7. The Disk Manager can be used to create a new partition.

   a. True

   b. False

8. Auditing cannot be used for a disk volume.

   a. True

   b. False

9. Which RAID level provides disk striping only?

   a. Level 0

   b. Level 1

   c. Level 2

   d. Level 3

10. Which type of fault tolerance requires two disk controllers or adapters?

   a. Disk mirroring

   b. Disk duplexing

   c. Disk swapping

   d. Volume redundancy

11. Which RAID level is the same as disk mirroring?

   a. Level 0

   b. Level 1

   c. Level 2

   d. Level 3

12. In RAID level 5, a disk can be replaced without stopping the other disks in the array.

   a. True

   b. False

13. Power fluctuations are prevented from damaging electrical equipment by which of the following?

   a. Power conditioning

   b. Power monitoring

   c. Power array

   d. Creating a floating ground

14. A _____ disk is one where there are many small pockets of unused space scattered throughout the disk.

   a. Formatted

   b. RAID Level 3

   c. Fragmented

   d. Failed

15. Information about the percentage of disk in use is available through what tool?

   a. Disk Reader

   b. Disk Manager

   c. The Windows DIR

   d. All of the above

   e. Only a and b

16. Which type of UPS has no battery switch-over period when the power goes out?
    a. Inline
    b. Online
    c. Offline
    d. Stand-by

17. Information about communicating with a UPS is provided where in NT Server?
    a. System icon on the Control Panel
    b. Server icon on the Control Panel
    c. UPS icon on the Control Panel
    d. Server Manager

18. Which type of backup is not used to enable restoring selected files or directories?
    a. Image
    b. Normal
    c. Incremental
    d. Differential

19. What type of cable is normally used for communications between a server and a UPS?
    a. Null modem
    b. Parallel
    c. Serial
    d. SCSI

20. _____ is used to spread data over multiple volumes in a disk array.
    a. Formatting
    b. Linking
    c. Striping
    d. Sectoring

21. What server component is especially susceptible to damage due to a power failure?
    a. CPU
    b. Disk drive
    c. Tape drive
    d. Modem

THE HOLLAND COLLEGE PROJECT: PHASE 11

Like Sara, you are very close to releasing the Holland College servers. Before you do, you want to set up maintenance and backup activities for both servers. Also like Sara, you will be focusing on the following:

- Event log maintenance
- Fault tolerance
- Backups
- Tape rotation
- Connecting a UPS

You will be working on all these tasks in the assignments that follow. As you work, keep in mind the different purposes of each server and how these affect your maintenance work.

ASSIGNMENT 11-1

In the following table, show how you would accomplish the specified task for the security log on the administrative server.

Task	Explanation of How the Task Was Completed
Set the maximum log size.	
Do not overwrite events.	
Save the log contents to a file and name the file.	
Clear the log.	
Record all audited activity on drive C to the log.	

ASSIGNMENT 11-2

Explain any differences in how you would maintain the three logs on both servers. Answer the following about each:

- Would you automatically overwrite entries in the security log?
- Would you keep old copies of any of the logs? Which ones and for which servers?
- How often would you check the contents of each log?
- Where would you store old logs that you choose to save?
- For how long would you keep logs?

 ASSIGNMENT 11-3

In the following table, explain what each type of backup does and what happens to the archive bit in each.

Backup Type	Purpose	Archive Bit Changed?
Normal		
Differential		
Daily		
Incremental		
Copy		

ASSIGNMENT 11-4

Explain the backup schemes you would establish for each server at the college, answering the following questions:

- How often would you back up the server?
- What type of backup would you use?
- Would you use tape rotation? If so, how would you rotate tapes?

ASSIGNMENT 11-5

In a lab, perform each of the following functions associated with tape management and note how you completed the task.

Tape System Activity	Explanation of How the Task Was Completed
Install a tape system driver.	
Format a tape.	
Re-tension a tape.	
Erase a tape.	
Back up only the files in the Plus! directory.	
Restore the files you backed up from the Plus! Directory.	

ASSIGNMENT 11-6

In a lab your instructor has prepared, practice the following:

- Partition a drive.
- Delete a partition.
- Mirror a drive.
- Stripe a RAID array.
- Back up all files on a drive (not the drive with NT Server system files) and then restore all files.

Explain what precautions you would take before starting each activity.

 ## ASSIGNMENT 11-7

Would you attach a UPS to both servers at Holland College? Explain why or why not. If you do propose a UPS, what other devices would you attach to it? Why? What type of UPS would you recommend? What features would you recommend?

 ## ASSIGNMENT 11-8

Connect a UPS to a file server in a lab your instructor has provided. Using the following table, explain in step-by-step fashion how you connected the UPS.

STEP 1:
STEP 2:
STEP 3:

STEP 4:
STEP 5:
STEP 6:
STEP 7:
Additional steps or comments about the installation:

ASSIGNMENT 11-9

Use the Internet to find additional maintenance tools for NT Server. Describe the function of each tool you find.

ASSIGNMENT 11-10

Research backup software that is available for NT Server using the library, references from your instructor, the Internet, or other resources. Find two examples of backup systems and briefly describe their features.

TROUBLESHOOTING

Sara and Kristin spend lots of time training the office users and find the returns are worthwhile. The network and file server have been available to everyone for more than a week, with most of the problems related to the users learning the new system. There have been many questions about logging on, mapping drives, printers, and other basic issues. The training has addressed many of the questions as everyone settles in.

Sara watches the system through the Performance Monitor, gathering information about peak use and slow times. Also, she regularly checks the event logs for any problems. So far, Nishida and McGuire has barely taxed the new server. Sara's backup scheme is working well, using normal NT Server backups and rotating the tapes. Mark is taking the tapes to the safe-deposit box, because the bank is on his route to work. The UPS has already gotten a live test during a one-minute power failure, sounding an alarm and protecting the server.

Sara is reading her newsgroup and forum information about troubleshooting, so she is better prepared to address problems. She gathers information about how to diagnose CPU overloading, memory problems, disk problems, and network problems, all topics explored in this chapter.

AFTER READING THIS CHAPTER AND COMPLETING THE EXERCISES YOU WILL BE ABLE TO:

- LOCATE SERVER PROBLEMS USING THE WINDOWS NT DIAGNOSTICS TOOL.
- TROUBLESHOOT SERVER PROCESSOR PROBLEMS.
- DIAGNOSE SERVER MEMORY PROBLEMS.
- TROUBLESHOOT SERVER DISK PROBLEMS.
- ADDRESS WORKSTATION PROBLEMS.
- IDENTIFY NIC PROBLEMS.
- TROUBLESHOOT PRINTING PROBLEMS.
- DIAGNOSE NETWORK PROBLEMS WITH THE NETWORK MONITOR AND PERFORMANCE MONITOR.
- USE THE EMERGENCY REPAIR DISK UTILITY TO FIX A SERVER.
- REBUILD A SERVER AFTER A MAJOR SYSTEM FAILURE.

PROBLEM PREPARATION

Sara is finding there are steps she can take right now to resolve problems quickly. One is to train users to accurately report problems. As they train, Sara and Kristin ask the users to take the following steps if a problem occurs:

- Save their work.
- Carefully record information about a problem, such as error messages or effects on their workstation.
- Record background activities before the error occurred.
- Quickly report a problem to Sara or Kristin at the time it occurs.

Another process Sara began in Chapter 9 is to gather performance information, continuing to build her knowledge about the network. For example, she already knows that the legal time software uses a high percentage of the processor and memory resources when Terry Norton creates reports from its database. It's not a problem now, but it might be if all managers generate reports at the same time.

PASSWORD PROBLEMS

The first few days after she released the server for use, Sara found that several people in the office could not remember their passwords. When she set up the user accounts, Sara put in the requirement that each user change his or her password the first time he or she logged on to the server. She did this so she would not know the account passwords and also to encourage each user to create customized passwords of his or her own. Although it is a good practice in terms of security, this step has meant extra work for Sara. For example, Mark Jackson was on vacation for the past two weeks and is now in Sara's office because he cannot remember his password.

As a security precaution, NT Server does not allow Sara to look up Mark's password. But, as administrator, Sara has the ability to change Mark's password through the User Manager. To change his password, Sara uses the following steps:

1. Start the **User Manager** from the **Administrative Tools menu**.
2. Double-click Mark's account name.
3. Enter a new password for Mark in the Password text box.
4. Confirm the new password in the Confirm Password text box.
5. Click the box to require Mark to change his password the first time he logs on.
6. Click **OK** to save the change.

Sara later checks with Mark to be certain he successfully logs on to the server. She likes to follow up on each problem encountered so users feel comfortable with the support she provides.

WINDOWS NT DIAGNOSTICS

A central place to determine whether there is a server problem is the Windows NT Diagnostics option on the Administrative Tools menu. This program has information about the server hardware and software, as presented in Table 12-1.

Table 12-1

Windows NT
Diagnostics
functions

Windows NT Diagnostic Function	Purpose
Display	Shows information about the display adapter card and its driver
Drives	Lists all known drives including floppy, hard, and CD-ROM drives
Environment	Lists all environment variables and environment information, such as the default path for system files
Memory	Presents information about available RAM, paging file use, and the location of the paging files
Network	Lists information about the domain and server names, number of logged on users, and administrator access level
Resources	Shows IRQ (interrupt) assignments, the bus in use, and the bus type
Services	Lists services and devices and shows whether they are running or stopped
System	Displays information about the processor and BIOS version
Version	Shows the NT Server operating system version level and the software registration

All information is arranged by tab, as shown in Figure 12-1 on the next page. The Services tab is particularly useful to quickly locate a service or device problem. The Services button shows all services and whether they are running or stopped. The Devices button shows information for hardware, protocols, and hardware-linked activities. For example, if LAWYER has trouble loading a file from the floppy drive, Sara would use the Devices button to quickly determine whether the drive is recognized by the server. If the server printer refuses to communicate, Sara would use the same button to check the parallel port.

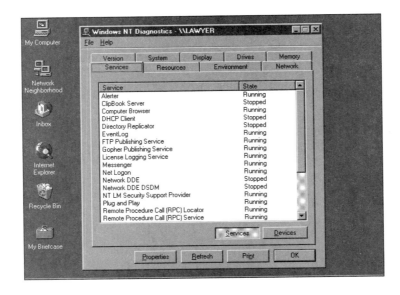

Figure 12-1

The Windows
NT Diagnostics
dialog box

SERVICE DOES NOT START

Occasionally one of the NT services does not start properly or goes into a suspended mode. Sara could go to the Windows NT Diagnostics to determine the status of the service or to the Services icon. The advantage of using Windows NT Diagnostics is that Sara can determine whether the service is dependent on another service or whether other services are dependent on it. If there are dependencies, then she might need to restart more than one service. For example, if Net Logon fails, it may be necessary to stop and restart the Server service as well.

When she determines a service is not started, Sara would next go to the Services icon to start the service. Sara recently experienced a problem in which NT Server sent a message to the console warning that a service had not started. Sara took the following steps:

1. Check the system log for a stop sign indicating a problem with a service, and open the event to find out what service has failed. There will be a message such as, "The Server service hung on starting."

2. Start the Windows NT Diagnostics and click the **Services tab** (see Figure 12-1).

3. Find the service that has stopped and highlight it.

4. Double-click the **Properties button** on the Services tab and click the **Dependencies button** on the next screen to determine whether the service is dependent on any others. Click **OK** to exit. Click **OK** again to exit the Windows NT Diagnostics utility.

5. Click the **Services icon** on the Control Panel and check the Status column to verify the service is stopped. Check the status of any dependent services.

6. If the service is stopped, highlight it and click the **Start button**.

7. If the service is not stopped, use the Stop button to halt the service and then start the service.

8. Start any dependent services.

If a service still does not respond after these steps, another option is to shut down the server after all users are off. Then reboot the server, checking on the service and its dependent services to ensure they are started after the server is back online.

USING EVENT LOG FILTERING TO LOCATE A PROBLEM

All three event logs in the Event Viewer have a filter option to help locate a problem quickly. For example, Sara could designate a filter to show only events associated with the disk drives or only events that occurred on the previous afternoon. The events can be filtered based on the following criteria:

- Date range
- Time of day range
- Event type, such as information, warning, or error
- Source of the event, such as a particular service or hardware component
- Category of event, such as a security change
- User associated with the event, including LAWYER
- Event ID, which is a number assigned by the Event Viewer to identify the event

For instance, to build a filter to view only the error events for the Server service, Sara would use the following steps:

1. Start the **Event Viewer** and display the system log.
2. Click the **View menu** on the menu bar and click **Filter Events**.
3. Click the **Error box** on the Filter screen under Types.
4. Click the **Down Arrow** in the Source box and click **Server**.
5. Click **OK** to view the system log showing only those events specified by the filter.

SERVER CPU TROUBLESHOOTING

A failed processor is rare, and is indicated by a system failure message or a message when the server is booted. Far more common is processor overload, which results in slow server performance. The most apparent symptoms are logon delays, delays in loading application files, and overall sluggish performance. Sara plans to watch processor performance closely as the network load increases. If there are frequent system slowdowns, she will have performance information to determine whether there is CPU overload. Often this is the first area a network manager investigates when server response is slow.

NT Server's Performance Monitor is used to diagnose processor overload. There are three important components to studying the processor load: 1) the percent of time the processor is in use, 2) the length of the queue containing processes waiting to run, and 3) the frequency of interrupt requests from hardware. The Performance Monitor has processor counters to measure each type of processor load.

When Sara monitors the processor load, she starts by observing the processor with the % Processor Time counter. This counter measures how much the processor is in use at the present time. It is normal for the processor use to fluctuate between 50% and 100%. If the processor constantly remains at a high percentage, such as between 90% and 100%, this indicates a problem.

Don't base your assumptions solely on processor use until you've checked some of the other indicators. A high level can simply mean that the currently running processes are efficiently using the processor.

When processor use is high, it's time to collect additional data by monitoring the number of processes waiting in line for their turn on the processor. Sara uses the Processor Queue Length counter for the object called "system" to determine whether there is a queue of waiting processes. If the processor is often at 100% but no processes are waiting in the queue, the processor is handling the load. If four or five processes are always in line, this suggests it is time to consider a faster processor.

Before making a decision to purchase a new processor, Sara has read that it is prudent to be certain the processor load is not due to a malfunctioning hardware component, such as an NIC or disk adapter. When she monitors the processor load, Sara adds two counters, % Interrupt Time and Interrupts/sec for the processor object. A high frequency of interrupts indicates a problem with a hardware component. It does not locate the component, but it does show the overload problem is unlikely to be solved by a new processor. If Sara encountered a high level of hardware interrupts, she would check the system log for information about hardware problems. Figure 12-2 illustrates the troubleshooting steps Sara would take to determine a CPU problem.

Collect benchmarks on the level of hardware interrupts so as to have comparative data for diagnosing problems later.

Figure 12-2

Testing processor load

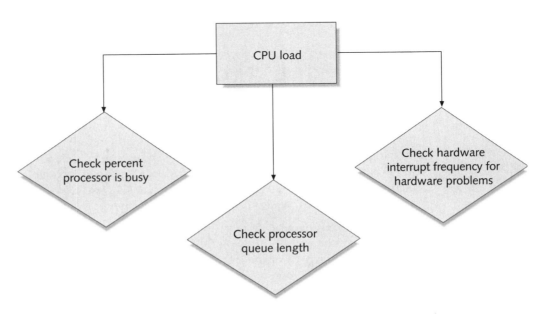

SERVER MEMORY TROUBLESHOOTING

In Chapter 10, Sara took several critical steps to ensure efficient memory management by increasing the page file size to match the amount of memory in the server. She also created page files for each server disk. Now, if there is slow server response and the processor is not busy, Sara would check memory utilization and paging performance. She monitors paging by using the Performance Monitor with paging selected as the monitor object and the counters, % Usage and % Usage Peak. The counter % Usage shows the amount of the paging file used at given points in time, and % Usage Peak shows how often the paging file is at maximum use. If Sara's benchmarks show that paging frequency is on the rise, she plans to add more memory to the server.

If a slowdown is suspected each time a particular application is run, Sara plans to trace the problem by using the Task Manager. As shown in Chapter 10, the Task Manager Performance tab has information about the memory and CPU use of all applications that are running. Some applications may need to be set up for optimum performance on a network.

If an application is causing server problems, check the documentation or call the vendor. Environment variables, swap files, and other parameters may need to be adjusted.

Memory is divided between server functions and network connectivity functions. The server functions include software applications, printing, and currently running services. Network connectivity is related to the number of user connections at a given time. Server functions use RAM and paging. The network connectivity only uses RAM. If the server performance is slow because memory is busy, the network memory parameters should be checked.

Network memory is adjusted from the Network icon on the Control Panel. Sara double-clicks the Network icon and then clicks the Services tab. She highlights the Server service and clicks the Properties button, as shown in Figure 12-3.

Figure 12-3

The Network
Services tab

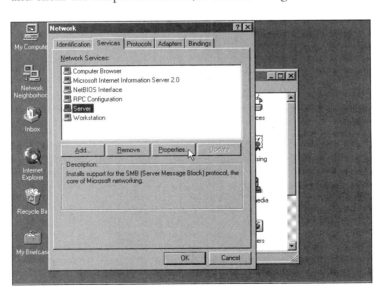

The memory optimization settings on the Server properties screen are described in Table 12-2.

Optimizing Settings	Purpose
Minimize Memory Used	Optimizes the memory used on servers with 10 or fewer simultaneous network users
Balance	Optimizes memory use for a small LAN with 64 or fewer users when NetBEUI is the main protocol
Maximize Throughput for File Sharing	Used for a large network with 64 users or more where file serving resources need more memory allocation to make the server efficient
Maximize Throughput for Network Applications	Used on dedicated database servers in a client/server application environment, such as those using Microsoft's SQL Server database
Make Browser Broadcasts to LAN Manager 2.x Clients	Used for networks that have both NT Server and Microsoft's early server operating system LAN Manager

Sara discovers that the selection Maximize Throughput for File Sharing is set on the screen. This selection does not optimize server memory for use by the firm, which has far fewer than 64 users. The server will have better performance if Sara changes the parameter to Balance. Sara clicks the Balance radio button and clicks OK (see Figure 12-4).

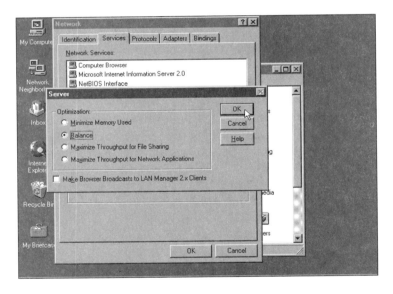

Figure 12-5 summarizes troubleshooting steps for memory.

Figure 12-5

Assessing
memory load

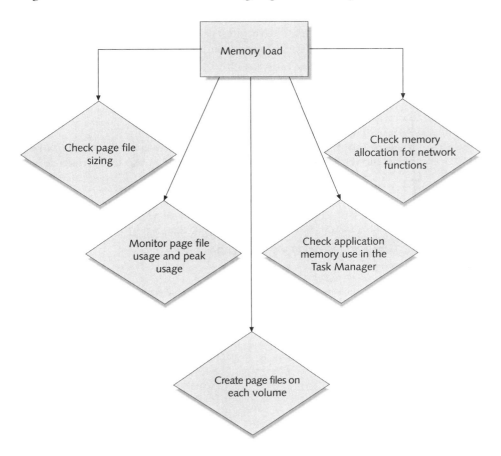

MEMORY HARDWARE PROBLEMS

Failing memory is often an intermittent problem in a server. When Sara checks the system log, she frequently looks for indications of hardware problems. But memory problems are difficult to track without software designed to search for failing memory. Sara purchases a test program recommended to her through her forum group. She plans to run the program on Thursday nights to check for memory problems.

SERVER DISK TROUBLESHOOTING

Another cause of slow server response is overloading a disk. For example, Sara initially placed all the firm's applications and data directories on one drive, but later moved half of them to be shared on the second drive. Spreading the load across multiple disks reduces the wait to access data, and extends the life of the server disks. Disk load balancing is just as important in small server environments as on large mainframes.

Sara uses the Performance Monitor to watch disk activity by selecting Physical Disk as the monitor object. She watches two counters, % Disk Time and Current Disk Queue Length. The first counter shows the amount of activity on a disk and the second shows the number of waiting requests to access the disk. If one disk frequently is busy at the 100% level, information on the number of waiting requests helps to diagnose the problem. If there are 0 to 1 requests normally in the queue, the disk load is acceptable. If the queue generally has 2 or more requests, it's time to move some files from the overloaded disk to one that is less busy. The best way to determine which files to move is to understand what applications and data are on the server and how they are used. If all of the server disks are constantly busy, it may be necessary to purchase disks with more **spindles** or to add data paths (see Figure 12-6 for disk troubleshooting ideas).

A **spindle** is a rod attached to the center of a hard disk platter and to a motor used to rotate the rod and disk.

Individual drives typically have one spindle; RAID drives have multiple spindles within the disk array. A RAID array is a good investment for growing servers because of the combined performance and redundancy features.

Figure 12-6

Troubleshooting
disk overload

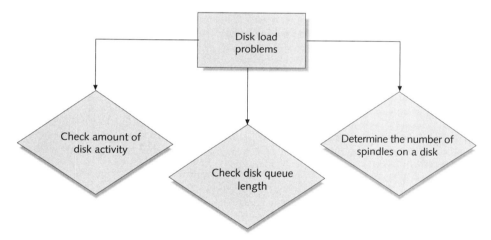

When a disk drive, controller, or SCSI adapter fails, the problem is made apparent through messages from the Alerter and problems running services. Sara asks Ryan whether he has experienced disk problems, and he responds that one drive failed on his server. The services stopped on his server and users received messages that they were disconnected from the server. The server console showed a message showing a system failure. Ryan determined the problem was a disk or its controller, because another drive attached to the server's SCSI adapter was still functioning.

If a particular disk is having trouble accessing certain files or directories, Sara has two options to test the disk. One is to run CHKDSK from the Command Prompt available on the Programs menu. This utility works for FAT or NTFS file systems, although it provides better error checking for NTFS. It checks the integrity of volume indexes, security descriptors, total disk space, user files, system files, and other information.

Another way to test for problems is from the Disk Administrator (refer to Chapter 11). For example, if Sara is concerned that drive D has a bad sector, she would select that drive in the Disk Administrator and click the Tools menu. Next, she would click Properties and select the Tools tab. This tab has a Check Now button to perform a lengthy analysis of the disk surface to detect problems.

WORKSTATION TROUBLESHOOTING

A workstation may have problems connecting to the server or accessing server applications for several reasons. Sara has a list of troubleshooting ideas for a workstation that cannot connect to the server while others can. These include the following:

- Check that the NIC driver is properly installed and is a current version.
- Use the NIC test software to determine that the NIC is functioning and re-seat or replace the NIC if it fails the test.
- Verify the protocol setup through the Network icon.
- Check to ensure the correct packet type is in use for the NIC setup.
- Check the cable connection into the NIC or reconnect the cable.
- Examine the network cable to the NIC for damage.

For example, when she first began testing workstations on the network, Sara had a problem with Kent McGuire's connection because the wrong Ethernet packet type was selected in the software setup. There are two Ethernet packet formats: frame type I and frame type II. The first is the Ethernet 802.3 format and the second is the Ethernet DIX format, which are similar but not identical. Sara used the workstation's Network icon from the Control Panel to change the frame type from Ethernet to Ethernet II. All workstations and the file server on an Ethernet network should use the same frame type. Another problem to check is the cable media setting in the software. An NIC set for coaxial media will not communicate if it is connected to twisted-pair cable.

If a workstation has problems executing software or accessing files, check directory and file permissions on the server. Another place to check is the user's group membership and related permissions. Sometimes a user has permission to execute a program but no permissions to write to setup or temporary files required by the program. Also, check that there are enough software licenses to accommodate all the users. Figure 12-7 summarizes workstation troubleshooting areas.

Figure 12-7

Troubleshooting workstation connectivity

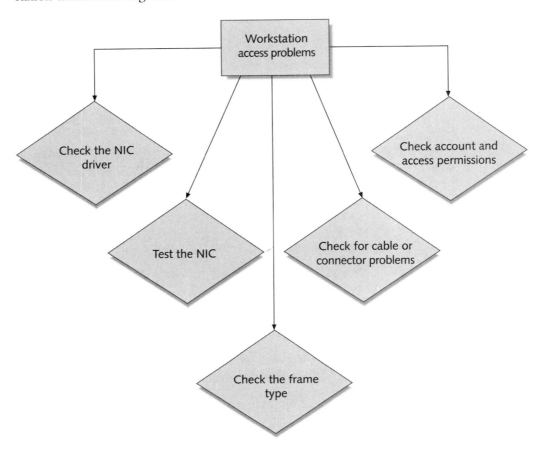

ADDITIONAL NIC PROBLEMS

Sometimes an NIC malfunctions and broadcasts continuously, causing the entire network to slow down. A good way to locate this problem is to use network management software or network analyzing equipment. These packages are beyond the price range of the firm, so an alternative is to look for a workstation having problems communicating or one that is receiving notices it is disconnecting. If Sara encounters this problem, she can check the transmit light on the workstation's NIC. If it is on constantly, the NIC may be malfunctioning. A way to solve the problem is to reseat the NIC in the computer. If this does not work, the next step is to replace the NIC.

PRINTER PROBLEMS

So far, most server- and network-related problems at the firm are printer-related. Sara's rule for these problems is to start with the simple solutions, because they are most common. Sara looks for the following:

- The printer is not connected to the wall power.
- The printer is offline (online printer button is not active).
- The printer lights indicate a reset problem.
- The printer is out of paper.
- The printer data cable is not properly connected to the printer or computer interface.

These are obvious problems but are not always checked first. Perhaps the most overlooked solution is to press the reset button on the printer. When several people share one printer, it may be printing documents with different fonts and formats. A slight misqueue at the printer or in a printer connection may cause it to miss the software reset instruction sent at the beginning of each document.

Another possibility is that the software may have omitted a form feed instruction on the last page of a document, causing it to stay in the printer's memory without printing. The last page is printed by pressing the form feed (FF) button on the printer, if one is available. If there is no form feed button, it may be necessary to press reset.

If the problem is related to the server or workstation, the most likely areas to check are the following:

- The printer driver is improperly installed and selected for the print job.
- The printer share is not enabled.
- The printer share permissions are set incorrectly.
- The software used to produce the print job is incorrectly installed at the workstation.

Figure 12-8 summarizes how to troubleshoot network printer problems.

Figure 12-8

Troubleshooting
network printer
problems

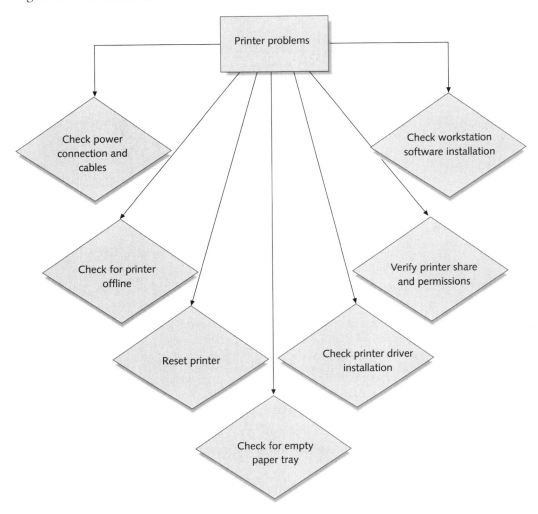

NETWORK PROBLEMS

NT Server has a Network Monitor Agent that can be installed to view network activity and trace problems from the Performance Monitor. Ryan tells Sara about this utility, which Sara decides to install. She double-clicks the Network icon from the Control Panel and clicks the Services tab (see Figure 12-3). Next, she clicks the Add button. She highlights Network Monitor Tools and Agent and clicks OK (see Figure 12-9). The install program notifies Sara it will need files from the NT Server CD-ROM, which she inserts in the server. She clicks OK to load the software. After the software is loaded, she clicks Close on the Services tab.

Figure 12-9

Loading the
Network
Monitor Tools
and Agent

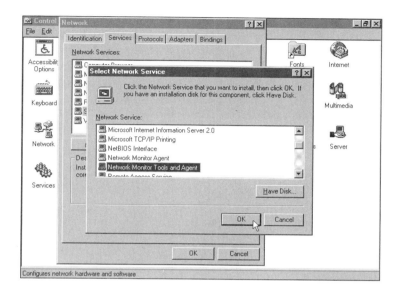

The installation has added a new tool onto the Administrative Tools menu called Network Monitor. Sara opens the Network Monitor as in Figure 12-10 and clicks Start under the Capture menu to begin monitoring. On the left side of the screen, she sees the current network utilization measured in percent. The % Network Utilization graph is a powerful tool, enabling her to check for network problems. On a network the size of the firm's, network utilization should normally be 30% or less. If utilization regularly climbs to over 40%, there may be excessive packet collisions on the network caused by a damaged cable, a malfunctioning NIC, or an outdated NIC driver. Continuously high utilization, such as over 70%, indicates a serious problem, such as an NIC flooding the network, a problem with the hub, or a very inefficient program. If Sara discovers continuously high network utilization, her next step is to narrow the possible sources of the high utilization.

Figure 12-10

The Network
Monitor

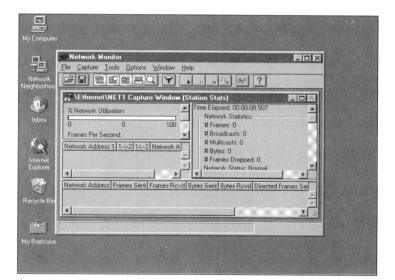

The statistics on the right side of the screen provide additional troubleshooting data. They include network statistics, captured statistics, per second statistics, and network card statistics. On the lower portion of the screen the monitor can be set to view data for Lawyer or another network monitoring station. For example, to determine if LAWYER has a malfunctioning NIC, Sara would use the Down Arrow in the statistics box to view information about **CRC errors** or **dropped frames**. If there are many errors, Sara would have a strong indication to replace the NIC.

Cyclic redundancy check error (CRC) is an error-checking technique used in network protocols to signal a communication problem.

Dropped frames are those that are discarded because they are improperly formed, such as failing to meet the appropriate packet size.

When she finishes watching the network activity, Sara clicks Stop from the Capture menu. Next, she opens Performance Monitor to view the new network object she installed, Network Segment. This object enables her to collect many of the same statistics as in the Network Monitor, such as network utilization, number of frames received, number of bytes received, and total frames received. The advantage of viewing the data in the Performance Monitor is that Sara can graph network information along with server data, such as monitoring the processor utilization with network utilization. Figure 12-11 summarizes network troubleshooting options.

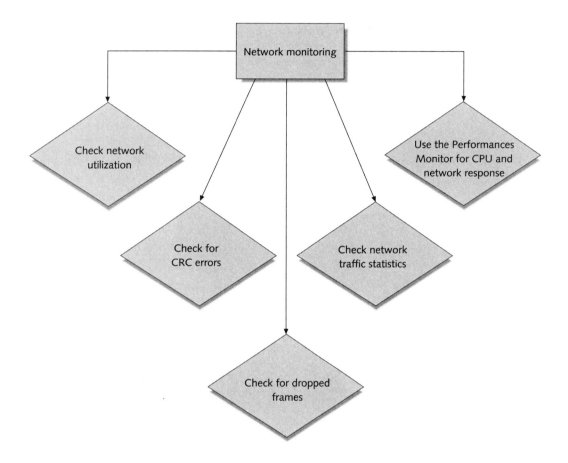

Figure 12-11

Monitoring for
network
problems

NETWORK CABLE

Many network problems are caused by faulty cable or cable connections. These may show up on the Network Monitor as dropped frames, CRC errors, or other error conditions. On a small network such as the firm's, it is good practice for the network administrator to periodically inspect the visible cabling for damage. Cable may be pinned under a table leg, excessively bent or knotted, or damaged from exposure to a portable heater. Also, cable connectors may be broken or have an exposed wire. The best solution for damaged cable is to replace it immediately. On large networks, cable problems can be traced through the use of network test equipment or by means of network monitoring software, such as Hewlett-Packard's OpenView.

NETWORK TEST EQUIPMENT

There is a wide array of network test equipment, but most of the equipment is more appropriate for networks larger than the firm's. The equipment ranges from inexpensive multimeters to very expensive network analyzers. The simplest place to start is with a multimeter to measure cable voltages and impedance. The multimeter can be used to verify that cabling is within the specifications for Ethernet. For example, the impedance of coaxial cable should be 50 ohms and the impedance of twisted-pair should be 100 ohms. A multimeter can be purchased for less than $100 and would be of use to Sara in locating damaged network cable.

The next step is to obtain a cable scanner for several hundred dollars. A cable scanner transmits an electrical signal, which it times to determine the cable length. Scanners also show if there is an open or short on a cable, along with the distance to the problem. They provide help in determining if the cable length meets Ethernet specifications.

Another network testing device is a time domain reflectometer (TDR). This device works like an oscilloscope to show the signal pattern on network communication cable. It shows cable distance, signal strength, electrical interference, impedance, and other information about cable communications. TDRs can record cable data to be played back later for analysis. These devices are more expensive than cable scanners because they have better analysis features.

Protocol analyzers are very expensive tools that provide an impressive range of data about network performance. They supply information about protocols, packet collisions, CRC errors, dropped packets, addresses of network nodes, network bottlenecks, broadcast problems, and many other kinds of information. Some vendors offer network protocol analysis software that can be installed on a server, workstation, or in network equipment. The software is a low-cost solution for protocol analysis, but creates performance overhead in its host.

The most economical solution for a small network like the firm's is to use the Network Monitor and Performance Monitor along with a multimeter. If a network problem cannot be found immediately, it's more cost-effective to hire a network professional than to purchase equipment and spend many personnel hours locating a problem. The network professional will likely have equipment to help quickly locate and solve a problem.

EMERGENCY REPAIR

A power or server hardware problem can damage one or more files on the server so it will not boot. For this reason, Sara created the Emergency Repair Disk when she installed NT Server in Chapter 5. This disk contains repair utilities and information about the server's configuration. If there was a problem, Sara would use the following steps to repair the server files:

1. Power off the server and insert the floppy disk Setup Disk 1 in the server.

2. Power on the server.

3. When Setup asks whether to install NT Server or repair files, press **r** to repair.

4. Insert the Emergency Repair Disk in drive A.

5. Follow all instructions provided by the repair disk.

6. When the repair is completed, reboot the server.

UPDATING AND CREATING AN EMERGENCY REPAIR DISK

Sara has read that the Emergency Repair Disk should be updated when the server configuration is changed. The program used to update information for the Emergency Repair Disk is located in the directory \Winnt\System32 and is called rdisk.exe. Sara uses NT Explorer to locate the program, and double-clicks to start it, as shown in Figure 12-12. If Sara adds a new disk or a RAID drive, she would first click the Update Repair Info button to update the files used for the repair disk. Next, she would insert a floppy disk and click Create Repair Disk to have the updated information on her repair disk.

Figure 12-12

Emergency disk repair utility

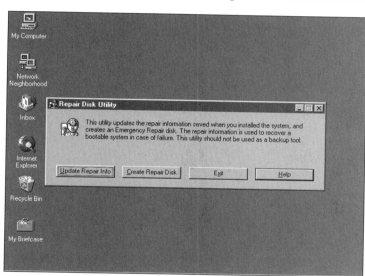

RESTORING A FAILED SYSTEM VOLUME

Sara's backup design gives her strong protection against a failed system drive or complete server failure. For example, if both drives fail or she has to replace the server, Sara would reconstruct the system using the following steps:

1. Replace the failed hardware.

2. Follow steps 1 through 6 to perform an emergency repair (see the previous section).

3. Restore using the last normal backup set.

Sara's restore procedures are straightforward because she only creates normal backup tapes. If she had designed her tape backups to combine normal and incremental backups, then she would have additional steps after restoring from the last normal backup. She would need to restore from each incremental taken that week, starting with the oldest to the most recent.

KEY CONCEPTS SUMMARY

Sara learns three new terms associated with diagnosing problems. These are presented in the review definitions which follow.

cyclic redundancy check (CRC) An error check performed at the protocol level of network communications to determine if a transmission or packet formatting error has occurred.

dropped frames Frames that cannot be used because they are incorrectly formatted, contain errors, or are the wrong size for network communications.

spindle A rod or shaft with a hard disk platter at one end and a motor at the other to rotate the platter.

SUMMARY OF WINDOWS FUNCTIONS

In this chapter, Sara learns about three essential tools for diagnosing server and network problems. Each is described in the following paragraphs.

Network Monitor This tool enables the network administrator to monitor and locate network problems through analysis of network usage, performance statistics, and packet error data.

Performance Monitor When the Network Monitor Agent is installed, the Performance Monitor contains a network object to view network performance data and graph it against other server objects.

Windows NT Diagnostics This Administrative Tools utility provides one place to quickly find a problem on the server. It is a central information resource about the server's display adapter, drives, environment, memory, network, resources, services, system, and operating system version level.

REVIEW QUESTIONS

1. CHKDSK is used for the following purpose:

    a. To test volume indexes

    b. To verify a FAT formatted disk only

    c. To verify an NTFS formatted disk

    d. None of the above

    e. Both a and c

2. Network connections use the paging file.

    a. True

    b. False

3. What would a network manager check to determine whether a particular program is overloading a CPU?

    a. Task Manager

    b. Page file size

    c. Dropped packets

    d. Security log

4. When monitoring the processor, a high number of hardware interrupt requests suggests which of the following?

    a. All hardware components are functioning at 100%.

    b. A hardware component problem

    c. An IRQ conflict

    d. The processor should be upgraded.

5. RAID drives have how many spindles?

    a. One spindle

    b. A main spindle and a backup spindle

    c. Multiple spindles

    d. RAID drives don't use spindles

6. Which of the following are common printer problems encountered by a network administrator?

   a. Printer is out of paper

   b. Printer needs to be reset

   c. Printer cable needs to be reversed

   d. All of the above

   e. Both a and b

7. The Windows NT Diagnostics can be used to determine the number of users on a server.

   a. True

   b. False

8. Where would you look in the Windows NT Diagnostics to determine whether the server's CD-ROM drive is not recognized?

   a. Services tab

   b. Drives tab

   c. System tab

   d. All of the above

   e. Both a and b

9. Which of the following continued percent-network-use statistics would cause you to suspect a problem?

   a. 10%

   b. 20%

   c. 30%

   d. 40%

10. A process can be stopped from the Services tab in Windows NT Diagnostics.

    a. True

    b. False

11. Which Performance Monitor measures help to determine whether a processor is overloaded and needs to be upgraded?

    a. Percent in use

    b. Queue length

    c. Interrupts

    d. All of the above

    e. Both a and b

12. One way to improve disk response is to

    a. Reduce the number of spindles.

    b. Spread data and files more evenly among multiple disks.

    c. Move all disk fragmentation to the boot disk.

    d. Periodically stop and restart the server disks.

13. Memory can be tuned for improved balance between network connection services and file services.

    a. True

    b. False

14. A CRC is

    a. A measurement of CPU queuing.

    b. A test available in the Windows NT Diagnostics.

    c. An error related to network communications.

    d. A memory test.

15. Which of the following tools has a utility to verify a disk drive?

    a. Disk Administrator

    b. Resources tab on the Windows NT Diagnostics

    c. User Manager

    d. Services icon

16. When diagnosing a problem at an NIC, which of the following would you check?

    a. Media type setting

    b. Merge setting

    c. Protocol booster

    d. Driver/CPU linkage

17. To enable network monitoring you need to install

    a. The Network Node Doctor.

    b. The Network icon.

    c. The Network Monitor Agent.

    d. The Network Tools.

18. The Emergency Repair Disk contains server configuration information.

    a. True

    b. False

19. Which of the following network parameters would you set on memory for a dedicated database server?

    a. Balance

    b. Maximize Throughput for File Sharing

    c. Maximize Throughput for Applications

    d. Minimize Memory Used

20. What Performance Monitor counters would you check to determine the load on a disk drive?

    a. % Disk Time

    b. Current disk queue length

    c. Disk rotation time

    d. All of the above

    e. Both a and b

21. Dropped frames are

    a. An indication of network problems.

    b. A processor counter in the Performance Monitor.

    c. Network packets used for high-speed communications.

    d. Network packets stored in an NIC buffer.

HOLLAND COLLEGE PROJECT: PHASE 12

Your network has been running for two weeks, with both servers online and available to users. The student lab is very popular and heavily used by classes and students working on assignments. The administrative users have gotten off to a slower start, but their use of the network is picking up. Because you have a very active network, there are occasional problems to troubleshoot. The assignments that follow provide you opportunities to solve a variety of problem situations.

ASSIGNMENT 12-1

Use the Windows NT Diagnostics tool to perform the following tasks, and record how you completed each task.

Task	Explanation of How the Task Was Completed
Determine whether the server recognizes drive C.	
Determine whether the spooler is running.	
Find the path used for ComSpec.	
Determine the amount of memory on the display adapter card.	
Find the peak use of the page file.	
Determine the version level of NT Server.	
Find the BIOS version of the server.	
Determine the number of logged on users.	

ASSIGNMENT 12-2

You have checked both servers and there is no capability to monitor the college network. What steps would you take to implement a network monitoring capability?

ASSIGNMENT 12-3

Jackie Herrera reports that her workstation periodically disconnects from the network and she has to reboot to make it connect again successfully. Describe what steps you would take to determine the source of her problem.

ASSIGNMENT 12-4

Each morning, the president's assistant, Steve Gaudio, runs several large reports on his FoxPro database on the server that seem to slow down the server or network. In the following table, outline the steps you would follow to diagnose the problem.

STEP 1:
STEP 2:
STEP 3:
STEP 4:
STEP 5:
STEP 6:
STEP 7:
Additional Steps or Comments:

Hands-On

ASSIGNMENT 12-5

Start the Network Monitor and describe how you would accomplish the tasks in the following table.

Task	Explanation of How the Task Was Completed
Record the current network utilization.	
Record the number of frames sent across the network.	
Find the number of CRC errors.	
Show the number of bytes sent per second.	
Find the network status.	
Stop the capture of data and save it to a file.	

ASSIGNMENT 12-6

Describe how you would determine that one of your server disks is overloaded. What steps would you take to resolve the problem?

ASSIGNMENT 12-7

One of the lab printers is printing pages with only one character on each page. How would you address this problem?

ASSIGNMENT 12-8

Bob Watson just called to report he cannot access the administrative server. When you get to the server, there is an abort message on the screen and you determine that the main system drive has failed. You try to reboot, but the server cannot find the drive. Explain in the following table the steps you would take next.

STEP 1:
STEP 2:
STEP 3:
STEP 4:
STEP 5:
STEP 6:
STEP 7:
Additional steps or comments:

ASSIGNMENT 12-9

You are interested in tracking network utilization, CPU utilization, and paging information. Explain how you would set up all three.

ASSIGNMENT 12-10

The administrative server seems to be slow, but you have determined the problem is not with the CPU utilization. What other factors would you check? How would you check each one?

INDEX

response, monitoring, 293–294
server performance and, 65–66
spindles, 346
storage, 62–66
striping, 314–315, 327
troubleshooting, disk load, 345
disk shadowing. *See* disk mirroring
disk storage, 62–66
disk capacity, 62–63
disk contention, 63–66
Setup tests of, 129–130
upgrading, 87–88
%Disk Time counter, 346
DLT tape, 68
Domain Administrators, predefined global group, 188
Domain Guests, predefined global group, 188
Domain name entry screen, Add User Accounts Wizard, 201
domain names
checking, 201
defined, 98
entering in setup, 141
selecting, 120
domain resource management, *See also* groups; resources; users
by group, 186
by individual user, 186
by resource, 186
domains, 155–175
adding with Server Manager, 172–173
defined, 98, 102, 144, 158, 159, 175
defining server relationship to, 119–120
multiple, cross-domain access in, 188–189
multiple master model, 166–167
names, 98
selecting with Server Manager, 173–174
server, 119
single master model, 165–166
single vs. multiple, 159
synchronizing, 174
trusted, 160–164, 169, 171, 175
trusting, 160–164, 169, 170, 175
trust relationships, 160–167, 169–171, 175
User Manager for Domains, 168
value of, 167
Domain Users
adding accounts to, 195
predefined global group, 188
drivers
defined, 10, 18
enhanced mode NDIS, 93
NT Setup, 123–124
printer, 253, 257–259
drives, *See also* disks
mapped, defined, 19
drop-down menus, 19
dropped frames, 353, 356
duplex setting, 94

E

ECC memory, 67, 72
80486 computers, 60
EISA bus, 61–62, 72
electromagnetic interference (EMI), 34, 35, 49

electronic mail, 15–16
emergency repair, 354
Emergency Repair Disk, 354
creating, 120, 143, 355
creating in NT Server Setup Wizard, 134
updating, 355
End Task button, Task Manager, 289
Enhanced mode NDIS driver radio button, 93
Enhanced Small Device Interface (ESDI) disk controllers, 64
error checking and correcting (ECC) memory, 67, 72
EtherExpress card, Windows 95 settings, 93
Ethernet, 36–38
bus topology, 40, 43, 44
defined, 36, 49
fast, 38, 39, 67
network interface cards (NICs), 67
packet formats, 347
reliability of, 39
star topology, 41, 42, 43
transmission speed, 38
troubleshooting, 347
event logs, 297–299, 300
filtering, 341
maintaining, 310–313
EventLog services, 282, 283
Event Log Settings dialog box, 311
Event Viewer, 167, 311, 328
filter option, 341
expiration dates
for accounts, 198–199
for passwords, 184
Extended Industry Standard Architecture (EISA), 61–62, 72

F

fast Ethernet, 38, 39, 67
FAT file system, 114–116
disk partitioning, 127
file recognition, 116
file size support, 115
security, 115
fault tolerance, 313–316
defined, 8, 9, 18, 313, 327
Disk Configuration, 319–320
disk duplexing, 314, 327
disk mirroring, 313–314, 327
redundant array of inexpensive disks (RAID), 314–316
fiber-optic cable, 32
File Allocation Table. *See* FAT file system
file-by-file backups, 320
file compression. *See* compression
file lock, 285, 300
files
activity information, NTFS, 115–116
permissions, 227
recognition, NTFS vs. FAT, 116
sharing, 99
size, NTFS vs. FAT, 115
structure, 220–221
file servers. *See* servers
File Transfer Protocol (FTP), 47
folders, *See also* directories

creating, 222–223
defined, 13, 18
formatting
defined, 114, 145
hard disk, 114, 117
form feed (FF) instructions, for printers, 349
486 computers, 60
frames, dropped, 353, 356
FrontPage, 12
full backups, 320, 321, 327

G

Games, NT Server components, 135
General directory properties, 223, 224–227
General printer specifications, 263–264
General tab, Volume Information, 317
global accounts, 199, 211
global groups
characteristics of, 188
creating, 206
defined, 186
purpose of, 188
Graphical User Interface (GUI), 9, 18
graphs, monitoring performance, 295–296
Group Management Setup Wizard, 207–209
Group Memberships screen, 195
groups
adding members to, 208
adding users to, in Add User Accounts Wizard, 203
assigning rights to, 209–211
creating, 206–209
creating using Group Management Setup Wizard, 207–209
defined, 195
description of, 207
global, 188–189, 206
local, 186–187
naming, 207
network access management by, 186–191
planning, 190–191
policies, 186–191
specifying type, 208
troubleshooting, 347
Groups button, 195
Guests, predefined local group, 187
GUIs, 9, 18

H

half duplex setting, 94
hard disk drives. *See* disks; related disk entries
hardware. *See* server hardware
hardware compatibility list (HCL), 59–60
hardware interrupts, problem diagnosis and, 342
Hidden directories, 224, 226–227
hidden files, 226
HKEY_CLASSES_ROOT, 236, 237
HKEY_CURRENT_CONFIG, 236, 237
HKEY_CURRENT_USER, 236, 237
HKEY_LOCAL_MACINE, 236, 237, 240
HKEY_USERS, 236, 237
"Hold mismatched documents" option, in printer Scheduling tab, 265–266
home directories
creating in Add User Accounts Wizard, 203–204